METHODS FOR MEASURING QUALITY OF LIBRARIES

M Bavakutty
K C Abdul Majeed

Ess Ess Publications

4837/24, Ansari Road, Darya Ganj,
New Delhi-110002
✆ : 23260807, 51563444
Fax : 011-51563334
E-mail: info@essessreference.com
url:http://www.essessreference.com

First Published 2005

ISBN: 81-7000-439-X

Rs.650/-

Published by:
Ess Ess Publications
4837/24, Ansari Road, Darya Ganj,
New Delhi-110 002.
Phone: 51563444
Fax: 51563334
E-mail: info@essessreference.com
url: http://www.essessreference.com

Printed in India at:
Printline, New Delhi

CONTENTS

PREFACE

The libraries have transformed drastically from the storehouses for books and journals to the powerhouses of knowledge and information since the middle of the 20th century. The information and communication technology, which is responsible for this revolution has drastically changed the organization, management and functioning of modern libraries. But, the libraries are still facing problems of survival and crisis of development due to heavy competition from mass media, online services, vendors, publishers, Internet etc. The very existences of libraries are fully depended on the satisfaction of users. Therefore, libraries are now more concerned about the library customers, their satisfaction, the quality of library and information products and services, and their proper marketing.

A user is get satisfied when the library is able to rise to his/her expectations or meet the actual needs. A customer who had an unpleasant experience from the library will tell it to many people, but a good experience will be told to very few. The human nature is that people remember bad experiences more than the good ones. Customers have also started to voice their opinions readily and will no longer accept substandard services. These resulted in the introduction of quality concepts in libraries and information centers, re-definition and re-organization of all the activities in the libraries to meet new challenges.

The library and information professionals have to properly understand the customers, what they want, how they want, and when they want documents and information from the library. Remember that the new generation of customers has high value on self-reliance, adaptability and survival under difficult conditions and they have the ability to do things on their own way. So the libraries have to consider the individuality of the customers, responsiveness of staff and the relationship of the customer with the library very seriously, as it affects the quality of library products and services heavily.

Every library exists to satisfy the needs of the customers, and aimed to achieve hundred percent customer satisfactions. However, there may be some discrepancy between what libraries provided and what their customers actually need. This mismatch results from the failures of the library to meet customer needs and from unrealistic expectations of customers. Therefore, it is necessary to have some system through which the customer needs are heard and these must be used to improve the quality of the services.

A quality service is said to be one, which satisfy customer expectations. Quality is connected with customers' satisfaction and experience. A good quality library service is one, which offers users an experience with which they are satisfied. Therefore quality of service can be measured through assessing customer satisfaction. Regular users of a library will have a realistic set of expectations than new comers, as expectation may be the reflection of what the service provider has been willing to offer in the past. One of the powerful influences on customer expectations is the previous experience of using the service.

Perceptions are the impressions formed from personal experience. Initial impressions are very important in setting customer perceptions. As there are multiple interactions in libraries, a single unfortunate incident may greatly lower the level of perception of customers about the library. Though there are several ways of improving the customer perceptions, the best way is to provide consistent and efficient service to the customers.

Throughout the history, libraries were mainly concerned with collection developments and processing, and engaged almost exclusively in themselves.. Unfortunately, the attitude of most of the professional librarians was that they know the needs of the customers and they always tried to meet their requirements in ways, which the librarians feel, were right for the customer. In this process the views of the customers were never weighed. The library professionals gave less concern to quality in products and services. No attempt was made to check whether the services provided to the users were appropriate from the users viewpoint and was delivered according to users requirements.

The social and economic changes have prompted the libraries to develop services and programmes that are more in tune with the needs of the users The library staff has a vital role in the satisfaction of customers. Provision of efficient and courteous service together with a willingness to help ensures a satisfied customer. On the other hand, a bad customer-staff contact will result in a low satisfaction to the users of the library. Library being a service organization, its prime objective is to provide the right documents and appropriate services to its users. User satisfaction surveys will facilitate the assessment of their satisfaction with the products and services offered.

There are several methods or tools or techniques to measure, control and improve the quality of a library. The quality can be perceived from the organizational level or user level or both. But, perception of the library users is the most important, as the quality of a library has been defined as the gap between the expectations and perceptions of users about the library.

The main objective of writing this book is to make the practicing librarians acquaint with various methods of measuring the quality of libraries. This book will also be useful to researchers, students and faculties of Library and Information Science. The book has thirteen chapters. The first chapter 'Introduction' discusses the changing role of modern libraries in the context of the new challenges faced. Highlighting the importance of employing modern management and marketing technique in libraries, the second chapter describes various methods of marketing of library and information products and services.

The third chapter elucidates the importance of introducing the quality concept in libraries and methods of conducting user satisfaction surveys. The fourth chapter discusses the Total Quality Management and its application in libraries. International Standards Organisation has pronounced several standards for service organizations. Chapter five describes the use of such standards in libraries to maintain quality.

Chapter six explains the concept of service quality, the role of library users in deciding service quality, dimensions and the components of service quality. The Gap model is also described in this chapter as a conceptual model for measuring service quality.

Quality measurement and evaluation assumes great importance in modern libraries, as it brings immense benefits to the library as well as users. Chapter seven elucidates the evaluation and quality measurement in libraries. The methods of collection of data for measuring the performance and quality of libraries, both quantitative as well as qualitative are discussed in chapter eight and the methods of analysis of data, namely mathematical and statistical methods, system methods, specialsied management methods etc. are explained in chapter nine.

Chapter ten elucidates the SERVQUAL method, a multiple item scale used in service organizations for measuring the service quality and application of this tool in libraries. It also includes the criticisms against this method. Chapter eleven explains the LibQUAL, a tool developed based on SERVQUAL instrument for measuring the quality of library products and services. This chapter also describes the LibQUAL+™ 2002, the latest instrument used for measuring quality in libraries.

Chapter twelve contains a review of significant studies on library quality reported in professional literature. Two case studies on library quality conducted using SERVQUAL instrument and suitably modified SERVQUAL tool are given in chapter thirteen. An elaborate bibliography on Library quality is provided at the end of the book.

We are indebted to many authors for conceiving this book

and gratefully acknowledge their intellectual contributions. We express our sincere thanks to Mr. Sumith Sethi, the Managing Director of Ess Ess Publications, New Delhi for taking all the troubles for bringing out this book with in a short period.

We tried to make this book as comprehensive as possible, yet there may be omissions and errors. We would welcome comments, views and suggestions from professional colleagues for further improving this book.

Calicut Uniersity Campus **Dr. M Bavakutty**
May 2005 **K C Abdul Majeed**

1
Introduction

The world has witnessed several information revolutions in the past. The first one was 6000 years ago when writing was invented, which made the way for the development of manuscripts. The second information revolution took place in 1300 BC when the first written book was published. The third information revolution 'the invention of printing press' in 1455 AD initiated a new form of revolution called the document revolution. The Guttenberg's invention brought vast quantities of uniform inexpensive reading materials to the mass. This led to the development of agencies to collect, store and circulate the printed materials to the needy public. These agencies are called libraries.

Libraries began as a place where all the cultural and scientific records of the early societies were kept. Archives (record rooms) and libraries (information dissemination centers) were maintained from as far back as third millennium BC. The greatest library of the ancient times was the one at Alexandria, which had precious copies of Aristotle's famous collection founded for scientific research. If royal patronage made libraries possible there were also marauding kings who destroyed the priceless collections in libraries to erase the memory of the culture they conquered.

Libraries once known primarily as storehouses for books and journals have changed drastically since the middle of the 20th century. From their historical beginnings as places to keep the business, legal, historical and religious records of a civilization, libraries have emerged as a far-reaching body of information resources and services that do not require any physical entity. They are considered as the collections of books, manuscripts, journals and other sources of recorded information. Although libraries have changed significantly over the course of history, their cultural and social role has not been transformed. They remain responsible for acquiring or providing access to books, journals, and other media that meet the educational, recreational, and informational needs of their users. They continue to keep the business, science, social, legal, historical, and religious records of a civilization.

A library can be defined as a collection of documents so organized and arranged in a suitable physical plant by the staff as to facilitate their easy use by users. It is the repositories of information and knowledge embodied in books and other information sources. Information is indispensable for any human activity aiming at social progress and economic development. All people need information to equip themselves better for the fruitful pursuit of their respective vocation. They have to use suitable information resource to acquire needed information. As the information resources are costly and not easily accessible, they depend on libraries to get required information.

Barua[1] defined a library as "an organized collection of books and periodicals and of other reading and audio-visual materials, and the services of a staff able to provide and interpret such materials as are required to meet the informational, research, educational or recreational needs of its users. A library is often classified and designated from the point of view of needs or objectives and the category of readers intended to be served. Whatever may be the types of libraries, collection, organization and dissemination are the primary purposes and functions of all libraries."

In the words of Barbara Kyle[2], 'libraries preserve knowledge so that nothing is lost; libraries organize knowledge, so that nothing is wasted; and libraries make the knowledge available so that none may be deprived of it.' Thus, libraries are the essential ingredients of civilized society, which acquire, store, arrange, and process knowledge for its easier, quicker, and better use. Knowledge is meaningful only when it is translated in to social action. The libraries accelerate the translation of knowledge in to social action and enable the individual to obtain the spiritual, inspirational, and recreational activity through reading. This is possible only when there is libraries to collect, preserve, and provide the recorded knowledge to each individual in the society who is ready to read and acquire needed knowledge.

A library has many social and educational functions. It is an instrument to improve the quality of life of the people giving them education, information, recreation, intellectual stimulation and enriching their life in all respects. A library well equipped and organized and with services and activities imaginatively planned and executed can learn from a society into a well-informed, educated and creative one contributing to its own cultural and economic progress. It is the means for communicating information between different generations and between the people of same generation. The creation of new knowledge is possible only on the firm foundation of the existing knowledge access, which is facilitated by the libraries.

The libraries and information centers are indispensable intermediaries for collecting, organizing, maintaining and disseminating the information to those who are in need of them. The worth of libraries depends upon the collection of useful, easily understandable forms of information and the effective techniques of retrieval of information. Today the information is appearing in variety of forms and the users are also having different approaches to the information. Unless the users are well aware of the different ways and means of obtaining information the objectives of the library cannot be met with.

In the words of Rabindranath Tagore[3] a library can bring into the fullest use by way of bringing the contents clearly and specifically to the notice of the users. Otherwise it is difficult for the user to find his way about them and the library is left as a city of vast accommodation that lacks sufficient means of communication. The library alone can be called hospitable which shows an eagerness to invite users to the feast at its disposal. It is such hospitality that makes a library big, not its size.

Changing Role of Libraries

Library is a service organization designed to preserve and facilitate the use of graphic records. It is concerned with the communication of knowledge, ideas and thought. Traditional role of a library was to collect, preserve, use and disseminate recorded information to the needed people. They offer books and journals to their users and concentrate on basic library and information activities, namely collection development, processing, organization of the collection, and provide services to the right person, in the right form and at the right time. The basic aim of a good library is to disseminate knowledge recorded in different medias. Library is the temple of knowledge and people visit the library to acquire knowledge. It helps the people to develop the ability of learning some thing without a teacher.

The library has changed tremendously from the storehouse of knowledge to the powerhouse of knowledge and information. Information is the input of knowledge, which is the building block of knowledge forming the basis of insight and judgment. What is knowledge for one may be information for another and vice-versa. The information or knowledge is increasingly becoming the basic national resource for all round activities. The varieties of information, which are recorded in a wide variety of documents, are essential for all purposes. As a result, collection, processing, organization and dissemination of documents containing information are recognized as essential elements in all educational research and development, social as well as personal development and like programmes. The free flow of information requires efficient handling of sources of information and the libraries alone can do this. The libraries also facilitate proper and timely utilization of information.

Modern society is known as information society. The society has recognized that information is most valuable to the success in any field. Information is treated as an economic commodity and the society treat it as the prime mover of the society. Investments in information generation and dissemination are becoming an engine of economic growth. Production, distribution and consumption of information have increased enormously. Information is now an international public good and its benefits extends to all those who can access it irrespective of geographical boundaries and time.. It is said that the investment in information generation gives much higher returns than in the production of industrial goods. Information generation is mainly brought by institutions of higher education and research through research and development activities. The libraries help to generate more information by disseminating it. The free and fast flow of information has made the world into a global information village.

Major features[4] of the modern information society are:

1. Information/knowledge creation and transfer leads to creation of wealth
2. Information is a superior substitute for the conventional factors of production, namely land, labour, capital and materials.
3. Electronic information has become fine medium of exchange

4. Managers, researchers and information professional are the new heroes of the information society.

Information is the most valuable commodity and the asset of the modern society. The information industry employs more than 65% of the labour force in developed countries. There are various new methods and policies for the acquisition and free flow of information and overcome the barrier of space and time. Now information is a social commodity, which needs a producer and consumer. The printed documents, radio, television, news channels, cell phones, Internet, intranet etc. ensure needed information for the mass. Nevertheless, modern libraries have the specific responsibility of meeting the information requirements of the present day society.

Modern libraries and information centers are the warehouses of information, their special features[5] are:

1. Highly compact storage of information.
2. Ease of reproduction, multiplication and manipulation of information
3. Contents can be easily detached from its container/ media, and put into other media without trace of the previous one.
4. Ease of transmission, communication and storage of information
5. Hyper-text and non-linear format allows a text to be fragmented and organized in a new mode
6. Heavy integration of print and electronic media and the integration of audio, video, text and animation in multimedia.
7. Sophisticated and complex searches through keywords, free text, boolean operators, class numbers, thesauri and their permutations and combinations
8. Removal of the distance barrier through virtual libraries

9. Remote and wireless access removing the barrier of space and time
10. Heavy use of information technologies
11. Decreasing cost of technologies and increasing power of information.

The value of information and the nature of new media of information have made serious impact on the shape, content, functioning and services of present day libraries. A modern library is quite different from the libraries of the past. It collects, processes and maintains a wide variety of information sources, like books and journals, microforms, audio-video cassettes, motion pictures, CDs, other electronic and online information resources and disseminate information recorded in any form and available anywhere in the world. The information use pattern has also changed enormously due to computerization of libraries, introduction of information networks and establishment of digital and virtual libraries. To recapitulate the recognition of information as the power of a society and a nation thus influenced and affected the libraries in great deal.

The computer and communication technology together have revolutionized the work and services of modern libraries. Many of the house keeping operations is now computer-based. Ordering of documents, preparation and maintenance of library catalog, circulation of documents, maintenance of records and statistics, information/document access, information storage and retrieval, information search, information transfer, etc. are presently computerized. Computers have became the basic necessity of a modern library because of its fantastic speed of handling data, unlimited storage capacity, ability to give different access points based on a single record, ability to access other computers and networking capability, the ability to transfer/send information to any computer interlinked and kept in any part of the world. Information and communication technology facilitates the accessing and retrieval of information from local, regional, national and international textual and bibliographic databases, online libraries and information services. It is the medium through which advanced information services like bibliographic service, indexing and abstracting services, CAS, SDI services etc. are offered even to the distant users through telecommunication and satellite communication systems. The emergence of information and communication technology and its wide applications in libraries has thus resulted in the development of novel activities and services, and new needs of users for advanced information services.

Modern libraries and information centers have to undertake several activities in order to attract potential as well as new customers:

1. Create and distribute service brochures and information kits
2. Improve the signage
3. Extend hours of operation
4. Provide more convenient material return
5. Simplify check out methods.
6. Cooperate with other leading libraries
7. Conduct material demonstrations by vendors.
8. Create quality advisory cell
9. Improve physical layout into more feasible and attractive.
10. Provide suggestion box and track complaints
11. Develop library outreach program
12. Develop digital library
13. Offer free internet access

14. Publicize new and changed services
15. Target services to specific groups of users
16. Offer CAS, SDI, Inter Library Loan, Document delivery service etc.
17. Offer customer care services
18. Conduct user surveys about the library services

But, presently the libraries face crisis of survival and development due to the introduction of modern information managing systems and competition from vendors, publishers, mass media, online services and the Internet. Hence the libraries have started to introduce business styles and techniques in all their activities including marketing of library and information products and services. In business, everything like input, production process, machines and employees, the final product, its cost of production, market, distribution process, selling price, the customers and their satisfaction, etc. is evaluated. Similarly libraries have also started to evaluate the input (collection, user facilities, etc.) process of service (technical and service process), machines used (computer, xerox machine, printer, binding machine etc.), employees (front-line, technical and supporting staff), quality of the product or service offered, method of distributing the product or service (service delivery system) the market where the information products and services can be sold, and the customers or users and their satisfaction.

Library users usually have wide choice of information (General / specific), its source (newspaper / general periodicals / subject journals / textbooks / reference books / websites), its physical formats (manuscript / printed / electronic), its access (direct and remote), its delivery (print / electronic / see / hear / read) its use etc. Knowledge of these choices increases the expectation level of users about library and information centers. If the users do not get satisfactory service from the library, they may go for the alternatives, which will result in the lowering of library user base.

In the present world of tight competitions, according to Snoj and Petermanec[6] the libraries face many challenges:

* Rising user expectations
* Rising user sensitivity and reactions
* Rising use of information technologies
* Rising generation of information
* Globalization of information supply
* Quality measurement of services, Customer / user satisfaction studies etc.
* Rising needs of users
* Rising user awareness about library services
* Increase in the cost of information, information technology, information processing and retrieval.
* Reduction in financial support and need to find alternate sources of income
* Complexity in identifying the users, and their requirements

So present day libraries are more aware about the fact that their existence depends on the satisfaction of users. Therefore, libraries are now more concerned about the library customers, their satisfaction, and the quality of library and information products and services, and their marketing. Libraries have to go to the users and offer the products and services to them. They should publicize their presence among the user community and attract them to the libraries. All these necessitate the librarians to have the knowledge of the business and marketing for managing the libraries in this world of free marketing and offer quality library and information services.

References

1. Barua, B.P. 'National policy on Library and Information Systems and Services for India'. Bombay. Popular, 1992. p1
2. Sonal Singh and Surendra Singh. 'Role of Librarianship in eradication of illiteracy'. In *Libraries and Information services in the electronic era.* Ed by J.L. Sardana. Delhi. ILA, 1999. p25.
3. Rabindranath Tagore. Library and its use. In Information and society. Ed by L.S. Ramaiah and others. New Delhi. Ess.Ess. 1997. p4.
4. Toffler, Alvin. Power Shift: Knowledge, wealth and violence at the edge of the 21st century. New York: Bantam Books, 1991. p232-234.
5. Satija, M.P. Five Laws in Information Society and Virtual Libraries. *SRELS Journal of Information Management.* 40 (1), 2003. p93-103.
6. Snoj, Boris and Petermanec, Zdenka. Let users judge quality of faculty library services. *New Library World.* 102 (1168), p314-324.

2

Marketing of Library and Information Products and Services

Information has been recognized as a significant component for the development of an individual, society and nation, which has necessitated the libraries and information centers to use modern information and communication technologies in the processing, re-designing, storage and retrieval of information. This enhanced the cost of collection, storage and retrieval of information, that compels the libraries and information centers to fix a reasonable price and sell their information products and services using modern marketing techniques.

Marketing is a management process responsible for identifying; anticipating, and satisfying customer needs profitably. Kotler[1] defines that 'Marketing is the process of planning and executing the conception, pricing, promotion, and distribution of goods, services and ideas to create exchanges with target groups that satisfy customer and organizational objectives'. Bell stated four essential features[2] of marketing:

1. It starts with customers
2. It has a long run perspective
3. It makes full use of all the resources, and
4. It is innovative

According to Sreenivasa Rao[3] marketing involves the following process:

1. Analysis of the environment in which the organization works. It is necessary to understand whether the parent body support the marketing of products and services, and ready to accept changes needed in the organization
2. Develop marketing strategy. Marketing strategy is an overall statement of the activities to be carried out in order to achieve the aims and objectives of marketing. It begins as a set of objectives and list out the means through which the objectives can be met economically. The marketing planning will make the strategy possible through more detailed, manageable, and measurable processes.
3. Assess the strengths, weaknesses, opportunities and threats of the marketing through SWOT analysis. The strengths and weaknesses are related to the internal matters of the organization and opportunities and threats are from the external part of organization.
4. Conduct a product analysis to know how heavily the products have been used and how much income it can generate through marketing. The analysis should include cost-benefit analysis, time study, motion study, user satisfaction analysis etc.
5. Conduct a customer study and understand the existing and potential user needs, tastes, interests, behaviour, services used and not used, etc. It will help to target the activities and services to be carried out to widen the market.
6. Study the geographical area to be covered and the service delivery method to be adopted. Manual and computerized delivery methods are suitable for marketing services internally, but computerized or mailing methods should be required to market information products and services outside to the campus.

7. Advertise and promote the information products and services marketed. It is good to begin in a small scale and increase it gradually to cover larger area or maximum number of customers.
8. Introduce customer care service to attract and satisfy the customers. The dissatisfied customers will go for other choices.
9. Measure the satisfaction of customers, quality of the information products and services regularly to maintain the market. It is necessary to keep the quality of the product and service higher to the customer expectations.

Though application of modern marketing technique is very important, the libraries and information centers have failed to adopt this concept for a variety of reasons[4]:

1. The library and information professionals misunderstand marketing and they believe that marketing is synonym to public relations and publicity
2. There is a real or perceived lack of resources to devote to marketing process.
3. Marketing may move the focus of control from the librarian to the users
4. Lack of expertise in marketing leads to difficulty in introducing the marketing concept
5. There are difficulties in promoting their information products and services that can be marketed.

Marketing is proved to be one of the important means through which all library and information products and services can be made in to effective use. But, it is not much popular among the libraries in developing countries as[5]:

1. Library professionals have no clear knowledge about marketing of library products and services.
2. There is no national level marketing policy of library

and information products and services.

3. Non-availability of reliable market research and segmentation studies in Library and Information service field.
4. Lack of initiative on the part of library users to pay for the service.
5. No timely and proper evaluation of library and information products and services
6. Lack of interest on the part of library and information centers to market their products and services.
7. Lack of enthusiasm on the part of librarians to introduce new concepts like marketing in Libraries and Information Centers.
8. Library and information professionals are not trained in marketing at library schools.
9. Libraries are not generating value-added library and information products and services that can be marketed easily.

There are also certain barriers[6] for the marketing of library and information products and services in the developing countries.

1. Library and information professionals are inward looking, as they are satisfied with what they have.
2. There is no library staff to capture the views and interests of users and there is no culture of marketing existing in library and information centers
3. Libraries and information centers are more storage, security and audit conscious and they are not ready to change them to user oriented or service oriented.
4. Information is considered to be free and should be sought by the users themselves. It is assumed that there is no need of going to the user and market the information for the benefit of users.

It is convinced that marketing of library and information products and services is the need of the day especially to those libraries that face shortage of funds. Therefore knowledge of modern techniques of marketing of library and information products and services has become essential to the library and information professionals, due to many reasons[7]:

1. Libraries and information centers invest huge funds on collection, processing and storage of information resources. These resources are put to very minimal use, which implies the wastage of funds. Marketing of these information resources are necessary for the promotion of its use.
2. Marketing of information resources are needed to create demand for the products and services.
3. Information is considered as the lifeblood of planning, directing and controlling an enterprise. Their information need is very intensive. Marketing of information products and services ensures proper information use eliminating its evils.
4. Marketing generally promotes the use of available information resources and services of the library by publicizing them.
5. Marketing creates and increases demand for information resources and services, which increase the image and status of the library.

The library and information professional need not be a marketing expert, instead the professional has to acquire special knowledge and skill in certain significant areas of marketing[8], such as:

1. Perception of the information requirements of users.
2. Knowledge of the ways of accessing information
3. Promotion of information skills through various

marketing strategies, distribution, advertising, and user satisfaction etc.

4. Skills of obtaining feedback from the users.
5. Coupling of new information with the already existing information sources.
6. Customer interest analysis
7. Understanding the reasons for potential users not seeking service.

The library and information professionals with sufficient knowledge and skills in marketing can bring, directly or indirectly, many benefits to their library and information center. The modern methods of marketing of products and services helps the libraries and information centres to[9]:

1. Develop new services
2. Modify and improve existing services
3. Satisfy users in a better way
4. Improve organizational status
5. Improve the image of the library among its well wishers and authorities
6. Improve the performance of the library.

Besides the marketing helps the library and information centers to mobilize additional fund. The major library and information products and services that can be marketed are: Bibliographies, Current Awareness Service, Indexing and Abstracting services, Literature search, Digest extracts, Descriptive reviews, State of the art reports/ trend reports, Compilations, Translation service, Editing service, Publishing service, Reprographic service, Reference/ information service, Online service, Inter-library loan service, SDI service, User education, Loan of Documents, Access to CD Rom databases, Document supply, Mobile library service, Reservation of Documents, Exhibitions/ workshops, and Reading / reference facilities.

According to Rama Rao and Jain[10] marketing of library and information services and products involves the following processes:

1. Analyze the marketing opportunities
2. Research and select target markets
3. Design the marketing strategies
4. Plan marketing programmes, and
5. Organize, implement and control the marketing process

While planning for marketing of library and information products and services, there are certain basic factors[11] to be kept in focus:

1. The total cost of the information generated, processed and distributed to a customer cannot be afforded by the customer alone
2. The impact of information on the development of the individual, organization, and the nation is increasing
3. Innovating information products and services (packaging and repackaging of information) are necessary to suit the needs of various customers
4. Library and information center is a service organization, and it is obliged to provide all needed services to the customers.
5. As marketing requires personal interaction, library and information professionals require orientation, acculturization, and training in marketing
6. Information technology can add four more properties to information, namely concentration, dispersion, circulation and feedback
7. Demonstrating the need to use information for and

its impact on development is necessary to make the customers to bear the part of the cost of information.

It is also good to remember that the basic aim of the library is to provide service, and its service is aimed to serve, to help or to satisfy users, and without user there is no library or its services and marketing. So a thorough knowledge about the users is necessary for the librarian to manage the library successfully and market its products and services to the maximum. For that, libraries and information centers have to get answers to the following questions[12] on their users.

1. Who are their users?
2. What they need?
3. Why they need information/document/assistance etc.
4. In what way they need it?
5. Why they choose our library instead of other libraries.
6. Why they choose a particular service instead of other services in the library?
7. What component of the service is important to them and why?
8. How far they satisfied with the component of the service?
9. What is the value of the service components to them?
10. Which factors influenced them in their evaluation?

As the library services are the combination of physical things (documents) and processes (technical processes, procedures and methods), the library professionals have to understand the specific characters[13] of the library:

1. Nature of the process carried out in the library
2. Intangibility of the services provided
3. Perishability of information contained in documents
4. Variability of user needs and their satisfaction
5. User Involvement in service process and its delivery

6. Personnel as part of the experience of users and their satisfaction
7. Lack of ownership to the documents or the information to the users, which they use for getting needed information.
8. Importance of users' time, as the users are very busy and their valuable time has to be saved by providing needed documents and information in time.

At the same time, the library users may not have a clear idea about the service and its features. They may use the physical or tangible clues to assess the quality of the service. These cause may include the physical evidence, library image, impression made by the contact employees, knowledge, ability and quality of the service providers like courtesy, friendliness, politeness, empathy, promptness, accuracy, attention, ability to convey confidence etc. Therefore, libraries have to consider the factors that are important in the formation of user perception about the library or information center and its services which may directly affects the marketing of library and information products and services. For that, the library and information center has to :

1. Understand and satisfy user needs
2. Learn about the process of information access and search
3. Facilitate mutual understanding among the service providers and users

It is also found that the service providers, user.contact personnel in libraries and those who has frequent contact with the user community have serious impact on the formation of users' perception about the library and its products and services. So, these contact personnel should be able to[14]:

1. Deliver services at a professional level
2. Perform services on time
3. Recover when there is a service failure
4. Monitor, detect and satisfy user expectations.
5. Act as supervisors of the colleagues who co-produce the service etc.

In marketing of any product or service, the four concepts (4Ps), namely Product, Place, Price and Promotion (called marketing mix) are very important. The marketing of a product or service is greatly affected by these factors. Therefore, it is very significant to a library to properly decide what product is to be marketed, in which geographical area it is to be marketed, on what price and how it is to be promoted among its users. The marketed library and information product and service must be in good quality, easily accessible and usable to the users.

Place is an important factor that affect the marketing of a product or service greatly. It is the channel that links the products and services with the customer. The major channels of distributing library and information products and services are[15]: Person-to-person delivery; Group personal delivery; Strategic placement; In-house delivery; Broadcasting; Telephone; Mail, and Computer networks. It is good to use a combination of distributed channels for library and information products and services delivery.

Pricing is another essential factor in the marketing of information products and services as price of the product or service greatly affect its demand and use. Pricing of information services and products is important, but with the increased emphasis on accountability and self-sufficiency in relation to resources, it is necessary to sell, on certain price, the information products and services and recover as much income as possible. While pricing the library and information products and services, it is necessary to decide the cost involved in the generation of the information product and service, and the demand of the products and services.

Promotion is the mechanism by which the target groups are informed about the library and information products and services offered by the library and information center. The promotional activities include public relations, advertising, incentives and atmosphere. Public relation is the interaction between the information agency and its current and potential target markets. Advertisements are for publicity. Incentives are offered to attract customer attention towards the products and services. The atmosphere consists of the environment of the distribution channels. All these promotional activities are aimed to facilitate the communication between the library and information agency with its target groups. The library can contact their target groups either directly or indirectly. Through mail or in person a customer can be directly contacted. They can also be indirectly contacted through news letters, news conferences, annual reports, photographs, posters, brochures, pamphlets, handbooks, guides, news releases, advertisements, video and radio transmission, websites etc. Whatever be the channel used, the promotional activity must be a continuous process.

Library and information products and services are the axel of library marketing. It is associated with the materials like, books, non-book materials, e-resources, etc, access to channels like reference assistance, computer searches etc, and programmes like instructions, demonstrations, etc. While planning, designing, and development of a library and information product, the following parameters have to be bear in mind:

1. Type of the library
2. Users requirements

3. Purpose of the information product
4. Periodicity
5. Sources of information
6. Presentation of information
7. Coverage
8. Distribution of the product
9. Pricing and promotion
10. Manpower required for making the product
11. Finance required and
12. Technology (computer, communication, reprography)

The marketing audit is also highly necessary for the success of library and information marketing. It is the independent examination of the entire marketing effort, namely objectives, programmes, implementation, organization and control. It consists of the following activities.

1. Evaluating the marketing environment of the organization, namely markets, customers and competitors.
2. Evaluating the marketing system through which the products and services are marketed. The marketing objectives, programmes, implementation and organization are to be evaluated seriously.
3. Evaluating the major areas of marketing activity in the organization. The major areas include the products, pricing, distribution, personal contact, advertising, publicity and promotional activities.

In the modern world, customers including library users are interested in latest, improved, most cost effective and cost benefit products and services. It is always remembered that dissatisfied users will not visit the library again. So innovations are needed to develop new products and services. Publicity is the key method of marketing the information products and services. The mass media will help the libraries to publicize their products and services. Changing the nomenclature of the information product and services catchy, expressive and impressive will attract more users to the library for needed information and documents. The staff requires necessary skills, tacts and imaginations to market information products and services. Therefore, proper training is necessary to acquire needed skills. They should also be motivated to market the products and services. In order to increase the information resources available in the library, it is highly necessary to develop and participate in information networks.

It is true that the very survival of modern libraries depends upon their use of management and marketing techniques. But, one should be aware that there are certain major elements in political and legal environment[16] that affect the library and information marketing:

1. The patent and copyright laws meant to safeguard intellectual property rights.
2. Import restrictions on electronic data transfer
3. Import duties on equipments and software
4. Government policies in relation to ownership and funding to educational and research institutions.

Economic environment is an important determinant of demand for any type of product or service. The demand for information products and service is greatly influenced not only by the change in income of customers, but also by changes in the requirement of information. Changes in income would give rise to different levels and types of information needs, wants and requirements.

References

1. Kotler, Philip. Marketing Management. New Delhi: Prentice-Hall of India, 1994. p7.
2. Bell, Fiona. Marketing the information service. In Hand Book of Information Management. Ed by Scammell, Alison. London; Aslib, 2001. p354.
3. Sreenivasa Rao, S. Introduction to Marketing of Information Products and Services. In Marketing of Information Products and Services. New Delhi: Tata-McGraw-Hill, 1999. p9.
4. Bushing, Mary C. The library product and excellence. *Library Trends*, 43(3), 1995. p19.
5. Chopra, H.S. Marketing of Information Services and Indian Scenario. In Infornmation Marketing. Ed by H.S. Chopra. New Delhi: Rawat Publications, 1996. p167.
6. Sreenivasa Rao, S. Op. Cit. p14.
7. Viswanathan, V. et.al. Information Marketing. In Infornmation Marketing. Ed by H.S. Chopra. New Delhi: Rawat Publications, 1996. p16.
8. Mishra, B.N. Information Marketing and Libraries in Bihar. In Infornmation Marketing. Ed by H.S. Chopra. New Delhi: Rawat Publications, 1996. p140.
9. Snoj, Boris and Petermanec, Zdenka. Let users judge the quality of library services. *New Library World*. 102(1168), 2001. p314-324.
10. Rama Rao, T.P and Jain, Abhinandan, K. Key Concepts in Marketing of Information Products and Services. In Marketing of Information Products and Services. New Delhi: Tat-McGraw-Hill, 1999. p42-47.
11. Sreenivasa Rao, S. Op. Cit. p17.
12. Snoj, Boris and Petermanec, Zdenka. Op.cit. p316.
13. Snoj, Boris and Petermanec, Zdenka. Op.cit. p315.
14. Rowley, J. Quality Management in the Public sector: some perspectives from the service quality literature. *Total Quality Management*. 9(2/3), 1998. p321-335.
15. Jagga Rao, N.V. et.al. Marketing of Library and Information Services. In Infornmation Marketing. Ed by H.S. Chopra. New Delhi: Rawat Publications, 1996. p39.
16. Rama Rao, T.P and Jain, Abhinandan, K. Op.cit. p38.

3
Quality Concept in Libraries

There is a shift in the focus of libraries now, from processes and outcomes to user satisfaction and quality. A user gets satisfied when the library is able to meet his/her expectations or actual needs. It resulted in the introduction of quality concepts in libraries and information centers. This resulted in the re-definition and re-organization of all the activities in the libraries to meet new challenges. So social and economic changes aroused due to the globalization of information, computerization and networking, competition from other information providers, demands of funders, new alternatives and choices of users, etc. have prompted the libraries to develop services and programs that are more in tune with the needs of the users.

Today, libraries and information centers are accountable to the parent body, funders, and users. So there is a strong need for assessing the quality of libraries. The major objective for libraries, in an environment of increasing economic pressure, structural change, and technological innovation, is to align themselves with the criteria by which the parent institutions and users are judging the quality of the library.

What is Quality?

The word 'Quality' has several definitions. The conventional definition is 'one that wears well, is well constructed and will last for a long time' and the strategic definition is 'meeting customer requirements'.

According to Webster's New World Dictionary, Quality is 'physical or non-physical characteristic that constitute the basic nature of a thing or is one of its distinguishing features'.

Quality is 'conformance to requirements' according to Crosby.

Quality is 'fitness for purpose' for Juran.

Deming considers Quality 'synonymous with customer needs and expectations'.

According to Robinson, Quality is 'meeting the (stated) requirements of the customer-now and in the future'.

The British standard 4778, of 1987 defined Quality as 'the totality of features and characteristics of a product or service that bear on its ability to satisfy stated or implied needs'.

According to Sarkar[1] Quality of a product or service is the ability of the product or service to meet customer's requirements. Here customer is the real authority who can clearly dictate the quality of a product or service provided.

Quality of a product or service may be of three types, namely[2]

1. Quality of Design
2. Quality of Conformance and
3. Quality of Performance

The quality of design is related to the development of a product or service that suit customer needs at a given cost, and the development of specifications. Quality of conformance refers the extend to which the organization can produce a product or service with a predictable degree of uniformity and dependability at a given cost. Quality of performance deals with how the quality characteristics determined in quality of design and the quality of conformance are performed in the products and services offered.

Quality can be viewed from different angles, like

product, user, manufacturing, value etc. The product-based quality is viewed as 'the per use and measurable variable' which facilitates ranking of products based on the desired attributes or characteristics which a product possesses. The economists defined the quality based on durability, how long a given product held up over time. But, this approach is not suitable for service sectors.

The manufacturing approach to quality is based on technological process carried out in the organization. Total quality management is developed on this approach. It is reported that process control will reduce the cost of product and improve its quality. As services are processes, the service quality approach is similar to manufacturing approach to quality. A user-based approach is used to define service quality. It is based on the premise that quality is a subjective perception, which can be best evaluated by customers. It equates customer satisfaction to quality. Now it is assumed that service quality is decided on the basis of customers' expectations and perceptions. The value-based approach to quality is based on cost of service and customer perceived performance. It integrates the manufacturing based view and user based view on quality.

The different approaches on quality stresses that all approaches require some standard for deciding the quality. In product approach, the quality standard is based on the inherent characteristics of the material components and the degree to which the final product compares favorably with established specifications. In manufacturing approach, the quality standard is based on the process used to create a final product or service. The quality standard in user-based approach is based on customers' perception of satisfaction and met expectations. Finally, the value-based approach uses the price and cost of the product or service to establish the standard for measuring quality. All these approaches/ definitions suggest that quality must be viewed from the side of customers and they are the apt judges for deciding the quality of a product or service. Therefore, it is necessary to understand the basic features of services compared to that of manufacturing products.

Assessing the quality of a product is easy compared to that of service due to its inherent features. Services are performances rendered by one party for another. It often has a physical product component, but it is secondary to the delivery process that makes the service unique. The performance part of service is a great challenge to the organization and it is responsible for certain characteristics, which make the measurement of service very difficult. These characteristics are[3]:

1. **Intangibility:** Services are performances that are largely intangible and cannot be physically felt, seen, tested, smelled or heard in some concrete manner. It leads to the assumptions that the nature of service is too elusive to be amenable to measurement.
2. **Heterogeneity:** It refers to the state of being different. No two-service performances are exactly alike. People provide services and different people may perform it with some variability. The physical and emotional aspects of employee influence the delivery of service, and so it is not amenable to measurement.
3. **In-seperability:** The production and consumption of services are inseparable, as the providers and customers of services engage in direct interaction. Customers entry into the service provides the service providers an opportunity to overcome some of the ambiguity associated with the actual service performance process.
4. **Customers' involvement in service process:** Customers participate in the service process by providing the service providers the information

needed to initiate and perform the needed service. Some times, customers actually perform some of the tasks associated with the service. Here the customers are the quality controller for both highly visible and tangible aspects of service.

5. **Precise Quality Standards** cannot be prepared and so correct quality measurement is not possible as the services are non-measurable.

Library is regarded as a service organization aimed to offer documents and information services to its users/ customers. Compared to the services of other service organizations, the services offered in a library have its own features[4]:

1. There is a direct interaction between the user and service provider. In libraries, services are offered through service personnel. Now IT enables the service to move from user-provider relationship to the user-service direct interaction
2. Users are also participants in service delivery. In a library, users search, locate and bring the document to the counter to get them issued out on loan. As such, this is a type of self-service system.
3. Services cannot be stored for future use. It is the user interaction that provides the key service issue. For a library, a day spent by a book untouched is a day wasted and that cannot be recovered forever. A library with a good collection would get maximum usage if all the documents in the collection are loaned and each time the document is returned, another user takes it again.
4. There is limited substitutability of library services, as the purpose of each library service is different. A user, who searches for a particular document may not be ready to accept another document either written by the same author or discusses same topic/subject. At

the same time, the user may be ready to a substitute when he/she searches for information on a topic/ subject.

5. Libraries have a monopoly of service provision with in their parent institution. Academic libraries and special libraries have a monopoly of service provision with in their campus.
6. Library services have an indirect competition from bookshops, private libraries, Internet etc, as they are also the sources of information and documents.
7. The users interact with library services on a regular basis. A library visit generates two or three interactions with different services.
8. Library services are the combination of the service process and its delivery. In a library, the service offered from the acquisition section, technical section, maintenance section, etc are the processes carried out there. Therefore, processes itself is treated as a service.
9. Library services are not aimed to make profit. So the services are offered either on free of cost or on a nominal charge. Quality is seriously considered on heavily charged services.

The library services are aimed to satisfy the information needs of the user community, who have to be considered while thinking about services in libraries. In order to satisfy the users, it is necessary to find out what they actually need from the library. It is necessary to understand that[5]:

1. Users are the most vital people to be served in a library
2. They are not dependent on the library, but the library depends on them
3. They are the most important part of the library, without them there is no library at all.

4. They are not mere statistics, but human beings whose feelings are to be considered
5. They are the people who bring their needs to meet through libraries

A user who had an unpleasant experience from the library will tell it to many people, but a good experience will be told to very few. The human nature is that people remember bad experiences than to the good ones. The new generation of users is even prepared to voice their opinions readily and will no longer accept poor services. Therefore, it is necessary for the librarians to understand the users, what they want, how they want, and when they want documents and information from the library. They have high value on self-reliance, adaptability and survival under difficult conditions, and the ability to do things on his/her own. So present day libraries have to consider the individuality of users, responsiveness of staff and the relationship of the user with the library very seriously, as it affects the quality of library products and services heavily.

The primary concern of a library is to meet the needs of existing users rather than meeting the needs of future generations of users. User needs must be central to the operation and development of library services. Different users will have different needs. No library can meet all the requirements of users. Sometimes, a user's need may be not met because of the failure of the user to use the library resources and services effectively. Therefore, a user must be educated to use the library effectively. A user should have[6]:

1. Knowledge of what facilities and services are available in the library.
2. Knowledge of how to access these facilities and services.
3. Knowledge of how to use these facilities and services effectively.

Every library exists to satisfy the user needs. However, there may be some discrepancy between what libraries provide and what the users actually need. This mismatch results from the failures of the library to meet user needs and from the unrealistic expectations of the users. Therefore, it is necessary to have some systems through which user needs are heard and used to improve user satisfaction.

User satisfaction is defined as the result achieved when service features respond to user needs and when the library meets or exceeds users' expectations over the lifetime of a service. It is the leading criterion for determining the quality actually delivered to the users. It refers to different areas of the relationship with the users, including the satisfaction with the quality of the service, satisfaction with the business relationship, satisfaction with the performance of the service, and satisfaction on the service that met users' expectations. So researchers are now focusing on users satisfaction with the quality of services delivered, the ongoing business and the users' expectations.

The users' views and opinions with regard to their satisfaction can be solicited in the following ways[7]:

1. Liaison with colleagues and experts
2. User groups
3. Encouragement of users' comments
4. Focus groups
5. User interview and
6. User satisfaction surveys

A liaison with colleagues and experts will enable the librarian to get their views with regard to user needs and preferences. User groups as forums will give their opinions with regard to what is being provided and to be provided from their library. Encouraging users to comment on the services offered to them through suggestion boxes, complaint boxes etc. will provide user needs and their expectations. Discussion with focus groups of users gives an opportunity to comment on what is being provided and to be provided from the library. Interview with individual users will also give a chance to the librarian to know their needs, preferences and expectations. User satisfaction surveys can be conducted to assess their satisfaction with the services offered to them.

User satisfaction surveys

User satisfaction survey is the survey of users to have quantifiable data about their satisfaction with the services offered in libraries. This is often used as a tool to assess service quality and user satisfaction in libraries. It can cover a large number of users and will enable the researcher to make valid judgments on the services offered. It is inexpensive, easy to conduct, and easy to understand. It is considered as the earliest and most enduring method of research on libraries.

User survey is a tool to evaluate the quality of library services from the side of users satisfaction. Out of the components of a library, users are the most important component to be considered while evaluating the quality of library services and that can be assessed through assessing the level of satisfaction attained to the users from the library and information products and services offered. Rapid changes in library services and operations, demands for internal accountability and assessment of expectations by funding agencies have necessitated the libraries to develop and apply new ways of user surveys.

The user satisfaction surveys can be designed and administered in a number of ways. If properly designed and administered, user satisfaction surveys can provide both quantitative and qualitative data related to the library service quality and their satisfaction directly. User satisfaction surveys are accepted as an important part of library's evaluative process and performance measurements. It can be conducted to evaluate the users satisfaction with respect to the services of the library as a whole and individual service or component of a service.

According to Cullen[8], the user satisfaction survey comprises the following stages:

1. Plan the investigation
2. Decide the purpose of the study
3. Read similar user satisfaction studies already conducted in similar conditions
4. Study the survey method of research
5. Decide the tool to be used.
6. Decide pilot investigation
7. Conduct sample survey
8. Process and analyze the data
9. Interpret and present the data
10. Report the results

The proper and systematic use of user satisfaction surveys will help the librarian in many ways[9]. It will give:

1. Detailed information about the users' opinion about the service,
2. Clarification to the librarian's concept of the service,
3. Librarian's assumption about user needs,
4. Apparent problems and suggested solutions.

It is assumed that satisfied users are the indication of good service quality and therefore, it is highly necessary to measure the users satisfaction about the library and information products and services for understanding the quality of the products and services offered from the library. Library services are supposed to be designed on the basis of the requirements and tastes of the present and potential users. The regular user satisfaction surveys will enable the libraries to understand the changes in users satisfaction and plan the services accordingly.

The users' satisfaction is based on many factors, like[10]:

1. Product-Credibility/ Understanding
2. Promotion-Availability
3. Place-Access/Security/Tangibles
4. People-Courtesy/Friendliness
5. Physical Evidence-Appearance/atmosphere/ cleanliness/comfort
6. Process-Reliability/communication

The credibility of a library is related to the reputation of the library as a source of up-to-date information, knowledge, learning facilities and assistance. The library should understand the users specific requirements and environment in which they are operating.

In order to promote the use of the library collection and services, the library should organize its facilities visible, well-signed and easy use. Every facility, collection, and services in the library developed and maintained for the users must be visible to them, otherwise they may not see it and get dissatisfied.

The library and its resources and services should be in an easily accessible location, and the library should ensure the personal security and well being of the users most. The tangibles of the library, namely the building, furniture and other physical facilities, collection, staff, machines etc. should be appropriate and useful for the users.

The library staff should be very courteous and friendly with the users. They should feel that there is some one to attend and help them while certain problem arise. The behaviour of the library staff greatly affect in the satisfaction of users.

The appearance of the library, its facilities, collection, staff and services should be attractive and pleasable. It should give a welcoming and friendly atmosphere for serious reading. The physical surroundings of the library, its furniture, floor, racks, documents, etc should be neat and clean, and should offer a good comfort and ambience to the users.

The library processes should be dependable and efficient and the services should have adequate quality that suffices the expectations of the users. The way of communication, assistance and guidance also greatly affect the satisfaction of the users. So the library has to convince the users that the library is capable of meeting their requirements in time in the way how they expect it.

While measuring the user satisfaction, it is necessary to consider both internal and external users of the library and their expectations. The internal users are the staff, working in the library, who produce interim out put/service and the external users are the users of the final product/ service. External users can be easily identified in a library as there is a direct interaction of the users and the service provider while providing a service, but it will be difficult when the library is accessible through Internet.

User satisfaction can be assessed on the basis of their expectations and perceptions. Expectation is the reflection of what the service provider has been willing to offer in the past. The expectations of the regular users of the library will be realistic. One of the powerful influences on user expectations is the previous experience of using the service. User expectations can be assessed with the help of user suggestions, benchmarking, focus groups, and user surveys. On the other hand, perceptions are the impressions formed from personal experience. Initial impressions are very important in setting user perceptions. As there are multiple interactions in libraries, a single unfortunate incident may greatly lower the level of perception of users about the library. Though there are several ways of improving user's perceptions, the best way is to provide consistent and efficient service to the users.

It is argued that the user perceptions are formed out of their actual experience with the library and therefore assessing the user experiences will give a good idea about users' perceptions. A good quality library service is one, which offers users an experience with which they are satisfied. According to Rowley[11], the useful criteria to measure user's experience in a library are:

1. Speed of service delivery (Access time, location, etc.)
2. Convenience (speed of delivery, location, working hours, range of services, suitability to requirements etc.)
3. Choice (options)
4. Life style (preciousness of time, priorities)
5. Value adding (CAS, SDI, Xerox Services etc.)
6. User Service (Interaction between user and staff)
7. Technology (Machines Used)
8. Quality

Based on the user expectations and perceptions/ experiences, the user satisfaction can be measured. It is assumed that provision of quality products and services satisfy the users, which means that the user perception is equal or above to his/her expectations. Therefore user satisfaction can be measured by identifying the gap between user expectations and performance perceptions.

It is observed that, if something goes wrong that can be very easily learned from the users. So, the user complaints can be taken as a good measure of user satisfaction. As only very few of the users report about their dissatisfaction with the library services, it has to be assessed directly from the users through user surveys. It will enable the library management to know how well the library functions, where to make changes; and determine whether the changes led to improvements or not. Therefore, it is necessary to make the library user focused, which require the following[12]:

1. **Every one in the library should serve the users**. Among the technical staff and front line staff in the library, front-line staff is the interface between the library and its users. At the same time, technical staff is involved with user services in an indirect way, like acquiring, processing, and organizing materials for the users in their desired manner. Therefore, both kinds of employees are responsible for the total service quality to the users.
2. **Services are inherently necessary** and it must be provided to the users in a most effective way. Not only that, the service should be presented and packaged in a good manner through front-line staff. A good service will give users a little more that to what they really expected.
3. **Meet individual needs efficiently.** Every user in the library is an individual and the library should respond appropriately to the expressed needs of each individual
4. **Customization.** It is the process of understanding the users, who they are, what they want, how and when they want the document and information services. Users participate well in a service delivery process. Good services satisfy the users and in turn a satisfied user brings new users to the library. It will strengthen the user base of the library.
5. **Provide maximum benefits to the users.** Users come to the library not for using a service, but for getting the benefits of the collection, facilities, staff and services in the library. If the interested benefit is not attained from the library, they may not visit the library again, resulting in a decrease in user base of the library.

6. **Interaction between service providers and users.** Services are provided to the users through front-line staff. It is a person-to-person contact that may make or mar the relationship between the staff and the user.
7. **Help users even when they do not demand it.** Users are reluctant to admit incompetence, inferiority and dependence on others even if they need help. Simply putting library resources at the disposal of users will not meet the objective of maximum utilization of library resources and services by users. Therefore, it is necessary to help the users as and when they need it even when they do not demand it.
8. **Stay close to users.** Users are to be considered well in libraries. Without users there is no library at all. Library products and services are developed for users and they must use it effectively. Without listening to users, library cannot understand their needs, tastes, interests etc, and services developed without considering the user will be a mere wastage.
9. **Communicate with users.** Two-way communication among the library staff and the users are primary for the success of a library. The library staff has to discuss with the users to get details of the user requirements, tastes, problems etc from the users. The front-line staff and the user should come in a dialogue/ discussion enabling the each group to understand the other.
10. **Introduce user service.** Users must be treated well, informed well, and acknowledged well about the service to the users. Satisfied users always strengthen the user base of the library.

Unfortunately, the attitude of professional librarian is that they know what the user needs and meet these needs in ways, which the librarians feel, are right for the users. But they fail to ascertain what the user actually requires. The library staff has a vital role to play to satisfy the users. Provision of efficient and courteous service together with a willingness to help ensures a satisfied user. On the other hand, a bad user-staff contact will result in a low satisfaction to the users of the library.

Library Quality

The concern for quality in library management was in vogue even in the days of classical Pergamon and Alexandria libraries when scholars in their quest for systematic knowledge became librarians, later when renaissance princes created magnificent collections of books in the same way as they gathered precious pieces of art and nature. It is true that the desire for quality has always been an attribute of librarianship, if a major shift of focus is taking place in this generation. The days when books themselves were very valuable objects, the librarian's perception of quality as residing in the book as a physical, intellectual or cultural object prevailed quiet recently. Another aspect of perceived quality was the comprehensiveness of collections. Along with that the intellectual functions like classification, cataloguing, documentation etc. were also treated as objects of librarian's thirst for quality.

The major shift in librarian's conception of quality may have been evolving over a long period. For instance, the King of Denmark opened his library to the general public in 1793 resulting in a redefinition of the library from a storehouse to an information service center. Throughout the history, libraries were mainly concerned with collection development, and processing and engaged almost exclusively in themselves. They gave less concern to quality in its products and services. The library professionals decide the service to be delivered or the services to be used by the users and provide them. No attempt was made to check whether the services provided to the users were appropriate from the users viewpoint and was delivered according to users requirements. A library with a loanable stock would get maximum usage if every one of those books was out of loan simultaneously and each time an item came back, another user arrived to take it again.

According to Ranganathan[13], the quality of a library can be evaluated in terms of whether or not it is able to provide the material sought by users at the time they are needed. His famous work 'Five Laws of Library Science', advocated that library collection and services are for use and necessary measures should be taken to connect the user with the information sources and services available in the library and save the valuable time of the user by providing quality services to them. All the laws are guiding principles for quality development and its improvement on a regular basis with a focus on the user in the library.

The Five Laws states the goals and the ways of storing, organizing, coding, and disseminating information in recorded materials in a traditional library. It helps in quality improvement of library services as the Laws are focusing the user very seriously.

The first Law 'Books are for use' is a direction for measuring the quality of a library. It implies that books and documents are not meant for storage purpose, but for usage, and so the documents acquired must be of good quality in terms of their physical conditions as well as contents. The quality of library collection not only depends on their content alone, but also on its accessibility and availability as and when needed. Besides, the opening hours of the library, physical facilities available, accessibility offered, helping mentality of the library staff, etc also affect the quality of information resources and their use in the library. In this age of information society, the required information should be easily accessible from anywhere in the world, for that the libraries should have an access to information recorded in any form and stored in any where in the world.

The second Law "Every Reader his/her Books' implies the need for giving greater emphasis to the users, who are not considered well in libraries earlier. Libraries perform many activities on the assumption that all the collections, facilities and services provided would be used by the user community. The users' actual requirements are not considered seriously while developing collections, providing facilities and services. In order to meet this law, modern libraries have to index all macro and micro documents available in the library very well so as to meet all possible approaches to the document in question, enabling the user to get his/her needed information/ document in time. Not only that, the library should participate in resource sharing programmes and thus increase its information and document resource to the maximum. The libraries also have to make use of the modern forms of information sources like electronic documents, bibliographic and textual databases, online information sources and services and the libraries on Internet. If the user gets his/her document or information in the form in which it is expected is a symbol of quality service in the library.

The third Law 'Every Book/Information its reader' implies the importance of documents and information available in the library, which are to be used to the maximum. It stresses that every macro and micro document in the library has to be used. It directs to identify the materials and match the same with the requirements of users. As unused document in the library is the mark of the failure of the library due to faulty processes and policies on collection development and management and its exploitation by the users. Therefore, the law advocates scientific document selection, subject based organization, advanced and in-depth indexing of macro and micro documents, efficient and effective searching and locating tools, personal help, open access, extension services, publicity programs, marketing of library and information products and services etc to get maximum users to the documents and information available in the library. All these lead to quality works and services.

The fourth Law 'Save the Time of Reader' indicates the importance of fast and efficient services to the users by using advanced technologies, methods and techniques, and tools. Provision of open access, classified arrangement of documents, location and directing guides, efficient and effective tool for searching micro and macro documents, personal help, easy and fast method of document loan, xerox facility, information technology, qualified and experienced staff etc. will ensure fast and effective services to the users. In order to have quality in libraries or to satisfy the users, the libraries have to focus and use modern methods of management like total quality management, system analysis, work-study, time study and motion study have to be made as part of management culture. Access to other library resources, electronic/ digital resources and online information resources and services are also necessary to satisfy the modern users. Personal assistance to the users for search, access and retrieve needed information from other library websites, databases, homepages, information service sights, etc. are considered as the need of the day.

Finally, the fifth law "library is a growing organism" implies that library is an institution that contains information resources and services aimed to meet the information requirements of the users. All the components of a library such as the documents, the users, the services, the methods and techniques, the technologies used etc. are changing. These changes give new phases to libraries such as computerized libraries, networked libraries, electronic libraries, digital libraries, online libraries, and virtual libraries. The world of documents and information is changing drastically. Now information is recorded not in papers alone, to many media, the latest being the electronic and digital form. The traditional libraries were mainly concentrated in printed documents, but the modern libraries deal not only with printed resources but electronic and digital resources also supported by advanced information and communication technologies. However, the new alternatives to libraries, such as private lending libraries, commercial information products and services, internet, etc. are considered as threats to the modern libraries.

Though Ranganathan suggested to focus on users very seriously while designing and measuring any library activity, the libraries tended to measure their success by easily quantifiable indicators, such as number of documents in the collection, number of users visited, number of documents circulated/referred etc. It is to be remembered that even a library with millions of documents in its collection will be judged poor when it fails to give a document needed for a user.

The presumption is that large collection of documents, staff, machines and premises and its development will improve the quality of library products and services that has to be changed urgently for getting the quality in the real sense. The users and managers are also well aware of the quality of the library, its facilities, collection, staff, services etc. than before. Therefore, an urgent look in to the quality matters in library and information services within the existing constraints is very much required.

The quality of a library can be perceived either from organizational level or user lever, or both. The level of perception of the organization may be different from that of users. Such a perception gap is not good for a library, as the organization perceive its services in a higher level than the level of actual users. Perception of library users is more important to the other. Therefore it is necessary to measure the expectations and perceptions of the users about the library products and services to assess the library service quality through the eyes of users.

Though quality aspect is considered in every action undertaken and every material acquired in the library, the ultimate quality of the library has to be judged by the users on the basis of the quality of the information products and service offered to them. The quality of an information product and service is influenced by[14]:

1. Environment;
2. Library resources;
3. Library aids; and
4. Library staff

The cozy and inviting atmosphere in the library attracts users, which will ensure better utilization of resources and service of the library. It enables and enthuses the library staff to work more efficiently. Such an environment can be created with the help of good and attractive building, adequate reader space, comfortable furniture, good lighting and ventilation, toilet and drinking water facility, temperature and noise control, friendly and capable staff etc.

Library resources should be capable of meeting the varied requirements of the users. No library can acquire all the information needed for the users, so they should have to access to other library resources and services, electronic and digital resources, online information resources and services etc.

Library should have proper aids such as comprehensive and easily searchable library catalogue, bibliographies, indexes and abstracts, access to other libraries, databases, online information resources and services, computers and other information technologies, etc. to help the users and staff to meet their requirements.

The library staff should be available in adequate numbers and have good qualification and experience in the field of library management, house keeping operations, information services and information technologies. They should be friendly with the users and always ready to assist them.

According to Ann Lawes[15] provision of quality products and services to the library users will bring several benefits:

1. Benefits to the users

Users get consistent quality services. The users have great role in the provision and delivery of information products and services. Library has more information about what users want and how much they are prepared to pay for it. Users have a good voice in the library products and services marketed. Implementation of quality standard will ensure the supply of necessary resources required to the standard implemented.The provision of consistent quality library and information products and services will increase users' loyalty to the library.

2. Benefits to staff

The quality processes help to break down the status barriers among the administrators, managers and other staff of the library in the process of quality implementation, management and its control. It leads to teamwork in the process of discussion, problem solving and control of quality. It leads to free communication between the administration, management and colleagues, as they work together, debate openly and solve problems. The evaluation of performance, the work manual and the standard of work help them to recognize what is expected of them and are able to participate in the achievement of library's goals. The work on quality leads to improved staff morale, as the quality clarifies employees' responsibilities and objectives, giving a clear idea about their accountability and areas of responsibility of staff at all levels. Staff become confident in knowing exactly what they are doing, where those tasks are fit into, and when and where to go for help when it is required. It increases their power and responsibility.

3. Benefit to organization and efficiency

Quality assessment is a powerful tool, motivator and focus for reviewing the performance of the library and the satisfaction of users. Measurement is the fundamental principle underlying quality assurance. It enables the works to be planned and conducted properly, and thus efficiency is improved. It eliminates or minimizes the waste and enables the library to control the cost of works and services and improve cost-effectiveness. The information from the evaluation of the library performance enables the manager to be aware of the changing needs and expectations of users and the strengths and weaknesses of the services offered.

The quality process necessitates detailed work manual for the library and information services, which ensure consistency and provide guidelines for staff in their works and services. It increases the efficiency of the library, its collection, services and staff. Not only that, it offers good management control over the works, services and staff.

4. Benefit to marketing and public relations

Quality program improves the image of the library. As the quality of Library and Information services are regularly evaluated, it sends the message that whether a first rate service is provided or not in the library. Improvement to marketing and public relation is inherent in the process of quality library and information services. It necessitates consultation with users to understand library and information service quality standards. Every member of the library staff and users will be the part of quality process, in the form of problem identification and its correction in library service quality.

To sum up, quality is vital to libraries and information centers and focusing on the user and the quality of library and information activities and services brings many benefits, such as[16]:

1. Quality service reduces problems and complaints from users and staff
2. It increases users loyalty through satisfaction, leading to increased business and attract potential users
3. It increases the opportunities for maximum use of services
4. It enables the staff to identify user needs, and suggest suitable services for users
5. It increases the job satisfaction and morale, commitment, good relation with employer, etc to the staff
6. It enhances corporate image, reduction of cost of service, and business performance.

References

1. Sarkar, Debashis. The managers handbook for total quality management. New Delhi: Sage Publishers, 1995. p1-2.
2. *Ibid.*
3. Lewis, B.R. Managing Service Quality. In Managing Quality. New York: Academic Press, 1991. p234-235.
4. Brophy, Peter and Coulling, Kate. Quality management for information and library managers. Aldershot: Aslib Gower, 1996. p14-19.
5. Coote, Helen. How to market your library service effectively. London: Aslib, 1994. p7.
6. Payne, Philip. User Empowerment. In Pinder Chris and Melling, Maxine, Ed. Providing customer-oriented services in academic libraries. London: Sconul, 1996. p69-70.

7. Ibid.
8. Cullen, P. Perspectives on user satisfaction surveys. *Library Trends*, 49(4), 2001.p662-686.
9. Ibid.
10. Cullen, P Op. Cit. p666.
11. Rowley, Jennifer. User Experience of Libraries. *Library Review*. 43(6), 1994. p7-17.
12. Gupta, Dinesh K and Jambhekar. Developing a customer-focus approach to marketing of library and information services. *DESIDOC Bulletin of Information Technology*. 22(3), 2002. p5-13.
13. Ranganathan, S.R. Five Laws of Library Science. Ed 2. Bangalore : SRELS, 1988.
14. Ann Lawes. The benefits of quality management to the library and information services profession. *Special Libraries*, Summer 1993. p141-146.
15. Ibid.
16. Ibid.

4
Total Quality Management and Libraries

Information is now considered as an important resource for socio-economic development of a society. So value added information service can only provide the conformance to the requirement of the users and their satisfaction. Libraries adopt management techniques to give their best in the form of services and products to its users. But it is very difficult to give best products and services, if there is no precise definition of what the best is in terms of library goals. There is no universally acceptable tool and techniques to measure, control and improve the quality of products and services in libraries. Total Quality Management (TQM) is one of such techniques used for the improvement and maintenance of quality or performance of the libraries. Therefore, it is necessary for the library and information professionals to understand the core concepts, methods and techniques used in TQM.

British Standard BS 7850 defines that Total Quality Management (TQM) is the management philosophy and company practices that aim to harness the human and material resources of an organization in the most effective way to achieve the objectives of the organization.

According to Tenner and Detoro (1992)[1] TQM is a basic business strategy that provides goods and services that completely satisfy both internal and external customers by meeting their explicit and implicit expectations. This strategy utilizes the talent of all employees to the benefit of the organization in particular and society in general and provides a positive financial return to the stakeholders.

According to Brockman[2], TQM is a management philosophy embracing all activities through which the needs of the customer and the community, and the objectives of the organization are satisfied in the most efficient and cost effective way by maximizing the potential of all employees in a continuing drive for improvement.

Features of TQM

Major features[3] of TQM are:

1. Everybody in the organization accepts ownership and responsibility for quality.
2. Quality improvement is the way of life
3. There will be good partnership with customers and suppliers.
4. Internal customers are properly acknowledged and given special attention to satisfy them, in return to satisfy the external customers.
5. Key performance indicators are identified to measure performance, assess improvements, monitor customer satisfaction etc.
6. Employee participation is stressed
7. Quality problems are solved through teamwork.
8. Internal barriers between sections and department are removed.
9. Simplify and standardize processes and procedures.

TQM in Libraries

TQM in the context of libraries is to provide the right information to the right user at the right place and time and also at the right cost. The goal includes ease, convenience, excitement, interest and fun that the library provides to the users. It has some relationship with the total experience of the user with the library in providing value adding solutions to the problems. The goals of libraries are keep on changing and these changes affect the manpower, product, user and environment in the library. In order to cope up with these changes libraries need to change their strategy, structure, leadership and human resource management. All these management constitute the goals, techniques, and elements of TQM.

TQM is a holistic, disciplined and continuous system approach which starts at the top of the library staff and goes to down the line. It is a planned organizational change based on mission, goals and objectives and requires total involvement of staff and calls for everyone to be skilled and knowledgeable. It promotes teamwork, focus on users, and considers quality as a strategic priority. It emphasizes the importance of performance measurement through the measuring rod of user satisfaction.

TQM involves defining the output to the requirement, assigning the process (action, methods, and operations) specifying input requirement (men, machines, materials, information, skills etc.) maintaining, monitoring/ controlling the adherents to user requirement, identifying changes in users requirements, communicating changes in process and inputs.

Objectives of TQM

According to Dobas[4] Total Quality Management of a library depends on a number of factors, which can be enumerated as the objectives / principles / elements ofTQM:

1. Initiate functions, services, strategies and action plan to achieve the basic objectives of the library.
2. Do things differently and document better processes, instructions and information
3. Identify user base to ensure optimum utilization of the resources and services in a cost effective manner.

4. Design and redesign systems and procedures of the library in an innovative way.
5. Educate and train library staff to make them more responsive and learn new ways and means of doing things.
6. Act the librarian as a role model to the members in the team.
7. Drive out fear from the mind of library staff so as to get the best out of them
8. Use the library as a holistic and integrated system
9. Do the work in the prevailing condition and don't try to raise the user expectation
10. Ensure that the reputation of library products and services match with the reputation of the parent body.
11. Use the hands and heads of all library staff to raise their confidence and contribution to the attainment of library objectives.
12. Provide a tool kit to support the systematic approach to understand and measure the performance gaps in their works.
13. Provide better avenues for career development and growth of the library staff.
14. Initiate a well thought strategy with full involvement of the staff

TQM requires continuous improvement of all operations and activities in the organization. It is recognized that customer satisfaction can only be obtained by providing a high quality product or service and continuous improvement of the quality of the product/ services is the only way to maintain a high level of customer satisfaction. As the product/output quality is the result of process quality, it must also be improved continuously, so measurement and monitoring of all activities and processes is necessary as part of quality improvement program. In addition to that, waste has to be eliminated properly. It is good to go for prevention rather than detection of errors and mistakes, at the beginning itself.

In library and information science field, the continuous improvement will be a six-step process[5]. These steps are:

1. Identify the value of products and services offered by the library from user point of view.
2. Map the processes used to deliver the library and information products and services.
3. Establish how improvement in these processes can be made.
4. Measure the effectiveness of the improvements made.
5. Communicate improved measures to the library staff, users and the management of the library.
6. Incorporate a benchmarking effort, to find out how other libraries accomplish the same task in a quality manner

Customer requirements are not restricted to the needs or functionality of a product or service, but may relate to ease of use, availability, delivery method, familiarity, reliability, time effectiveness, reputation, enjoyment, etc. It is necessary to understand what the users actually need and design the service and deliver them to satisfy the expectations of users. This is necessary for the successful implementation of TQM in libraries.

In the context of TQM, quality is defined as meeting the requirements of customers, both internal and external customers. The library user is placed at the top and the front-line staffs who directly contact with the user next, i.e. there are two sorts of customers/users, internal and external users in a library. Understanding the needs and requirements of both of these users are compulsory for the success of TQM in libraries. The recognition of work colleagues within the library as user is vital to the philosophy of TQM. The quality chain in a library comprises supplier-customer interaction from the external supplier, through numerous customer-supplier interfaces within the library. To meet the requirements of the external customer or the real user and to operate TQM successfully, the quality chain must be complete. The customer-supplier interface in a library is shown in the figure 4.1

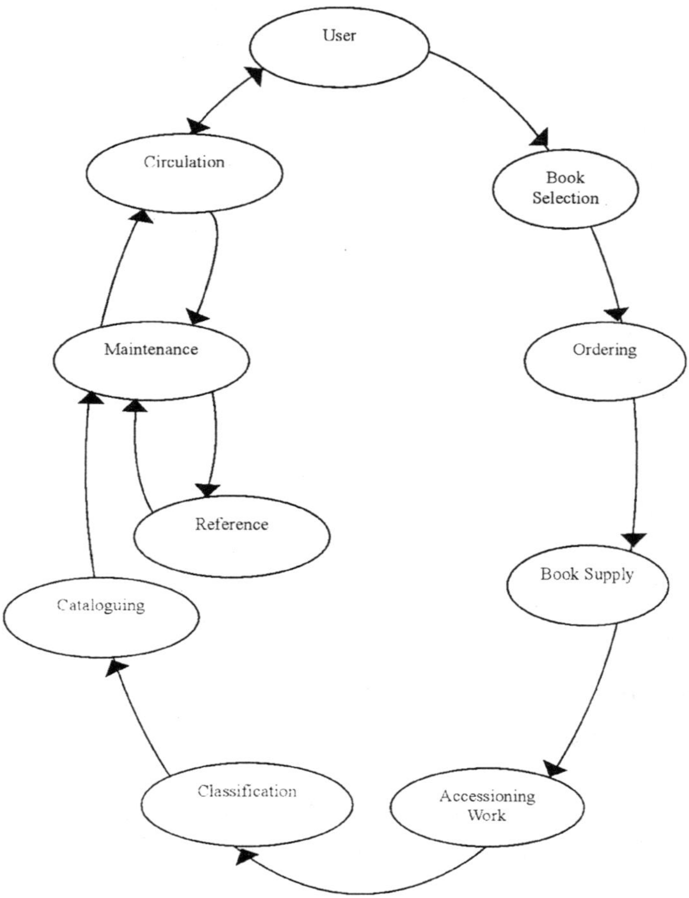

Fig. 4.1 User –Staff interface in a Library (Customer – Supplier Relationship)

Identification of the internal and external user is very important in TQM. In libraries, the external customer is the real user, but in certain situations the same user becomes a supplier as like the book supplier or the service suppliers or the library staff. Similarly, the library staff also becomes the user as like the original user in the library. For example, the library staffs who deals the book selection work is a supplier of book details to the order clerk, but at the same time, he is the user/ customer who receive requests from the original user. Both the library staff and the original user in a library play such customer-supplier roles. So satisfaction of the needs and requirements of these users is very important in TQM.

TQM maintains and improves all library processes automatically by a process of designing, controlling, detecting and implementing. The prevention of errors and wastages of resources, like material, effort, time, etc are vital to the success of TQM in any organization. TQM recognizes that the achievement of the right first time depends not only on management commitment but also on the involvement of all staff. Through setting clear objectives, making the employees properly trained and providing with good working facilities, the library can prevent wasted efforts and errors and target the services to meet the customer requirements, make the efficient use of the resources and increase the satisfaction of users.

The management commitment to the TQM is the key to its implementation, maintenance and success. The top management should ensure all employees commitment to TQM. It is an employee-focused approach that uses the creative energy of all employees and acts as a tool for innovative changes and problem solving techniques. A total employee involvement is possible through empowering the staff. An organizational system has to be used which draws all employees together for a common purpose and helps them to see their role, place and importance in the organization and the quality work.

The library management should concentrate on the staff, their empowerment, satisfaction and commitment to service quality. This will create a culture compatible with TQM. All library activities and processes must be defined, described and recorded in the form of staff manual, policies and programs etc. The managerial experiences of implementingTQM in libraries emphasized the need of well-defined quality policy, design and development of systems and procedure manuals in libraries. These manuals are the good source of information to staff, users, management, and auditors. to understand the services offered, procedures and programmes carried out, responsibilities of staff, systems used etc.

The librarian should be committed to the users, profession, basic human value and excellence and this has to be communicated to lower levels properly and clearly. The librarian should have a clear vision about the performance and quality of the library services provided and it must be recorded properly. It will equip the library staff with sense of purpose, confidence, determination and committed effort to produce good results.

Effective functioning of a library is vested on the trust between the librarian and the other library staff. A well-defined library system ensures optimum utilization of skills and knowledge of the library staff. An open system will ensure trust among the library staff and permit two-way communication between the staff and librarian. A well-designed library staff manual covering job description, role, duties and responsibilities, tools and techniques, etc. will relieve the librarian and the staff from most of the problems related to their work. Teamwork in libraries is essential for the success ofTQM. It enables the management to get diverse talents, skills, expertise, and experience of others to the problem solving tables.

TQM is a means of expanding organizational thinking and learning capabilities. Learning helps the library staff to understand the new needs of the users, which is necessary and essential for continuous quality improvement of the library products and services. Learning is possible through education and training of employees, which has a great role and importance in TQM. It enables the staff to perform present and expected future roles and enhances the capabilities for the development and exploitation of the inner potential for personal and professional development. It develops right attitude towards users, equips with knowledge of all the processes, procedures, practices and other related aspects of the job and develops competency, capability, responsibility and accountability for higher works.

Components of TQM

The major components[6] of TQM in a service organization like libraries are shown in the figure 4.2.

The library must be very clear about what they are trying to achieve. It is necessary to define adequately the fundamental values and purposes of the services and articulate it in to practice. The development and use of mission statement is the good way of defining the purpose of a process or service. Mission statement is the statement of the library's current activities. It differs from a statement of aims or objectives of the library, as it is developed to express the nature of the library and the place it seeks to occupy in its external environment. Mission statements can be treated as the starting point for the implementation TQM in libraries.

Similarly, the library has to develop a clear *vision* about what they should be. The librarian, through leadership, has to generate a good vision based on the hopes, aspirations and desires of employees and customers. In this context, it is necessary to understand the fact that the world in which

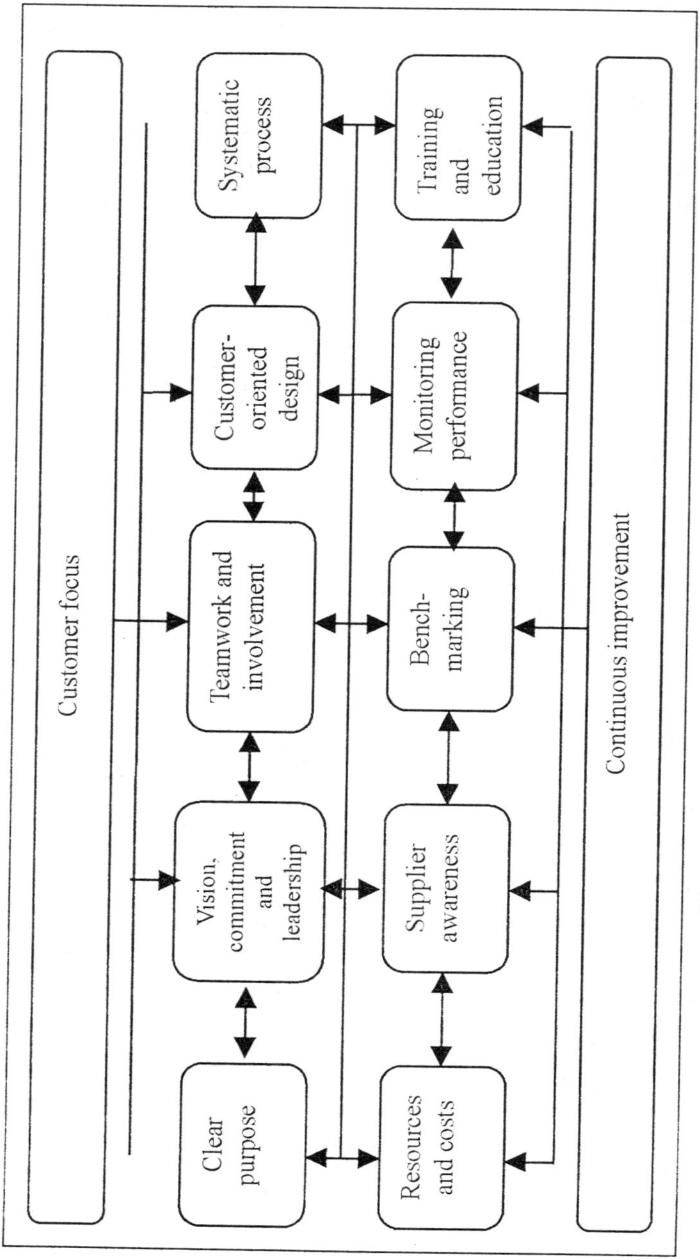

Figure 4.2. Components of Total Quality Management

the library operates changes tremendously, and it may necessitate a change in vision of the library also.

Team work and *Staff involvement* in the process of quality management is very significant. Teamwork enables the librarian to tackle the problems by more than one person at a time and allows a mix of skills and abilities to solve these problems. So, quality circles or quality improvement teams are constituted in quality management system of libraries.

The *design* of a library service must incorporate the user requirements at the initial stage. While designing a service, it is necessary to consider what is to be delivered and how it is to be delivered. Tebout (1991)[7] suggests that there are five principles to be considered while designing a service.

1. Provide quality services at all levels.
2. Recognize that customers of services experience a series of moments of truth.
3. Understand that there will be a variety of support services, which have direct effect on the customers.
4. There should be flexibility in the delivery of service as customers' demands are varied and dynamic.
5. Consider the total cost of the service and examine the value provided for that cost.

The processes carried out in libraries to turn the input into output should be a systematic one, which is a vital component of the TQM approach, as the process are central to what the library does, and what it delivers to the user. It is necessary to identify the individual processes, which together contribute to total performance and user satisfaction. In addition to that, the processes that have serious impact on quality are also to be identified. In order to find out the processes that have serious impact on quality, the following questions[8] are to be answered first.

1. Which services are most important to customers?

2. How are these services produced?
3. How is customer demand recognized and turned into a service?
4. Which processes are most visible to the customers?
5. Which processes have the greatest effect on performance standards related to customer requirements?
6. Which processes have greatest potential for improvement?

Similarly, it is found that the *resource* input of the library and information center have a considerable affect on the ability of the library to deliver various kinds of services, as every service requires financial investment in one form or the other. Therefore, the input resource of a library will decide its ability to deliver a service. It is to be remembered that the *cost* of quality should not go beyond the control due to the shortage of the required resources. Improper use of the resources may lead to increased cost of quality. The cost of quality[9] may be the total of the cost of following:

1. Cost of prevention of mistakes and failures;
2. Cost of assessment, audit and appraisal of quality;
3. Cost of internal failure resulting wasted works;
4. Cost of external failure leading to the dissatisfaction of users;
5. Cost of exceeding customer requirements; and
6. Cost of lost opportunities in the form of failure to attract new users or to retain existing users;

Libraries and Information services are largely based on the information sources supplied by the external suppliers and the libraries do not have any control over them. The quality of the information services offered in the library is totally based on the information supplied to them. As part of quality, the library has to assess the speed of supply, accuracy of transactions, and the added value of the supplier. Therefore, a good partnership between the information suppliers and the library is necessary for improving the quality of information services offered in the library.

Benchmarking is the process of comparing the operations, products and services of the library with a library doing quality processes and offering quality products and services to its users. It can be either internal or external. Internal benchmarking is the process of comparing a department or unit in the library functioning as per quality norms with another unit or department in the same library.

Performance measurement and monitoring is one of the important activities of Total Quality Management. This is necessary to identify the problems, if any and find new ways for improving the product or service. It requires both quantitative and qualitative data about the various operations carried out, and the products and services delivered to the users.

In service organizations, the staff is considered as one of the most important resource for the delivery of its services to the customers. The qualification and experience of the library staff depends upon quality of the service they offer. So, total quality management consider the staff, the internal customers, very seriously, learn them very well and necessary training is offered to them to improve their skill.

The TQM process of continuous improvement requires continuous performance measurement to ensure targets or standards are being met and to inform adjustments to processes to meet changing demands. The library staff collects statistical data about processes and services regularly for assessing the performance of the library. In TQM the use of statistical data forms the basis of decisions and actions taken by the staff themselves in controlling their works. Statistical process control is an essential part of the TQM strategy.

Statistical Process Control[9] is a set of techniques, which uses a tool kit of seven basic tools, namely, Process Flowcharting, Check sheets / Tally sheets, Histograms, Pareto Analysis, Ishikawa Diagram, Scatter Diagrams, and Control Charts.

Process Flow Charting is used to describe what is done and in what sequence. It is particularly useful for identifying and testing the steps involved in a new process or identifying the inputs needed for a particular process or to confirm the written instructions for an entry in the staff manual. Check Sheets are used to gather data, record actual events, or how often something happens. It is heavily used for collecting data about users and their use of library resources and services. Histograms are used to present the performance of a process pictorially or graphically. It is useful to present information to indicate the areas of strategic decision making is required. It is used to indicate the variations in the use of a service before and after its modification. Pareto analysis is used to present possible ranges of causes for a problem and the percentage of incidents attributable to each cause. It is found that a high percentage of a problem is attributable to one or two causes. It may help to identify the major causes for the serious problem in the library. By identifying the root causes of the problems and solving it judiciously will help to improve the service quality in libraries. Ishikawa Diagram or Fishbone Diagram or Cause and Effect analysis is a method of analyzing and identifying the causes and its effect on a problem through brainstorming process. It helps to identify the main and sub causes and their role in making the problem a serious one. Scatter Diagram is used to plot how one factor affects another and to determine whether there is any relationship between the two. It will also show the extreme level where the relationship disintegrates. Control Charts are used to record measurement of a particular process over a period of time.

These tools are intended to support problem solving and decision-making. Its use must be planned through the quality planning and quality improvement processes. They must then be built into the quality control mechanisms established supplying the data required to support the regular monitoring and review on which quality service provision depends. The quality assurance measures alone will not produce quality services in libraries. To ensure quality these tools need to be used appropriately. The ability and experience in using these statistical tools must be considered for implementing TQM in libraries effectively.

There are certain problems associated with the application of total quality management technique to libraries and information centers. These problems[10] are:

1. The organizations have less control over the factors affecting quality
2. As the services cannot be stored for later use, there is higher uncertainty in services.
3. It is difficult to set quality standards as services are intangible.
4. The expectations of customers about a service vary from customer to customer.
5. As the customer participates in the process, there is an impact on the quality of service provided.
6. As service quality is subjective, its measurement is difficult.
7. Difficulty in identifying and pursuing real goals, which are quantifiable and measurable.
8. Difficulty to measure administrative and managerial effectiveness.
9. Difficulty to change old practices
10. Resistance of staff against change

Application of TQM in a library will bring several benefits[11]:

1. It results in better quality of service
2. It creates a loyal user base
3. It develops a satisfied user base.
4. It attracts persons with high caliber to the organization
5. It increases staff morale

In the context of financial stringency, tremendous increase of documents, changing demands of users, escalating material prices, technological developments, etc., TQM may offer a suitable frame work within which libraries can re-think their service objectives, delivery mechanisms, and internal systems in order to meet user requirements and deliver quality services. Implementation of TQM in an organization is considered as the beginning step for the ISO certification.

References

1. Tenner, A.R. and DeToro, I.J. Total Quality Management: Three steps to continuous improvement. Reading, MA: Addison-Wesley, 1992.
2. Brockman, J.R. Just another management fad? Implications of TQM for Library and Information Services. *Aslib Proceedings*, 44(7-8), 1992. p283
3. Lascelles, D.M and Dale, B.G. The Road to Quality. Bedford: IFS Ltd., 1993. p18
4. Dabas, Drishan Chander. Application of Total Quality Management to the University Libraries in Punjab, Haryana and Chandigarh. Amritsar: Guru Nanak Dev University, 2001. Ph. D. Thesis. p20.
5. Dabas, Drishan Chander. Op. Cit. p21
6. Brophy, Peter and Coulling, Kate. Quality Management for Information and Library Managers. Hamshire: Aslib Gower, 1996. p71.
7. Teboul, J. Managing Quality Dynamics. Herts: Prentice-Hall, 1991. p31

8. Brache, A.P and Rummler, G.A. The Three levels of Quality. *Quality Progress*, 21(10), 1988. p46-51.

9. Brophy, Peter and Coulling, Kate.Op. Cit. p103-106.

10. Brophy, Peter and Coulling, Kate.Op. Cit. p90-97.

11. Raina, Roshan. Total Quality Management in Library and Information Services. New Delhi: Infuse Inc, 1999. p1-151.

12. Ibid.

5
ISO Standards and Libraries

Bringing quality in libraries is not an easy task. The implementation of total quality management technique or national or international quality standards like ISO 9000 can accomplish quality concept in libraries in a purposeful way. Even an attempt for quality standard certification itself will bring quality in an organization. There are many quality standards, at institutional, regional, national and international level, available today. Such quality standards are required to maintain quality consistently and to improve it continuously in an organization.

ISO 9000 is rapidly becoming the most popular quality standard in the world. Many organizations, including library and information centers, have already adopted this standard and many are in the process of implementation. This standard is suitable to all types of organizations. It is not a matter what is the size of and what the organization does. It is a tool to both product and service organizations to achieve standards of quality that are recognized and respected in an international level.

It is a statement of what the organization is doing to achieve quality, documented procedures which show how those actions are carried out consistently and how action is taken to amend the procedures when something goes wrong, and evidence of record keeping to enable compliance to the standard to be demonstrated.

It necessitates three sets of documentation, namely Quality manual, Procedure manual and Work instructions. The quality manual explains the organization's quality policy and objectives, responsible persons in the system, and the quality system. It demonstrates management's commitment to quality system. The procedure manual describes all procedures used in the organization. And work instructions include the instructions to staff to carry out specific tasks.

ISO 9000 is a series of international standards[1] on quality management issued by the International Standard Organization in 1987. This is developed on the British Standard BS5750. It consists of six standards with different purposes and scope. These are:

1. ISO 9000
2. ISO 9001
3. ISO 9002
4. ISO 9003
5. ISO 9004 and
6. ISO 9004-2

Among these, ISO 9001, ISO 9002, ISO 9004, and ISO 9004-2, are dealt with definitions and guidelines of a quality standard, and rest of the standards are meant for external quality assurance purposes.

ISO 9000 quality standard has to be considered in three levels of quality management, namely, strategic level, operational level and continuous quality improvement level. At the strategic level, an overview of the libraries performance and success in meeting strategic aims, which contribute to the achievement of library's mission, is needed. The key question here is 'what should we be doing?' At the operational level, an attention to the quality of service the individual user receives is needed. Here services are reviewed to see whether they are in conformity to user requirements or not. The key question to be asked is 'How should we be doing it?' At the continuous quality improvement level, an attempt is made to avoid losing relevance to current needs and be ready to meet the future. It indicates quality of change or future quality. It involves development of staff and other mechanisms to improve the quality of the services offered and the mechanisms to review the quality of service on offer.

ISO 9000 standard is offering a major ingredient in the successful delivery of quality at the operational level. It is important to recognize that the key to this standard lies in[2]:

— Establishing agreed procedures for all aspects of the operation;

— Defining who in the organization is responsible for each procedure;

— Documenting those procedures;

— Ensuring that staff are trained to follow the procedure;

— Auditing that the procedures are being followed;

— Monitoring the effectiveness of the procedures in relation to customer need.

This standard aims to build quality into the product, prevent poor quality occurring in the first instance and provide highest quality service every time. It is a checklist of requirements than a specification. It is a means to ensure that changes are introduced systematically and consistently. The standard is concerned with procedures, and procedure manual. To meet the standard, the basic procedures needed are to be uniformly applied for ensuring consistency of the service.

ISO 9001 contains 20 clauses[3] that require documentation and implementation:

1. Management responsibility
2. Quality System
3. Contract Review
4. Design Control
5. Document and Control
6. Purchasing

7. Control of Customer Supplied Products
8. Product Identification and Traceability
9. Process Control
10. Inspection and Testing
11. Control of Inspection Measuring and test equipment
12. Inspection and Test status
13. Control of non-conforming products
14. Corrective and preventive action
15. Handling storage and packaging
16. Control of quality records
17. Internal quality audits
18. Training
19. Servicing and
20. Statistical techniques

ISO 9004-2: 1992 Quality Management and Quality System element Part 2: Guidelines for Services[4] is an international standard to establish and implement a quality system within a service organization. The concepts, principles and quality system elements described in the standard are applicable to all forms of service provision.

According to the standard, a quality system should be the interaction between management responsibility, personnel and material resources and the quality system structure used. The management is responsible for establishing a policy for service quality and customer satisfaction. For that, the management has to document its objectives, policies, responsibilities and activities of the organization and its commitment and the involvement of staff to fulfill these commitments.

The standard considers the personnel and material resources in an organization as the major elements responsible for improving the quality system of the service provided. In the case of personnel, planning, motivation, rewards, communication, training and development are to be considered very seriously. In material resources, the information sources, stationary, equipment, work facilities, tools and techniques etc are very important. The efficiency of an organization greatly depends up on the job satisfaction of the staff. Teamwork, motivation, and communication are necessary to enhance the morale of the staff.

The quality structure requires documentation of all the works in the organization. It should include objectives and policies, scope, responsibilities, authorities and control of each activity. This will lead to a standard working practice in the organization. The structure gives much importance to quality manual, quality plan and documentation control, which will make a quality record of the organization and it can be audited for ISO certification.

For the purpose of certification, an approved agency examine, inspect and approve the quality system. The procedure[5] for certification of the ISO Standard is given in Figure 5.1.

Implementation of the quality standard and its certification is the responsibility of the top management of the organization. The management is committed to do the required process involved in certification in time. First of all the management has to formulate a strategic plan for the purpose. It should form a core group of managers who are well versed in quality matters as well as ISO quality standards. Based on the strategic plan, the core group has to identify suitable persons and form a taskforce particularly for the purpose. The management should take necessary arrangements to make aware all the employees about their attempt for ISO certification and sufficient training is to be given to those who do works that greatly affect the quality of products and services.

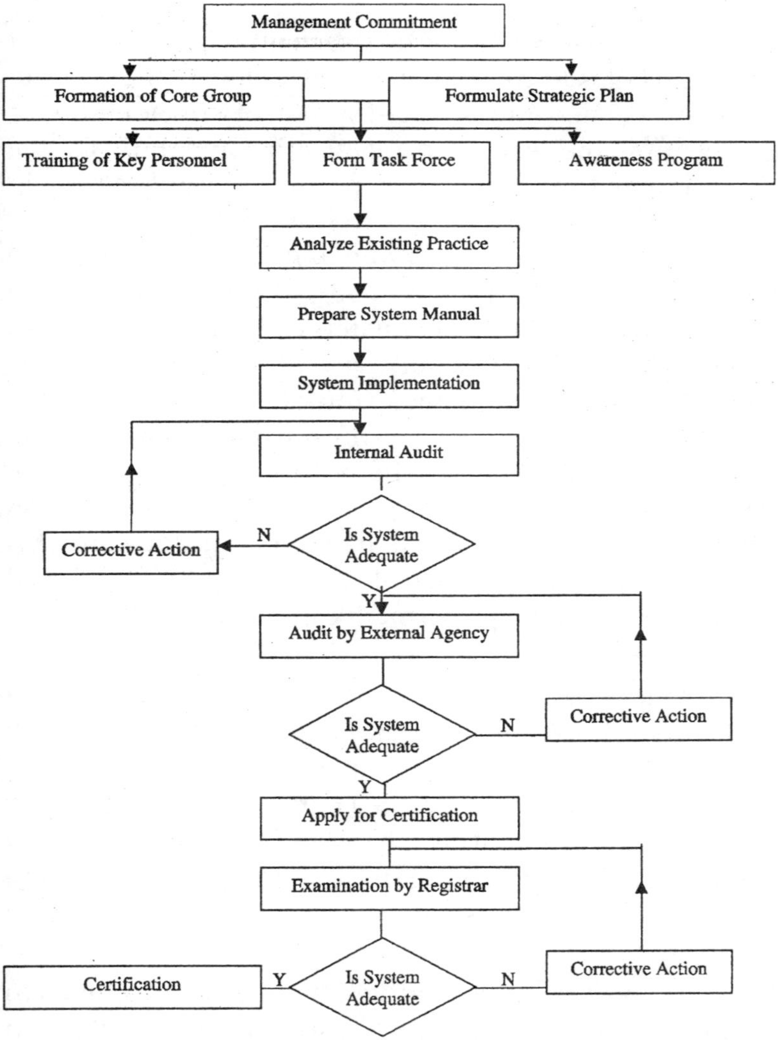

Figure 5.1 Procedures for Certification of the ISO Standard

Initially the taskforce should critically analyze the existing practice of doing works and delivering services in the organization to identify the problems that adversely affect the quality of products and services offered. Once the problems are identified and corrected, they have to prepare a system manual explaining how each unit of work is carried out and what is its role in the overall quality of the product and service. Then the corrected system of work and service is to be implemented in the organization and the taskforce has to audit its performance properly. If problems are again found, it must be corrected and re-implement the corrected system of work and service again. It must be continued till a problem-free system is identified and implemented. Once the system is functioning adequately, then the quality system implemented should be audited by external auditors. If any problem is identified by the external auditors, it must be corrected and implemented. This must follow an internal auditing to verify whether the problem identified by the external auditors still exists or not. If the system works adequately, external auditors have to audit it again. This process should be continued till the external auditors found satisfactory with the performance of the quality system in the organization.

Once the external auditors feel that the quality system in the organization is functioning properly and satisfy all the requirements of ISO quality standard, then the management can apply for ISO certification. The agency responsible for auditing the quality system for ISO certification will audit the system used in the organization, and if they are satisfied, they will recommend the organization for certification.

The process of ISO certification itself contributes to the improvement of quality in the overall functioning of an organization. It enables to streamline all activities and get rid of redundant practices. The quality manuals and activity manual make the functioning of the organization more transparent and enhance communication.

A quality system that meets the requirements of ISO 9000 standards is needed to use this standard. Once a quality system is introduced, the ISO standard will help to control the quality of the product or service, reduce the costs associated with poor quality or to make the product or service more competitive. Use of the ISO standard is necessitated because the customers expect it or it is mandatory for the regulatory body. Based on the ISO standard, any organization can develop a quality system that meets the requirements of any one of the standard included in the ISO 9000 standard series; it is also necessary to consider the ISO guidelines. The ISO's requirements include ISO 9001, ISO 9002 and ISO 9003. ISO's guidelines include ISO 9000, and ISO 9004. All these are translated into plain English. An internal audit system is needed to assess the working of the quality system; it is also necessary to select and appoint an external auditor (registrar) to evaluate the effectiveness of the quality system employed. If the necessary requirements are met, the external auditors certify that the quality system has met all of the ISO requirements and they issue an official certificate stating that the product or service of the organization is managed, controlled and assured by a registered ISO 9000 quality system.

In order to make the development of a quality system and the ISO certification process easy, ISO have created a quality system development plan, internal quality audit programs, defined ISO's concepts in ordinary English and developed a simple theoretical frame work that explains what ISO is all about. All these will enable the organization understand what is ISO? And how to proceed to get an ISO certification for the organization?

Benefits of Obtaining ISO Certification

Several tangible and intangible benefits[6] are accrued for an organization from obtaining ISO certification. These benefits are:

1. Increase the credibility of the organization
2. Better access to global markets

3. Reduction of cost through eliminating waste, reworking and redundancy
4. Boosting personal morale through the involvement of all employees in the organization
5. Ensures consistency in quality of its output, which in turn increases customer confidence.
6. Periodical audits as part of the quality system help in preventing deterioration and enhancement of quality
7. Effective use of manpower through procedure-task orientation
8. Easy training of new personnel and redeployment of persons to new tasks
9. Higher accessibility to documented procedures and it leads to improved efficiency, raises employee morale and results in effective communication

ISO Standards and Libraries

ISO standards are not generally applied in libraries and information centers due to many reasons. The usefulness of these standards to libraries is not evaluated well, as it depends on many circumstances and variables, especially how the standards are interpreted and implemented. The requirements of a standard for libraries are also not discussed in detail in professional circle so far.

However, quality standards enable the libraries to maintain quality consistently and to improve it continuously. It enables them to satisfy stated and implied needs of the customers, which leads to customer delight, loyalty and co-operation with library programmes, activities and services.

It is found that, ISO 9001 and ISO 9002 are largely implemented in the field of libraries and information service sector. ISO 9000 standard can be very easily used in libraries, as it contains several flexible clauses[7] like:

1. Define and select services and information products.

It gives a provision to include most important and essential services for quality assessment and also to focus on heavily used services and products.

2. Determine quality goals, objectives and policy. There is a provision either to use internal quality standards or the standards developed by the professional community for the purpose. It directs to have regular negotiation with the customers while determining quality goals and objectives of the organization. It allows using traditional user surveys and quantity analysis as part of quality evaluation. It insists that the quality goals and policies should match with the specific needs and culture of the customers and the staff in the organization.
3. Select necessary requirements. Though the ISO 9000 contains 20 basic requirements, only the appropriate elements needed to be taken for use.
4. Choose appropriate means and levels. There are different elements and means for ensuring quality in an organization. Detailed work instructions and procedures alone may not ensure quality. Sometimes education and training of the personnel may be more powerful than to other means. Based on specific circumstances, suitable means can be adopted. The primary goals included in the standard are: goals, objectives and policies, education and training, procedures, work instructions, and manuals and guidelines.
5. Write procedures and work instructions. It is a highly creative process based on knowledge of motivation and human management. Writing procedure includes what to do, who has to do, and when it has to do. It must be done in a scientific way based on professional knowledge and skill, and systematic collection and analysis of data. Cause and effect diagrams and Pareto

charts should be used for the purpose. It directs to prepare clearly defined job descriptions and provide materials and other required items to do the jobs properly. It also directs to entrust the staff with the responsibility for the quality of the work done.

6. Determine the structure of the quality manual. The structure of the quality be determined either by copying the structure of ISO 9001 or prepare a new one similar to ISO 9001.

The ISO 9000 has to be suitably modified while implementing to any organizations including library and information centers. The ISO 9004-2: 1992 guidelines[8], when applied to a library environment may contain the following clauses:

A. **Collection development practices** – Collection quantum, Acquisition policy, Acquisition procedure, Organization of collection, Strength and weaknesses in the collection, weeding out policy, etc.

B. **Circulation practices** – Timings, Reservation policy, Reference material policy, Fine policy, User friendliness of the library etc.

C. **Library services** – Value added services, Innovative services, Modification of existing services etc.

D. **Budget** – Budget strategy, Budget adequacy, Budget control, Information retrieval regarding budget matters, Budget accountability.

E. **Library administration and personnel matters** – Physical location, Space, Library automation, Communication with higher authorities, Staff training, Rewards, Job satisfaction, Work analysis, Library user manual, User feedback system, etc.

Implementation of quality concepts in libraries assists libraries' effort to meet the expectations of the customers. A good quality system ensures consistency of products and services and guarantees the utilization of same resources, equipments, methods and procedures every time in the same order. It ensures the following:

1. Define each activity
2. Set appropriate procedure
3. Document the procedure
4. Act as per the Document

The first major library known to have actually implemented the ISO 9000 standard on quality management is the library of the University of Central Lancashire[9]. In India, several libraries, especially special libraries, have obtained ISO certification as part of its parent organization.

References

1. Johannsen, Carl Gustav. Can the ISO standards on quality management be useful to libraries and how? IFLA Conference, Barcelona, 22-27 August 1993. p227-239.
2. Ibid.
3. FID. ISO 9000 for libraries and information centers: A guide. The Hague: FID, 1996.
4. Date, Danasree A and Gokhale, Pratibha A. Implementation of ISO 9000 in Industrial Libraries: A Case Study. *Library Science with a Slant to Documentation and Information Studies*. 36(2), 1999. pp65-72.
5. Jha, Kamal Narayan, et.al. Application of ISO 9000 for Library and Information Services. *Annals of Library Science and Documentation*. 44(3), 1997. pp81-85.
6. Ibid.
7. Johannsen, Carl Gustav. Op. Cit. p232.
8. Date, Danasree A and Gokhale, Pratibha A. Op. Cit. pp67-68.
9. Brophy, Peter, 'The quality programme of the library and learning resource centre at the University of Central Lancashire', ASLIB Information, 21, (6), 1993, p246-248).

6
Service Quality

Libraries and information centers are service organizations charged with the responsibility of providing various information and document services using a variety of resources like tangible assets such as the library building, furniture, equipments, information resources and staff and intangible services. These assets and services have to be evaluated in the light of changing faces of libraries and users. Today, the libraries are facing severe threats from the Internet, private lending libraries, commercial and non-commercial information products and services, escalating price of information resources, budget cut, competition from other libraries and information centers etc. Therefore the libraries have to adopt suitable strategies and techniques of the business and management and restructure everything in the most economical and attractive way. Adoption and strict application of quality in library and information products and services is a step towards this direction.

Libraries are now interested in and insisted for service quality because[1]:

1. Parent institution of libraries has made a commitment to be accountable for customers and compete for their loyalty.
2. Service quality is considered as a way to improve their ability to meet their mission of serving users.
3. An understanding of the benefits, the customers and the actions of the library is possible, which can be used for planning the improvement of services

4. It encourages the service improvement.
5. It establishes a closer personal contact between the library and the customer.
6. Staff gets more knowledge about user expectations, which can be used for satisfying the users.
7. Customers are better informed about libraries and their services.
8. It gives opportunities for improvement and raises the overall customer satisfaction with library services.
9. It enables the review of service goals and objectives in relation to customer expectation.

Service is intangible and a customer judges its quality only after its consumption. He/ she judges its quality by comparing his/her perceptions of what he/she received with his/her expectations of what they should receive. Both expectations and perceptions are experimental sensations and not real. Therefore service quality definitions are customer led. Services are more difficult to evaluate than goods. Due to impermanence of service the customer refer back to his/ her memory for future review of the experience. It is identified that both service personnel and customers have a direct role in the production and delivery process of a service. Services are consumed, as they are produced, with the customer playing an integral role in the process. In certain cases, the customer is required to contribute information or effort before the service is delivered.

Service quality is a measure of the extent to which the service delivered meets the customer's expectations. The principles underlying the concept of service quality are[2]:

1. Service quality is more difficult to measure than quality of a good;
2. Service quality is based on the customer's perception; and

3. Service quality is the difference between the outcome of the service and what the customer expected prior to the service.

Lewis[3] defined service quality as 'a measure of how well the service level delivered matches customer expectations. Delivering quality service means conforming to customers' expectations on a consistent basis'. According to Parasuraman et.al[4], service quality is 'the discrepancy between customers' expectations and perceptions'. But, attaining quality in services is very difficult due to the following reasons:

1. *Lack of visibility.* Problems of quality in services are not visible to its provider. Even if the customer understands it, it is reported that only 4% of them will complain to the provider about it. If the quality of the service is less than 25% of the quality expected normally he will not complain.
2. *Difficulties in assigning specific accountability.* The service delivery system greatly influences the customer's perception of service quality. But it is very difficult to account the exact position where a quality problem exists in the service delivery process.
3. *Long time requirement.* Once a problem is identified, it requires long period of time to resolve it, as it is more dependant on people than on machines or scientific procedures.
4. *Delivery un-certainty.* Persons are involved at both ends of the service delivery system. On one end the providers such as library professionals and on the other the customers. The service delivery is largely unpredictable due to the un-certainty of the nature of people involved in it, providers and customers.

However service quality is very important in service marketing as it affects both existing and potential customers.

Poor service reduces the potential customers. More and more people will hear about a poor customer service than a positive one. The positive service attracts more and more new customers to the service and so every service organization that markets their services is interested in positive service. Besides, the service organizations are interested to measure and understand the quality of the services offered to their customers. Since poor quality will adversely affect the organization itself, it is necessary to measure the service quality through the angle of the customers. Provision of good services will always continually satisfy the customers, inspire them to use the service again, and these satisfied customers will also refer the service to others. It helps the organization to retain existing customers and gain new customers through positive word of mouth,

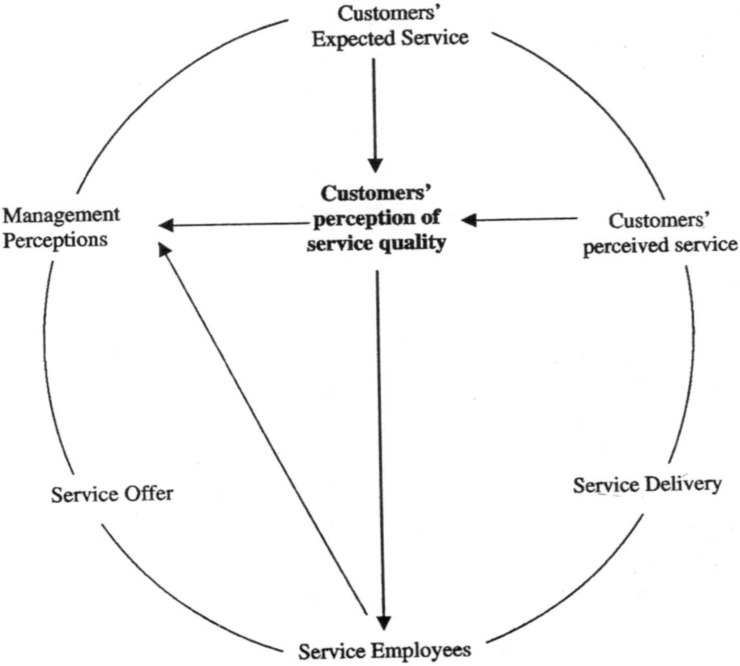

Figure 6.1. **The processes of Service Quality Development**

which increase the customer base of the organization. If the management perceives it well, decide the services to be offered, provide necessary training to the staff and deliver the appropriate services, then the customers' perception about the service will be good. This process is shown[5] in Figure 6.1. It is good to study the customer perceptions about the service, understand the reasons for low quality, if any and take corrective measures to improve the level of perception of customers.

Role of Customers in Deciding Service Quality

Customers are the end users of a product or service. They can very well measure the actual quality of a product or service from their experience. According to Parasuraman et. al.[6] the criteria that count in evaluating service quality are those defined by the customers. They have identified ten criteria that customers use to judge the quality of service that they receive. The first five are related to the quality of the final out come and remaining five are related to the quality of the process of service delivery. The ten criteria or dimensions of service quality are[7]:

1. *Reliability* indicates the ability of the service provider to perform the promised service dependably and accurately.
2. *Access* relates the accessibility and time of delivery of service.
3. *Security* indicates the freedom of service from danger, risk or doubt.
4. *Credibility* means trustworthiness and honesty possessed by the service provider.
5. *Understanding* the customer is related to the effort the service organization make to get to know its customers and understand their needs
6. *Responsiveness* means the willingness of the service

employees to help customers and deal with their specific problems

7. *Competence* indicates the extent of required skills and knowledge to perform the service the staff possesses.
8. *Courtesy* indicates the politeness and considerations given by staff to customers.
9. *Tangibles* mean the appearance of the physical facilities, equipments, personnel and communication materials used in service.
10. *Communication* indicates the effectiveness of communicating what is provided in the service and what roles are assigned to customers.

After further research on the topic, Parasuraman et al[8]. advocated that only 5 criteria are needed to customers to judge the quality of service they receive. The SERVQUAL instrument is based on these five criteria or dimensions. They are:

1. Tangibles
2. Reliability
3. Responsiveness
4. Assurance
5. Empathy

Here Assurance indicates the knowledge and courtesy of staff and their ability to inspire trust and confidence, that is, it is a combination of Competence, Courtesy, Credibility, and Security criteria mentioned above. At the same time, Empathy indicates caring, individualized attention the firm gives to the customer, which is a combination of Access, Communication and Understanding the customer.

Parasuraman et al.[9] identified that customers judge the quality of a service by comparing the service they actually receive with the quality criteria they have with what they expected to receive. Based on this understanding, they have defined service quality as the difference between customer's expectations and perceptions. If perceived quality exceeds expectations, the customers are satisfied and if performance falls below their expectations, they will be dissatisfied.

According to Gronroos[10] service quality comprises three dimensions, namely:

1. Technical quality of Outcome
2. Functional quality of Service, and
3. The Corporate Image.

Technical quality of outcome is the actual outcome of the service encounter. The customer can measure service outcome in an objective manner. The functional quality of service is concerned with the interaction between the service provider and the customer and it is often perceived in a subjective manner. It is highly related to the courtesy shown by the service provider to the customer. Corporate image is concerned with customers' perceptions of the service organization. It is related to the technical and functional quality, communication, location, appearance, competence and behaviour of employees.

Lehtinen and Lehtinen[11] had identified three dimensions to service quality. They are:

1. Physical Quality
2. Corporate Quality; and
3. Interactive Quality

Physical Quality is related to building, furniture, fittings, equipments used etc. Corporate quality is related to the overall image of the organization. Interactive quality is related to the interaction between the service providers and customers as well as the interaction between customers themselves.

There are seven[12] service quality attributes:

1. Security – Confidence as well as physical safety.

2. Consistency – Receiving the same each time.
3. Attribute – Politeness and social manners.
4. Completeness – Ancillary services available.
5. Condition – Of facilities (Clean, comfortable)
6. Availability – Access, Location, Frequency; and
7. Training – Propitious execution.

The attributes[13] of the service quality are:

1. Physical facilities and processes,
2. People's behaviour; and
3. Professional judgment.

According to Johnson et. al.[14] there are three common dimensions to service quality, namely:

1. Input Quality
2. Process Quality; and
3. Output Quality.

The input quality includes consideration of equipments and its working order, waiting areas and its furnishing, cleanliness and lighting, and service providers and their knowledge and skills. Process quality refers to the quality of the interaction between provider and consumer, i.e. how the service is produced. Service accessibility and availability and providers' courtesy, friendliness and willingness to answer questions are aspects of process quality. Output quality is a measure of what is produced as a result of providing the service. It includes intangible benefits as well as any tangible outputs of the service. A measure of overall service quality should include judgments of all dimensions of the service, i.e. inputs, processes and outputs.

It is admitted that dimensions / determinants / attributes of service quality may vary from person to person and from service to service. But the determinants identified by Parasuraman et al. are more prominent than to the others. According to Parasuraman service quality is the difference between the customers' expectations and perceptions.

Expectations are pre-trial beliefs about a product or service. It is defined variously as desires, what the customer hopes to receive and adequate service. Parasuraman et al[15] defined expectations as "desires or wants of the customer what the service provider should offer." The expectations are of three types[16]:

1. Customers' form expectations about what will happen in their next service encounter.
2. Customers' form expectations about what should happen, what they feel they disserve in their service encounter; and
3. Customers' ideal standard.

Any way, most of the customers enter in a service encounter with some form of expectations and these expectations have a significant bearing on perceived service quality. There are four key factors influence the service quality expectations of a customer. They are[17]:

1. Word of mouth communications
2. Personal needs and preferences
3. Past experiences; and
4. External communications.

Perceptions of service quality is defined as the discrepancy between what the customer feels a service provider should offer and his/ her perceptions of what the service firm actually offer. In effect, perceptions are reality as far as the customer and service quality is concerned. It is the mismatch between the customer expectations and the perceived service performance. If the performance does not match expectations, it is necessary to understand what influences expectations and perceptions of performance.

The expectations are influenced by the needs of customers, word-of-mouth communication, past experience and corporate image. It is shown[18] in the Figure 6.2.

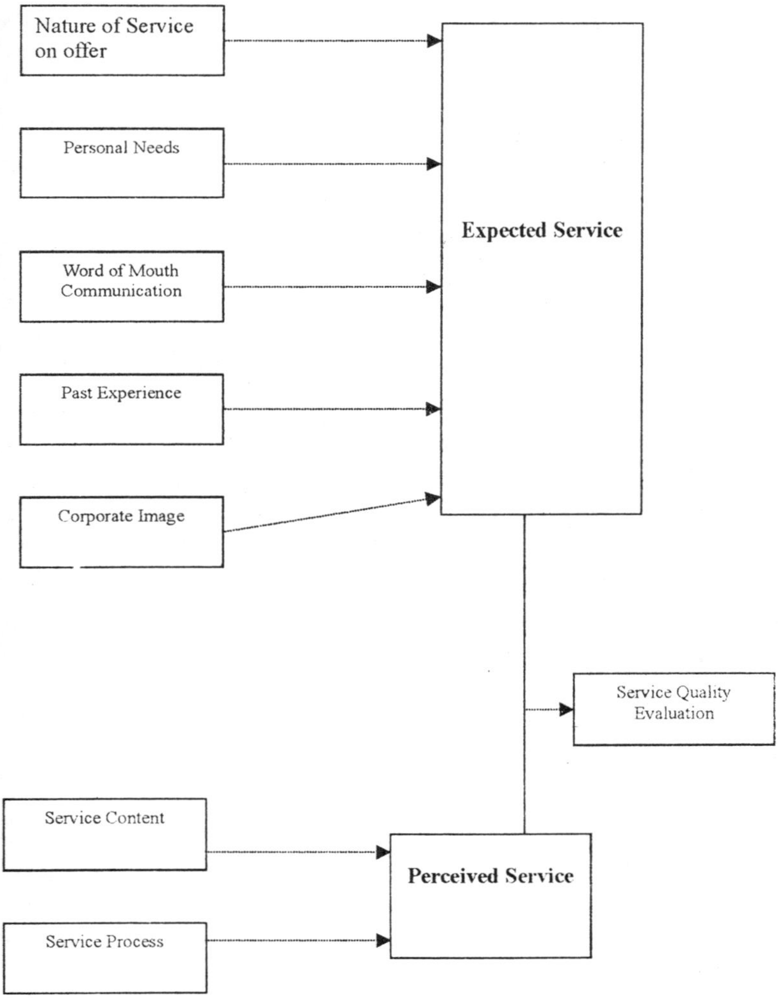

Figure 6.2. Components of Service Quality

At the same time, perceptions of performance are influenced by the content and the process of service availed. The Figure shows the perceptions of performance and its difference (gap) from expectations.

Customers' perception of service quality is influenced by service outcome and service process. It is the total of prior customer expectations, actual process quality and actual outcome quality. Actual quality is the real level of service quality provided. Perceived quality is the customers feel for the quality of the service. It determines the extent of customer's satisfaction and quality of the service. There may be 3 levels of perceived quality[19]:

1. Satisfactory quality
2. Ideal quality, and
3. Unacceptable quality.

Satisfactory quality is one when customer expectations are exactly met (customer expectations = customer perceptions). Ideal quality is that when perceived quality is higher than the customer expectations (customer perceptions > customer expectations). At the same time Unacceptable quality is one when perceived quality is very less than the customers expectations (customer perceptions < customer expectations).

The Figure 6.3 illustrates[20] how the customer expectations and perceptions of service quality are formed and get a final shape.

Gap model

A conceptual model of service quality was developed by Parasuraman et.al. It attempts to show the salient activities of the service organization that influence the perception of service quality. It shows the interaction between the activities and identifies the linkages between key activities that are pertinent to the delivery of a satisfactory level of service quality. These linkages are described as gaps. A gap represents a significant hurdle in achieving a satisfactory level of service quality. It identifies five potential gaps. The first four gaps are organization related and the fifth one is customer oriented and it is the sum of gaps 1 to 4. These are shown[21] in the Figure 6.4.

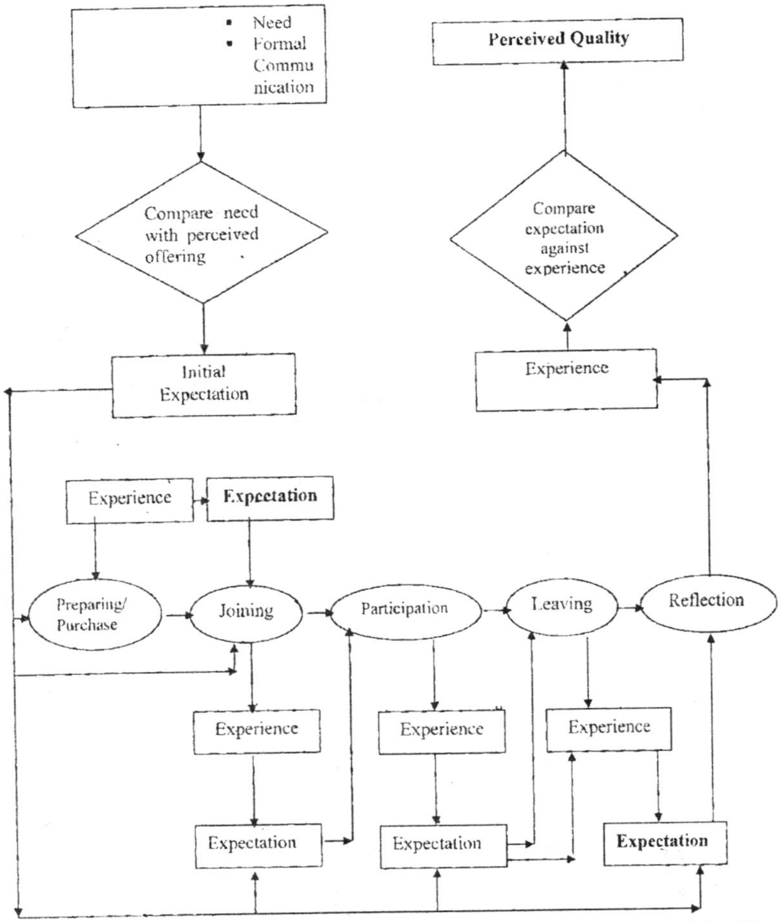

Figure 6.3. The development of expectation and perception of Quality

Gap 1 is the difference between what customers expected and what management perceived customers' expected. Management may provide service thinking that customers expect it when customers do not really expect it. The size of this gap can be reduced by identifying customer expectations either through communications with

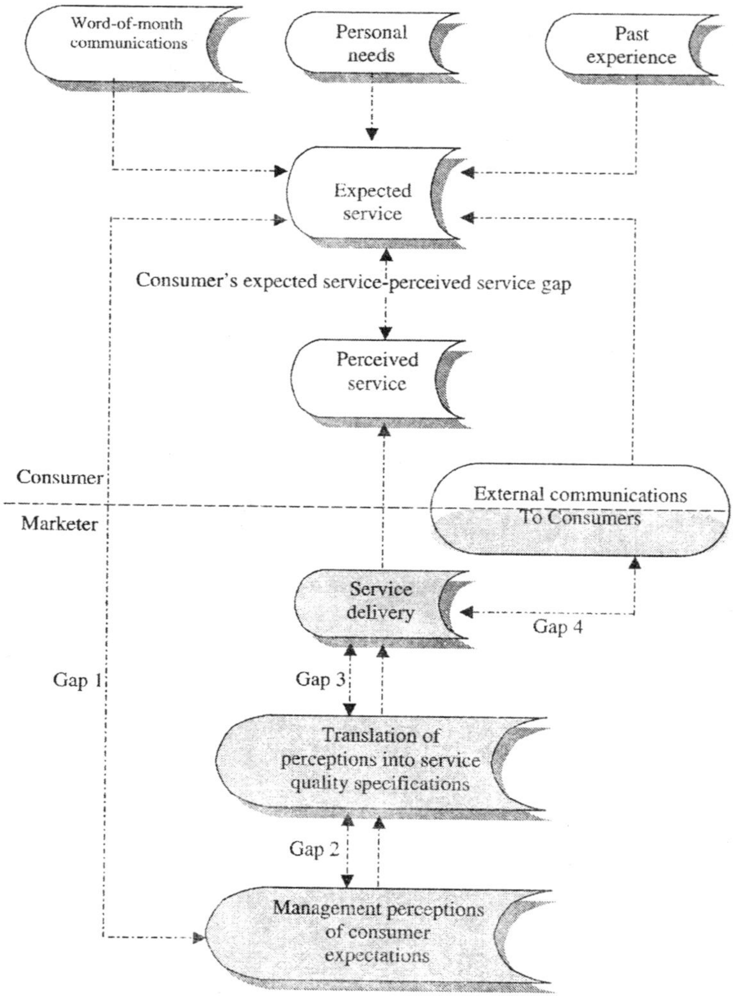

Figure 6.4. Diagrammatic Representation of Gap Model

customers, market research, and upward communications or by decreasing layers of management.

Gap 2 is the difference between management's perceptions of customer expectations and the translation of those perceptions in to service quality specifications. This gap arises when the management understands what customers actually expect but fail to translate the expectations in to correct service specifications. It may happen due to resource constraints, bad market conditions or management indifference. This gap can be reduced to the maximum by having top management commitment for providing high level of service quality developing customer oriented service quality goals for improving market conditions and standardizing tasks for improving work methods and providing a uniform delivery of service to the customers.

Gap 3 is the difference between the service quality specifications and the delivery of these specifications to the customers. It arises when employees do not provide the service as specified in the service quality specifications. It may happen when employees are unaware of the service quality specifications and do not have necessary skills to perform specifications properly. It also happens when employees are unwilling to perform according to service quality specifications. Such gaps can be avoided or reduced to the minimum by enhancing teamwork among employees, by ensuring fitness of employees and technology to jobs, and by developing a supervisory control system for ensuring their job performance.

Gap 4 is the difference between the service delivered and the external communications about the service. It arises when the organization fails to provide the service as they promised. It may happen when the employees lack information about the promise given to customers or when the organization intentionally gives over promise to customers. This can be avoided if the employees are informed well about the promises given to the customers. Giving promises in excess to the customers should also be avoided to reduce this gap.

Gap 5 is the difference between what customers receive

and what they expected. It is the sum of the gap 1 to 4 and it arises when any of the first four gaps exists.

There can be many reasons for the gap between customer expectations and perceptions. Some of them are the following[22]:

1. Service provider need to ensure that management appreciates exactly what service attributes are valued by their customers and in what order.
2. If the management fully knows the attributes valued by customers, but are willing, or unable to put resources to solve the problems.
3. If the quality standards are correctly set in accordance with customer expectations, but the attitude and manner of contact employees are not good.
4. When there is difference in the promise of organization about the services and the service delivered, it leads to a gap

Gap model enable the management to identify systematically all service quality shortfalls. It facilitates the identification of gaps between different aspects affecting service quality. It helps the management to identify the pertinent service quality matters from the perspective of customers. The SERVQUAL method of measuring service quality, developed by Parasuraman et.al is totally based on this gap theory.

References

1. Calvert,P. International variations in measuring customer expectations. *Library Trends*, 49(1), 2001.p732-757.
2. Parasuraman, A. et al. A conceptual model of service quality and its implications for future research. *Journal of Marketing*. 49, 1985. pp45-48.
3. Lewis, B.R, 'Service quality measurement', *Marketing Intelligence and Planning*, 11, (4), 1993, p4-12.
4. Parasuraman, A. et.al. 'SERVQUAL: a multiple item scale for

measuring consumer perceptions of service quality', *Journal of Retailing*, 64, (1), 1994, p12-40.

5. Randall, Lyn and Martin Senior. Training for service quality in the hospital industry. In Service Quality in Hospital Organizations. Ed by Richard Teare. New York: Academic Press, 1999. p174.
6. Parasuraman, et.al. A conceptual model of service quality and its implications for future research. *Journal of Marketing*, 49, Fall 1985, p41-50.
7. Parasuraman, A. et.al. (1994) Op.cit. p34
8. Ibid.
9. Ibid.
10. Gronroos, C. A service oriented approach to marketing of service. *European journal of Marketing*, 12 (8), 1978. p47-53.
11. Lehtinen, U and Lehtinen, J.R, 'Two approaches to service quality dimensions', *The service industry journal*, 11, 1991, p287-303.
12. Sasser, W.E et.al, Management of service operations. Boston MA: Allyn and Bacon, 1978. p52
13. Haywood-Farmer, J, 'A conceptual model of service quality', *International Journal of Operations and Production research*, 8, (6), 1988. p48.
14. Johnston, R et.al, 'Developing the determinants of service quality', In Langeard, E and Eiglier, P (Eds), Marketing operations and human resource insights in to services, Aix-en-provence: Institute d' Administration des Enterprises, 1990, p373-400.
15. Parasuraman, et.al. (1985 Op.cit. p48.
16. Boulding, W et al. A dynamic process model of service quality. *Journal of marketing research*. 30, 1993. pp 7-27.
17. Parasuraman, A et.al.(1985). Op.cit. p46.
18. Ibid.
19. Parasuraman, A et.al, (1994). Op. cit. p22
20. Parasuraman, A et.al. (1985). Op.cit. p48.
21. Ibid.
22. Ibid.

7
Library Evaluation and Performance Measurement

Library is a service organization, which requires constant transformation in order to exist in the fast changing world of today. The developments in publishing, research and development activities, education, information and communication technology, allied increasing number of users and their needs etc. have great impact on the management of libraries. Presently, the library professionals are very keen in assessing the library, its components, processes, services and their performance properly at regular intervals to make sure that the library meets its objective and satisfying their users with needed information in time.

The management of library and information services and their evaluation assume increasing importance throughout the world for various reasons. A profession's concern for the quality of its service constitutes the heart of its responsibility to the public. Improving service quality is paramount importance to all service firms. But, because of absence of proper research, no reliable and universal tool has yet been established for objective evaluation and measurement of library and information services and its quality.

Libraries assess their services with a vast amount of information collected on numerical data on expenditure, books added and journals subscribed, documents issued, referred and withdrawn etc. They assess their effectiveness to meet the document and information requirements of the users. They evaluate their operations and services and compare the results with stipulated standards to see whether their works and services are up-to a desired level. It was also made certain whether the users were satisfied with the library resources and services as a means for assessing the quality of library resources and services.

Libraries, even in the past, evaluated or measured the quality of their operations and services, in one-way or the other, based on quantitative data. But they did not measure the quality aspects like the role of friendliness of staff or attractiveness of building and furniture or cleanliness of library premises, or accessibility etc. in using the library effectively. Now librarians find themselves in a situation where they cannot just be satisfied with the traditional way of evaluating or measuring books and journals, its loan, use etc., but they also have to evaluate and assess their target users, their needs, interests and tastes, perception of service quality etc. Greater attention to evaluation, performance and measurement in libraries and information centers is needed today mainly because of growing demand for greater accountability in libraries. The other reasons[1] are:

1. To learn about customer perception. Customers are individuals who perceive services differently in the same situations. Identifying each customer's perceptions will help to improve the service quality. The perceptions may be related to:
   * What a customer looks for in a library?
   * Why a customer does visit a library?
   * What has caused a customer to change the library used last?
   * What might make customer change again in future?
   * What criteria are for acceptable service quality performance?

* What a customer must receive to be satisfied?
* What a library must do to make a customer extremely satisfied?
* What a library must do for a customer to continue as a regular user of the library?

2. To determine customer needs, requirements and expectations.
3. To close the gaps between customers and service providers. The gaps are based on the differences in perception between what the library believed it had provided and the customer's perception of what was received. The important gaps identified so far are:
   * Gap between what a library thinks a customer wants and what the customer actually wants.
   * Gap between what a library thinks a customer wants and what the customer perceives
   * Gap between the service quality the library believes it is providing and what the customer actually perceives.
   * Gap between customer's expectations of service quality and actual performance.
   * Gap between service premises and actual delivery of service.
4. To improve service quality and customer satisfaction. For that standards of performance, which will help to improve both quality and service, are set.
5. To improve performance and attract more customers.
6. To apply the process of continuous improvement. Otherwise the customers of one library will be the customers of another. Ask the customers, implement their suggestions, it improve service performance and retain the customers.

Therefore librarians are, willingly or unwillingly,

interested in evaluation or measurement of the library resources and services, tools and techniques, processes and machines, users and stakeholders, staff and management, and even the environment in which the library functions. According to Snoj and Petermanec[2], service minded librarians continuously ask themselves about the users of their services such as:

* Who they are?
* What they need?
* Why they need something?
* In what way they need it?
* Why they chose our service instead of others?
* What components of the service are important to them?
* How satisfied they are with these components?
* What is the value of components to them?
* Which factor influence their evaluation and choice of the service? etc.

It is reported that library quality measurement / evaluation is at present recognized as one of the important function of library management, as this will bring immense benefits[3] to the library:

1. It provides the organization immediate, meaningful and objective feedback.
2. It helps to understand how the organization is doing now.
3. It helps to compare with some standard of excellence or performance.
4. It helps to decide what the organization has to do to improve the service.
5. It helps the organization to have a sense of accomplishment or feeling of achievement

6. It can form the basis of a reward system based on performance of employees.
7. It provides a baseline standard of performance and a possible standard of excellence.
8. It motivates the employees to perform and achieve higher levels of service.

Evaluation of library effectiveness is concerned with the effect a library has on its users. A user is the judge, one who can assess the effectiveness of a library very well. Earlier, it was measured by assessing the value and usefulness of the collection to its users. Now it is recognized that the value of a library is dependent on a wide variety of factors. Evaluation or measurement of effectiveness must be undertaken from the point of view of those who receive the service. Some libraries evaluate their effectiveness based on standards for inputs; certain others approach it through internal processes without regard to the effects on customers. Some libraries measure their effectiveness according to the directions listed. Another way of measuring the library effectiveness is in accordance with professional standards and agreements. Libraries were also assessed considering their historical tradition. Lately systems approach and certain specialized management methods are used for assessing the library effectiveness. The libraries consider the effectiveness now very seriously due to the financial stringency and heavy competition from electronic networks, so the library and information management is ready to evaluate their resources and services and measure its performance regularly.

According to Abbot[4], it is necessary to distinguish between evaluation and performance measurement. Evaluation is the process through which the input, process, output, and their performance are assessed. On the other hand, performance measurement is the process of assessing the performance of the input, process, and output to see how far it meets the expectations of the management.

Though the performance indicators can be the basis of the process of evaluation, evaluation becomes a broader term to performance measurement. Lancaster[5] approaches library evaluation from the perspective of performance measurement and use a systematic approach for the purpose.

Library Evaluation

Every organization is aimed to attain its objectives efficiently, effectively, economically and timely. Evaluation is the process through which it is testified that whether the objectives are achieved and if so, to what extend. It also testifies whether the resources spent have properly resulted in the attainment of desired objectives. The changing needs of library management necessitate the library evaluation and enhanced possibilities of analysis. There is a culture of evaluation exists in libraries, but the methods of evaluation used are different. Evaluation of library and information services is an integral part of good library management. It is necessary to convince the funders and users that the service is delivering the expected benefits. It is an internal control mechanism to ensure that the resources are effectively and efficiently used.

Evaluation is basically a judgment of worth, assessing the value of the organization to the people for whom it is meant. It assesses the performance against users expectations, or it is the testing of an organization or system for effectiveness and efficiency. Lancaster[6] suggested three levels of library evaluation, namely measurement of effectiveness, cost-effectiveness and cost-benefit. Similarly Vickery and Vickery[7] have suggested the evaluation of effectiveness of economic efficiency and value of a system and Moore[8] evaluate the library in three levels, namely efficiency, performance and effectiveness.

According to Alemna[9], library evaluation methods may

be either subjective or objective. Subjective method is based on user opinions or attitudes. Questionnaire or interview method is used here to collect user opinions to measure the effectiveness of a library. It is assumed that user evaluations are the valid indicators of library performance.

The objective method of evaluation requires:

1. Specification of the purpose of the system,
2. Selection of a measure reflecting this purpose and specification of the units of measure, and
3. Construction of measuring instruments and the implementation of a measuring method.

The evaluation of a library will show how far the library objectives are met through the physical facilities, collection, information and services offered to the users. Evaluation or measurement of library effectiveness is a complex issue, as there are no universally accepted measures, measuring units or methods for this study. There is little agreement about what is to be measured. It is necessary to find out things, processes and phenomena that are measurable and where the measures would be valid indicators of effectiveness and benefits.

The rationales[10] for evaluating the performance of a library and information center are:

1. Collect information to facilitate decision-making and justify increasing expenditure or defend existing expenditure.
2. Assess and improve the quality of service provided
3. Identify the extent to which problems can be solved.
4. Identify differing or contradictory needs of different user groups
5. Plan public relations work and information dissemination

6. Provide feedback to service managers for correction and improvement.
7. Involve users in management through their voices in evaluation
8. Provide the basis of further improvements
9. Close the gap between the library and user through giving the results to them.

The major steps[11] involved in the process of library evaluation are:

1. Decide whether the evaluation is necessary or not
2. Decide the source of data for evaluation
3. Decide the performance issue to be evaluated
4. Decide the method to be used
5. Conduct the evaluation
6. Communicate the results to the higher authorities, staff and users.

The factors to be taken into consideration while evaluating the performance of a library are[12]:

1. Library input

The level of library input in the form of physical facilities, services, resources and staff can be taken as a measure of performance. The effectiveness of a library is directly proportional to the resources and services utilized. Library standards and statistics can be used to indicate the effectiveness and efficiency of the library.

2. Relationship between library goals and the tasks of employees.

Efficient use of library personnel resources will result in maximizing of library performance.

3. Library's interaction with users.

The user study can be taken as a measure for evaluating what is and what is not done for the user.

4. **Impact of total population on the outcomes of library service.**

The measure of the library and its environment will show the effectiveness of the library.

As the library performance can be evaluated in terms of its effectiveness and efficiency as well as the goodness of the library against the resources required, the criteria for library evaluation may include[13]:

1. **Effectiveness** - how well the service satisfies the demand of users?
2. **Efficiency** - how far cost is minimized in attaining the objectives.
3. **Cost** - cost of input used to provide a service.
4. **Cost-effectiveness** - how efficiently the library satisfies its objectives in terms of cost.
5. **Benefit** - how much benefits are derived to users, parent body and others from using the library.
6. **Time saved** - how much time of a user is saved by a library service.
7. **Satisfaction** - what is the attitude and behaviour of users against the library resources, services, staff and facilities
8. **Cost-benefit** - how far the worth of a library service is justified in terms of the cost.

Library evaluation faces certain problems, mainly due to the inherent features of the service organizations. It is generally believed that library services cannot be measured precisely due to many reasons. Services with a major qualitative component are very difficult to evaluate. The volume of activity in a service has to be related to the demand for it to understand its performance and the service must be appropriate to the need of the user. The other reasons[14] include:

1. Lack of generally acceptable definition of performance evaluation and criteria of evaluation.
2. The effects of library services are indirect and subjective, as users are the sole judge of its utility and effectiveness.
3. It is very difficult to develop a reliable, objective and empirical tool for measuring the performance.
4. There are problems in translating the desired goals to utilities and actions, which may hinder the evaluation process greatly.

It is good to start the library evaluation with mission statements, user committee reports, library committee reports, institutional direction, program of research etc. Besides, standard guidelines for library evaluation can also be used for conducting the evaluation.

Performance measurement

Performance measures are defined as 'a quantitative statement of the actual performance achieved'. It should include adequate means of specifying its range and limits. This is done partly by defining effectiveness criteria, but it also relates to an understanding of the underlying aim and objectives of the process or activity in question.

Performance measurement is a key management activity used to understand the effectiveness of a library or a service offered by the library. As services are intangible and depends on an act that is often variable, lacks consistency and depends on the interaction between client and the provider, it is very difficult to measure accurately. Measuring performance of a library is more complex as library services can be delivered in person or through electronic means.

According to Brophy and Coulling[15] performance measurement should satisfy: Relevance; Helpfulness; Validity; Reliability; Practicability; Comparability;

Affordability; and Sensitivity. It should include measures of inputs, outputs, and service effectiveness.

The major inputs in a library are human resource and financial resource. Library users evaluate the worth of human resource and financial resource in libraries. The over all performance of a library depends up on the effective coordination of these components. Therefore, cost measurement can be treated as a performance measure of libraries. For example, the input measures may include:

1. How much the library cost to acquire and process a document
2. How much it cost to catalogue a document
3. How much it cost per loan

Similarly, the outputs of a library may be of two types namely, intermediate output and final output. The intermediate outputs are the services offered in the library, like loan service, xerox service, reference service, etc. The final output is the impact of services offered on individual user and the parent body. Performance measures are normally derived from the intermediate outputs in libraries. The output measures may include:

1. Library membership/ visits per capita
2. Circulation per capita
3. Stock turn over rate.

The evaluation experts[16] view that performance measurement of libraries is the measurement of three Es, Economy, Efficiency and Effectiveness. Economy in acquisition of resources is a professional skill and its measurement is very important as library acquire, process, organize and make available information sources and the means of accessing them to users. Efficiency in the use of resources is related to the cost of providing various services. Based on the measurement outputs, it is possible to derive quantitative standards or norms for measuring efficiency of a library service. Effectiveness in the achievement of objectives is a good measure of library performance, as it will show the value of a service in terms of money. The document delivery capability of a library is treated as a measure of library effectiveness, which is related to the measure of availability and fill rate. It is necessary to value a service in terms of money, as information has value, documents are costly and heavy investment is required for making the necessary physical and reading facilities in the library. So the money income of a service can be taken as a measure of performance.

In order to develop performance measures for each operation in the library, a relationship between service goals and objectives and users' needs, and perceptions is necessary. As user needs and requirements are related to library quality, the users' can assess the performance of library services and its quality. So, it is treated as one of the key principles of service quality management. Continuous performance measurement of a process will help in developing performance standards. The performance standards will make the performance measurement easy and reliable.

The major performance indicators of the functions of a library are[17]:

Acquisition – Efficiency, Effectiveness, Cost productivity

Classification – Accuracy, Time factor, Co-extensiveness, cost

Cataloguing – Efficiency, Time Effectiveness, cost effectiveness, productivity

Technical processing – Efficiency, Effectiveness, cost, productivity

Collection development – Economy, effectiveness

Collection maintenance – Efficiency, Effectiveness, cost, productivity

User education – Market penetration, Effectiveness, cost, productivity

Information service – efficiency, effectiveness, cost

The performance measurement can be either quantitative, qualitative or both in terms of user satisfaction. The qualitative performance measurement is based on users' expectations and what is most important to them. Performance measure as part of Quality Improvement Program (QIP)[18] necessitates data collection to identify the performance measure for the process. Therefore, a data collection system is to be developed. The qualitative measures include, case studies, content analysis, focus groups etc. The case study is the in-depth exploration of selected service areas and target audience in the organization. The findings can be used in the quantitative data collection activities. The content analysis will enable the organization to gather documentation and reports to review the historical development and evolution of network related activities. Similarly, the focus groups will help to explore key issues like information content, service, management and performance. Once the data is collected, it has to be analyzed with statistical quality control techniques like Pareto analysis, Control charts, Cause and Effect diagram etc. It will help to identify the problem and its causes. Then it is easy to identify measures to solve the problems.

The quantitative measures include: mail or electronic surveys, traffic measures, web-log file analysis, and individual interviews. The mail or electronic user surveys will help to explore identified key issues of information content, services, management and performance with a large user base. The traffic measures are used to collect network or terminal traffic use statistics like, number of users, user access points, information and service content use, network server, etc. Web-log file analysis is used to measure web-based services. The user interviews are conducted to explore the content, services, management and performance with the users to assess the development of print and network environment. These qualitative and quantitative measures can be used to produce necessary performance indicators.

Developing measures for the libraries in an electronic environment are much more difficult than traditional libraries. For example, in a traditional library, the details of the user population and the document collection are easily available from the users register and the library catalogue, bibliographies or indexes. Such measures are not available in electronic libraries. Therefore, electronic libraries require alternative measures[19] like:

1. Technical infrastructure, which includes the hardware, software, equipment, communication lines, technical aspects like workstations, modems, servers, etc.
2. Information content that represent the resources available on the network
3. Information services, which includes all tools and services that the user can access on the system
4. Support services that include the assistance and help provided to the users like, training, guidance, help desks, etc.
5. Management of the network, which includes the human resource, planning and finance.

Similarly separate criteria are required to measure the performance of web-based library and information services and its use[20]:

1. Extensiveness, which represents the number of services offered in the network

2. Efficiency, indicating the use of resources and its access
3. Effectiveness, which represent the ability of the service to meet the objectives of the providers and the users
4. Impact, made in some part of the organizations activities or researchers
5. Usefulness of the service to the user
6. Adoption of the networked resources and services into individual activities of the organization or user

There are 15 measures[21] possible in library environments :

* General user satisfaction
* Number of items issued
* Number of items used inside the library
* Total material use
* Materials availability
* Requested material availability
* Attendance/visits
* Remote users
* Total uses
* Facilities use rate
* Service point use
* Building use
* Reference transactions
* Reference Satisfaction
* Online Search Satisfaction

The experts have grouped these measures into four sets[22]:

1. Library use measures like library visits, number of registered members, number related to total users.
2. Materials use measures like average number of circulation in relation to per-capita of the population

served, in-house use of materials, average number of circulations per volumes etc.

3. Material access measures concerned with how successful users are in finding the materials they want. It may include title approach rate, author/subject approach rate, browsing approach rate, document delivery rate etc.
4. Reference services measures–measuring the number of reference transactions per capita of the user population and a reference completion rate.

The Office of Arts and Libraries (1990)[23] has suggested 21 performance measures and 16 performance indicators to assess the performance of public libraries. They are grouped into 4 categories:

1. Service input cost measures
   * Amount of resources applied to each service
   * Amount of funding applied to each service
   * Attributes of the service which affect the cost
2. Service output measures
   * Quantitative of outputs for each service
   * Quality of outputs for each service
   * Timeliness of outputs for each service
   * Availability of service
   * Accessibility of service
3. Service effectiveness measures
   * Amount of use
   * Users perception of attributes
   * User expressed satisfaction
   * User indicated importance
   * Purpose of use
   * Consequences of use

4. Service domain measures
   * Total population size
   * Total population attributes
   * User population size
   * User population attributes
   * Size of geographic area
   * Geographic area attributes
   * Information needs

The performance indicators listed by the Office of Arts and Libraries, 1990 are[24]:

1. Operational Performance Indicators
   * Productivity
   * Cost per output
   * Cost by attributes level
   * Productivity by attribute level
2. Effectiveness indicators
   * Turnover rate
   * Amount of Use by attribute level
   * User satisfaction
   * User satisfaction by attribute level
   * Amount of use by satisfaction level
3. Cost effectiveness indicators
   * Cost per use
   * Cost per user
   * Cost per capita
   * Cost by satisfaction level
4. Impact indicators
   * Users as a proposal of the population
   * User per capita
   * Needs fill rate

IFLA and ISO[25] have also developed a standard set of performance indicators for libraries. They are:

1. Relevance in collection development
2. Degree of satisfaction of users
3. Hours of openings
4. Average delay between ordering and its availability on shelves
5. Percentage of requested items actually obtained by users.

United Kingdom, Standing Conference of National and University Libraries (SCONUL)[26] set out a five-fold approach to assess a library. These are:

1. Integration of the library to its parent body's objectives
2. User satisfaction
3. Effectiveness
4. Efficiency
5. Economy

These measures and indicators of performance would provide a comprehensive picture of the performance of a library. But, it is to be noted that performance measurement is often assumed that the libraries should use the same set of indicators for the comparison with other libraries.

In libraries, performance measures and metrics will be useful as an evaluative and analytical procedure to determine how well the library performs in a given situation and to identify major sources of weakness, failure and inefficiency. It is getting important consideration in the libraries in changing environments. It is due to the fact that libraries are suffering from sharp cuts in budgets and are being required to demonstrate that they offer value for money. Several studies were conducted on performance measurement for many years. The Public Libraries Research Group (PLRG)[27] in Great Britain had brought out many publications on this aspect. The American Library Association[28] had put forward a public library standard for performance measurement. It suggested that the right thing for libraries to do was to set their own objectives, in order to derive local standards of provision of service, and measure the performance based on the objectives. The Association of Research Libraries, USA[29] had also published a manual of measurement for academic libraries. All these indicate that performance measurement is a live topic in library and information science literature, and sufficient models and indicators of performance measurement are available for use.

However, it is significant to mention the innate problems for measuring the performance of the libraries[30]:

1. *Availability.* It is the percentage of items sought by users, which are available in the library when requested. It is reported that opinions of users are same in every year even if corrective measures are taken to improve the condition. So it is assumed that measuring availability of documents requested is not precise enough to detect small changes in collection and performance.
2. *Fill rate.* It is the proportion of items requested which are supplied within a given time period. It is related to availability.
3. *Service delay.* It is the length of time between a demand being made and a demand being satisfied. This cannot be measured precisely as there are many reasons in delaying a service delivery.
4. *Timeliness.* It is the proportion of items, which are delivered in time to be of use to the requester. It is reported that except on urgent cases and in the case of researchers, timeliness in the provision of a service is not a matter to users and so it does not affect the performance measurement strongly.

References

1. Snoj, Boris and Petermanec, Zdenka. Let users judge the quality of library services. New Library World. 102(1168), 2001. p314-324.
2. Ibid.
3. Rowley, Jennifer. Customer Experience of Libraries. Library Review. 43(6), 1994. p7-17.
4. Abbott, C. Performance measurement in library and information centers. London: Aslib, 1994. p2, 9
5. Lancaster, F.W. If you want to evaluate your library? 2nd Ed. London: Library Association, 1993. p6.
6. Lancaster, F.W. The measurement and evaluation of library services. Arlington: Information Resources Press, 1977. p4.
7. Vickery, B and Vickery, A. Information Science in Theory and Practice. London: Butterworth, 1987. p262.
8. Moore, N. Measuring the performance of Public Libraries. *IFLA Journal*, 15(1), 1989. p17.
9. Alemna, A.A. Library evaluation: Some options for academic libraries. *Aslib Proceedings*, 51(7), 1999. p244
10. Crawford, John. Evaluation of Library and Information Services. London: Aslib, 2000. p10-11.
11. Crawford, John. Op. Cit. p17.
12. Alemna, A.A. Op. Cit. p245.
13. Alemna, A.A. Op. Cit. p246.
14. Alemna, A.A. Op. Cit. p247.
15. Brophy, Peter and Coulling, Kate. Quality Management for Information and Library Managers. Aldershot: Aslib Gower, 1996. p146.
16. Public Libraries Research Group. Public Library aims and objectives. *Library Association Record*, 73(12), 1971. p233-234.
17. Meera, B.M. Performance measurement: a criterion for quality improvement in library and information services. *Library Science with a slant to Documentation and Information Studies*, 35(3), 1998. p153-156.
18. Meera, B.M. Op. Cit. p152.
19. Bertot, J.C, *et al.* Developing national library network statistics and performance measures for U.S. public libraries. *Performance measurement and Metrics : International Journal for Library and Information Services.* 1(1), 2000. p15-42.

20. Ibid.

21. Van House, N.A et.al. Output measures for public libraries. London: ALA, 1987.

22. Ibid.

23. Office of Arts and Libraries. Key to success: performance indicators for public libraries. London: HMSO, 1990.

24. Ibid.

25. Poll, R. Quality and performance measurement. *British Journal of Academic Librarianship*, 8(1), 1993. p35-47.

26. Winkworth, I and Rear, J. Draft proposals based on evidence to a subcommittee of the Higher Education Funding Council's libraries review. London: SCONUL, 1993. p25.

27. Public Libraries Research Group. Public Library aims and objectives. *Library Association Record*, 73(12), 1971. p233-234.

28. Palmour, V.E. A planning process for Public Libraries Chicago: ALA, 1980. p8.

29. Ford, Geoffrey. A perspective on performance measurement. *International Journal of Information and Library Research*, 1(1), 1989. p14-15.

30. Snoj, Boris and Petermanec, Zdenka. Op. Cit. P 320.

8
Methods for Collection of Data

There are several methods of collection of data for measuring the performance and quality of libraries. These methods can broadly be grouped in to two, namely Quantitative methods and Qualitative methods. The Quantitative methods include verification of library records, questionnaire and interview methods and qualitative methods comprise of focus groups, observation, and case study methods. But the latest trend is using of both the methods for qualitative study of libraries and information centers. According to Crawford[1] the qualitative methods of collection of data have certain special features:

1. It works well with small samples
2. It is appropriate for analyzing problems in depth
3. It is useful for tackling complex and poorly understood problems
4. The participant is an actor in the events being studied.
5. It is much looser compared to quantitative methods. It does not produce the tidy array of statistics compared to the other.
6. It allows users to participate in library management and gives a feeling that they are making direct contribution to policy formation.
7. It is less labour-intensive and time consuming.
8. Certain methods require special skills to operate the method.

Library evaluation and performance measurement is the need of the day. Therefore libraries and information centers have o collect required data regularly, process and use it for the betterment of library resources and services.

Verification of Library Records

Research data needed for studying a library can be collected from the library itself. The data inscribed in various records, files and registers of the library are good sources of library data. Researchers heavily use these records available in the library for various purposes. Verification of these sources provides the correct data relating to the organization, management, collection and services of the library.

User request file provide data relating to types of the documents needed, but not available in the library. This data can be used to assess the considerations given to the user's requests by verifying whether these books are procured later. Documents order file can be used to collect data for studying the types of the documents ordered – subject wise, language wise and physical nature wise, the performances of various suppliers, and the time taken for receiving a document ordered. The accession register can be used for studying the collection development of the library, strength and weakness of the collection developed in different subject areas, etc.

The circulation data can be used to study the use of various types of documents, category of users who use the loan service better etc. Similarly, the reservation register can be used to ascertain the types of documents in heavy demand, the membership records will contain necessary data related to the class of user, age, subject back ground, economic status, gender, level of knowledge and understanding, field of interest, needs and requirements etc. The visitors register is a good source for collecting data on the number and class of users visiting the library at different times, time spent in the library, frequency of visit, purpose of visit of the user etc. The user complaint register is an important source of information about problems faced by the users in using the library resources and services. It will also give data related to the staff performance. The financial records will give data on the budget, the source of income, the allocation of fund to various projects and programmes, its utilization, etc.

Verification of these records is treated as one of the common method of collection of data. These data can be used to cross check the data collected through questionnaire or interview method. In certain situations, this becomes the sole source of information for the researcher.

Questionnaire Method

Questionnaire is the most popular method of collecting data for an evaluation and assessment. It can be used to a whole range of issues from a sample overview survey to a detailed survey of a specific issue. The structure and method of administration of questionnaire may vary from survey to survey depending on the user group surveyed. The questionnaire method has got certain advantages[2]:

1. The views of many thousands of people can be collected.
2. It adopts a highly structured approach
3. It gives clear-cut answers to the questions asked
4. It is good for asking questions on counts
5. If limited number of answer options is given, the data can be analyzed easily and quickly.

However, this method has certain disadvantages too. They are:

1. As it is highly structured, it is highly inflexible.
2. Mistakes in questionnaire found during administration cannot be corrected easily.

3. It does not penetrate the attitudes, which inform the answers.
4. It answers only the questions, which have been asked.
5. If it does not address important issues related to the problem, then its quality will be low.
6. If all issues related to the problem are not included, it may lead to misleading results.

While designing a questionnaire, it is good to use standardized methodologies, as it will allow to benefit from the experience of others and to compare the results with similar libraries. The questionnaire should be short for larger user surveys where as a longer questionnaire can be administered to a small population with a high level of commitment to the library. It should be designed in a user-friendly manner from general to specific. The questionnaire may be either closed (pre-coded) or open (free response) questions. In closed questions, the questions follow choice of answers that can be ticked or circled. It is much easier to analyze these answers.

Following points require special attention while designing a questionnaire[3]:

1. Don't ask questions unless there is a need to know the answer.
2. Ask only questions which can be answered.
3. Ask only questions which can be truthfully answered
4. Ask only questions which the user is prepared to answer.
5. Ask only for information that is unavailable through other means.
6. Ask precise questions instead of general questions
7. Avoid double questions
8. Use simple jargon-free language
9. Avoid gift questions

The questionnaire should contain both open and close ended questions. The open-ended questions will help to assess the problems hindering their satisfaction. It should be designed in a user-friendly manner and should help to collect needed information about the users satisfaction on the services offered. It will help to produce a considerable amount of data that are of potential value in the evaluation of library services. It will indicate how far the users are satisfied with the services provided and not. But, the main problem with the questionnaire method is that most of the users dislike questionnaires and they fill it incomplete or carelessly.

If the user population to be surveyed is very large, it is good to go for sampling. The sample must be a certain minimum size, which should be accurate and representative. The bigger the sample, the longer the analysis, and higher the administrative cost.

There are chances of misinterpreting the questions by users. Therefore, before administering a questionnaire, it is advisable to conduct a pilot study, which will help to eliminate errors. It is not advisable to administer questionnaire among minors, instead interview method can be used for collecting data from them. It is not good to administer questionnaire at different times. Timing of the administration of the questionnaire is very important, otherwise respondents may not be available or not in a condition to answer the questions and the data obtained may also vary.

A questionnaire can be administered either directly or indirectly. In direct method, the researcher can go to the users and circulate the questionnaire. In indirect method, the questionnaire is administered through post. It is also possible now to administer the questionnaires electronically through Internet. As specimen, two questionnaires used to assess the quality of the resources and services available in a public library[4] and an academic library (web-based questionnaire)[5] are given at the end of this chapter.

Interview Method

Interview is a universal method of obtaining information from respondents in a direct manner. It is the verbal questioning of respondents for collecting data. It is a two-person conversation, initiated by the interviewer for the specific purpose of obtaining research relevant information and focused by the research objectives of description and explanation. It is a structured activity to probe in detail into the experiences and reactions of respondents. It is a good method for exploring sensitive and confidential issues. It is a skilled activity as it is the interaction between the staff/interviewer and user. It can be recorded either in paper or in audio-video tapes.

An interview may be structured, unstructured or semi-structured. A structured interview is based on a list of questions prepared. There is no such base of pre-prepared questions in unstructured interviews. However, sufficient skill is required to conduct unstructured interviews. A semi-structured interview is the one, which bases on a pre-prepared list of questions, but allows the users to express their views freely.

In in-depth interview, the users are interviewed in person or by telephone. Former is very effective than later. It requires much time for one-to-one encounter. The presence of the interviewer tends to ensure that the user correctly interprets all questions. The interviewer can also check the accuracy of the information or response given by the user. There is a chance for collecting unanticipated information from the users. It will allow the user to express the responses in his/her own words and language. The responses will be more complete and revealing than the questionnaire method.

The interview must be conducted in a relaxed and informal manner. The interviewer should prepare well for conducting the interview, other wise the interviewer may fail to get the needed data from the user interviewed. The interviewer should list out the questions to be asked and as and when needed, it can be modified according to the need of the situation. It is utmost necessary to record the interview in some ways, personal or audio or video recording. A well-planned and structured interview will give good results. It will also give insightful observations and opinions regarding the related matters of the problem in question.

Busha[6] highlighted the factors to be taken into consideration for conducting a user interview successfully:

1. Thoroughly prepare for the interview in advance. Know the purpose of the interview well and frame good questions suitable for getting required data from the users.
2. Conduct the interview in a friendly and relaxed manner. Keep the user ease throughout the interview.
3. Make the users understand that their views and opinions are significantly important for the study.
4. Assure the users that their opinions will be kept secret and used only for the purpose of the study.
5. Ask the questions clearly and concisely and one question at a time. Give the user sufficient time to answer it clearly.
6. Don't put words in to the users' mouth or add words while the user is answering to a question.
7. Don't react on the users' reply to questions and show a mark of approval or disapproval, surprise or shock etc.
8. Don't try to dispute with the user or cross their views.
9. Record the data correctly and neutrally so that the data will be objective and accurate.

10. Express gratitude to the user for his/her co-operation and assistance in getting correct views on the topic.

In interview method, compared to questionnaire method, the data collected will be more reliable, dependable and valid. It is superior to questionnaire method, as the verbal communications will elicit significantly more complete answers to questions than through the questionnaire. It depends upon the respondent's ability to answer the questions correctly and honestly. The interviewer must have the personal qualities like, honesty, interest, accuracy, adaptability, temperament, intelligence, education and other subjective and objective characters. However it is a time consuming and expensive process. Hence interview method is not suitable for collecting data from large number of users.

This method requires a neutral interviewer. The interviewer must be professional in the field of study. A tape recorder is useful to collect the data. It requires a great deal of time and emotional energy on the side of the interviewer to collect required data.

Interview method can be used in libraries to collect data from stakeholders, users and staff about their experiences, opinions and attitudes, reactions to changes, knowledge, satisfaction, expectations, etc regarding the library facilities, information resources, services and such other matters.

Focus Group

Focus Group is a research method used to collect useful data about a problem. It is founded on the premise that people interacting with each other, as a group, will contribute more useful information than personal interviews with them. The significance of this method of collecting research data are[7]:

1. Members of a group will be encouraged to express

more of their thoughts on a particular problem by the views and feelings expressed by others in the group.

2. The overall dynamics of the group will reveal how peer pressure contributes towards the adoption of a product or concept
3. People feel more comfortable to discuss a topic when they are involved in a group discussion on it.

Focus group method is treated as a superior method of appraising the marketability of new products and services. This method comprises the following requirements[8]:

1. Decide the objectives of the focus groups
2. Formulate a discussion schedule
3. Select the moderator who will lead the discussions
4. Form focus groups comprising eight to ten members. Give adequate representation to the customer groups to be covered
5. Decide the venue, where the discussion is to be held
6. Supply necessary stationeries, refreshments, honorarium, etc in time.
7. Start discussions with a welcome to participants, introduction of moderator, and objectives of the discussion. Lead the discussion from the general aspect to the specific problem in question.
8. Sum up the discussion
9. Record the discussion properly (audio or video recording)

The results of the discussion can be obtained in the form of moderator's report. The quality and reliability of the focus group depends upon the quality of the moderator and the participants in the focus group.

In this method, a group of 8 to 12 persons are formed and discuss a particular topic under the direction of a moderator. The discussion will start on the broad area of research and gradually narrow down it to the focus of the research. The researcher will select the participants of the focus group based on the topic of research.

It will help to elicit data and insights through a group interaction process. But it may not accurately reflect the attitudes of an entire population. The participants may not be a real representative sample. The success of the method depends upon the questioning skill of the moderator. It is an expensive method as moderator and participants are to be paid well.

The role of facilitator is very crucial, as he/she must encourage positive discussions without imposing control on the group. After an introductory discussion, the participants, in small groups, identify and prioritize key themes. Then all the groups come together and discuss their points with other groups. Thus agreement is reached on each point and a record is kept on the discussion for further verification. Focus groups as method of collection of data have several advantages[9]:

1. Participants use their own words to express their perceptions.
2. Facilitators ask questions to clarify comments.
3. It requires less time compared to questionnaire survey
4. It offer unexpected insights and more complete information
5. The respondents comment on the views of others
6. Design of a focus group discussion is flexible and can clear up confusions easily
7. It is a good way to collect preliminary information
8. It detects ideas, which can be fed into questionnaire design.

However, while organizing focus groups in libraries, Crawford[10] stressed the necessity of considering certain special points:

1. Use facilitators from outside the library
2. Select facilitators with expert skills
3. Recruit volunteers who are ready to participate in the discussion seriously
4. Include all aspects of population
5. Limit the participants 8 to 12.
6. Allow enough time for discussion
7. Develop a discussion guide based on the objective of the study
8. Use three to four groups for best results
9. Hold discussions in a convenient place
10. Reward participants appropriately
11. Trends or repeated comments have to be analyzed or summarized
12. Don't over generalize the results or use it for policy discussions.

This method can be used to discover why people do not use library services offered. It can reveal distinct gaps between the perceptions of library staff and the users. But, they are not very competent for discussing technical issues as they lack expertise in technical matters.

Observation

Observation is the direct surveillance and recording of dimensions of a phenomenon that is to be measured or evaluated. It is the close perception of a phenomenon, which facilitates a detailed and exact explanation of how the phenomenon behaves under known conditions.

Gardner and Elliot[11] define observation as 'selection, provocation, recording, and encoding of that set of behaviors and settings which are consistent with empirical aims'. It is a technique in which the investigator observes what the customers or user actually do in the library. It allows the investigator to observe the users in their natural setting, and get correct data. It is a systematic process of acquiring knowledge using sense organs. It is the process of recording non-verbal as well as verbal behaviour and communication. It is one of the most widely used method of survey research for direct surveillance and recording of a phenomenon that is to be evaluated. The close perception of subjects, objects and processes facilitates a detailed and exact explanation of how they behave under known conditions.

Observation involves sensation, attention and perception and employs vision as its main means of data collection. According to Krishan Kumar[12], observation is the most appropriate method only when other methods of data collection are found non-appropriate for data collection. It helps to get needed data directly. It will also give valid conclusions to the phenomenon observed.

The direct observation and recording of the phenomenon can be used to understand the situations, processes, developments, events or its related phenomenon very clearly. As events occurs in natural settings, the observer can record it properly, so the value of the data collected is very much reliable than to the one collected through questionnaire and interview.Observation can also be used to check the validity and reliability of data collected through questionnaire and interview. It is a good method for studying present conditions, existing practices, procedures, activities, processes, etc in libraries. It will help to collect data on the actions of staff, and how the phenomenon occurs in certain particular environments.

There are two types of observations:

1. Structured observation
2. Unstructured observation.

Structured observation is a pre-determined activity, in which a form is used to record whether the specific activity takes place, and if it takes place, when and how? It involves definition of categories under which information is to be recorded. It is used to provide systematic description or to test causal hypothesis. Generally it is considered as a quantitative method of data collection. On the other hand, in unstructured observation, the observer records any behaviour or action or event, which is relevant in the study. It is an open-ended approach, which is relatively flexible and heavily used in exploratory and qualitative research.

As observation is a skilled exercise, the observer must know much about the situation to understand and interpret what is going on. If the users understand that they are observed, they may change their behaviour. Not only that, whenever something relevant for the study is observed, the observer has to record it with its relevance, reliability and validity. If the observer is also participate in the event, he/ she can understand and observe the event very well.

In un-obstructive Observation, factual questions are asked to users and required information/ answers are collected. Once the staff is informed about the observation of a library service for evaluation, the library staff at service points does their duty better on the feeling that they are also going to be evaluated. This method will acknowledge the existence of service problems and so measures to improve the services can be easily derived.

There are six dimensions that can be observed[13]:

1. Physical actions
2. Verbal behaviour
3. Expressive behaviour
4. Spatial relations
5. Amount of time spent in performing jobs
6. Verbal records

Krishan Kumar[14] identified seven steps in observation.

They are:

1. Identification of the subjects to be observed
2. Definition of the activities to be observed
3. Time schedule for observation
4. Selection of instruments and form of recording to be used
5. Physical location of the observer
6. Special condition required for the subjects, and
7. Designing of forms for recording.

The major criticism against observation is that it is biased to the investigator. So the investigator has to conduct observation and recording objectively.

The observation of library facilities, processes, services, etc. offers excellent opportunities for the librarian to acquire correct and adequate data. It can also be used to see whether opinions or complaints of users regarding a library program are genuine or not.

Walk Through Audit

Walk-through audit is a method of collecting data and assessing the customer satisfaction in a service organization. It is a technique having potential application in library and information centers. It is a good technique to collect the experience of users in using a particular product or service offered in a library. The idea here is to identify the typical visit of a user and all that it entails first, followed by a similar visit by the librarian or other library staff to go through that experience stage by stage and understand and record all events taken place during the visit. It will enable the librarian to identify the easiness, problems, difficulties, etc in getting and using the product or service offered in the library. Such internal audits can be undertaken by the librarian or other responsible staff to understand what will be the experience of the users of a particular service. It can begin even from the entry to the library premises and progressing to the library tools, library facilities, library resources and services, and its use. This method is found very effective when other methods of data collection fail to collect needed research data on user's satisfaction. It also enables the librarian to get accidental information about the service, which may not be generally noticed by an ordinary user.

Mystery Shopping

Mystery shopping is an important method of collecting data about the satisfaction of customers on a product or service and very much used in marketing research. In this method, the researcher pretends to be the customer of the product or service and acts in exactly the same way how the customer approaches the product or service. As a customer, the experienced researcher can easily note down the problems, difficulties and other hindering factors that influence the marketing of the product or service in question.

Since libraries and information centers deal with users/customers, it can collect the users' experience with the library, its facilities, collection, services, tools and techniques, staff etc by conducting a 'mystery library shopping' in the library. It will enable the library researcher to understand the actual experience of the library users. It can also be used to measure the correctness of data given by the user.

Diary Method

Diary method of data collection is generally used in marketing and social research, in which the people to be surveyed is given with a diary to record their experiences, problems and opinions regarding the use of a specific product or service. In libraries and information centers, diary method can be used to collect data from library users with regard to their method of approach, search method, use of library catalogue, OPAC, Books and periodicals, services etc.

It is considered as one of the major methods for identifying the user problems relating to library tools and techniques, information sources and services. It is an important method of collecting data, which is difficult to collect by other means.

The major problems[15] of using the diary method as method of collection of data are:

1. Completing a diary is a tedious work. So all users may not interest in writing diaries. Therefore, the users who are ready to cooperate with the study are to be identified first.
2. Keeping diary for longer period may lead to heavy dropouts of users, and in completion rates. To be useful, the diary has to be kept for shorter period.
3. The data obtained will be highly varied and specific.
4. It is very difficult to identify performance issues from the detailed observations of the users.
5. There are chances for getting incorrect data. The users who are aware about the research study may write false details regarding a process, product or service.
6. It is treated as less casual and unstructured activity. There is no pre-determined structure for recording the data, which leads to difficulty in analysis.

In libraries and information centers, diary method can be used to understand the information seeking behaviour of library users. It can also be used to monitor library use, activities performed, areas visited and satisfaction levels, time spent for reading or browsing, actions taken after a book or reference had been found in the library etc. For example, Goodall[16] had conducted a diary research in the centre for research in library and information management at the University of Central Lancashire in 1994.

The major merits[17] of this method are:

1. It provide very specific data and is very close to the point of action

2. It is good at getting at users intensions and comparing them with the information outcomes
3. It helps to collect a lot of data over a relatively short period of time.

However, the diary method has certain problems too. They are:

1. There is a problem of authenticity and bias
2. There is a doubt about their accuracy and completeness
3. There is difficulty to obtain a representative sample
4. There is a big drop-out rate
5. Analysis of data is difficult and time-consuming, when an un-structured diary form is used.

Suggestion Boxes

Suggestion box is an important method for collecting user responses about the library and information processes, tools, collection, services, facilities, staff etc. The suggestions of users can be collected through registers, boxes or even through computer terminals. In the case of registers, the users write their problems, suggestions and opinions in the register, which will be verified regularly. In suggestion boxes, users write their suggestions in papers and insert in the box. The box will be periodically checked for collecting the suggestions. The computer terminals provided to the users can contain suggestion box, in which the user can input their suggestion, which in turn comes to the librarian's terminal.

The suggestion book or box must be prominently displayed and adequately communicated to the users. Similarly, the suggestion box should be visible separately on the computer screen. The users can put questions, which will be answered by the library staff regularly.

Case Study Method

Case study is a method of collecting extensive data about a problem or process showing all the relationships with the variables associated with the problem or process studied. It concentrates on a single phenomenon and aims to obtain comprehensive information about the phenomenon. It uses observation method of data collection. It can be supplemented with questionnaire and interview method of data collection.

The library itself or its components like staff, users, programmes, resources and processes can be taken for the case study. This method allows close examination of the phenomenon and collects detailed description about it. It can also be conducted to discover and describe what exists in the library. It is reported that case study is a time consuming and expensive process, and a single study does not give definitive results.

Busha[18] listed the steps to be followed while conducting case studies in a library:

1. Identify the object to be studied.
2. Describe the object to be studied in detail giving all information about the object.
3. Define and describe the relevant terms and variables to be studied (by analyzing the data about the object and the investigative task)
4. Formulate the research question to be studied
5. Choose an entity as the specific object to be studied with reference to the research question
6. Observe the object carefully and identify the causal factors associated with the observed phenomenon.
7. Analyze the data and test the research question
8. Conduct follow-up case study in the same problem area to support the research findings.

Methods of collection of data enable the libraries and information centers to collect necessary quantitative and qualitative data for understanding and assessing the performance and quality of the library and information works and services carried out, which can be used to take correct decisions leading to its improvement.

References

1. Crawford, John. Evaluation of Library and Information Services. London: Aslib, 2000. p48-50.
2. Crawford, John. Op. Cit. p29-30
3. Crawford, John. Op. Cit. p32.
4. Spiller, D et.al. Libraries in the workplace. Loughborough: LISU, 1999.
5. http://www.libqual.org/
6. Busha, Charles H. Research Methods in Librarianship. New York: Academic Press, 1980. p77-79
7. Young, V. Focus and focus groups. *College and Research Libraries News*, 54(7), 1993. p391-394.
8. Ibid.
9. Ibid.
10. Crawford, John. Op. Cit. p52-54.
11. Gardner, Lindzey and Elliot, Aronson. Handbook of Social Psychology. Ed2. New Delhi: Amerind Publishing Co., 1975. Vol 2 p535-537.
12. Krishan Kumar. Research Methods in Library and Information Science. New Delhi: Har-Anand Publication, 1997. p114.
13. Busha, Charles H. Op. Cit. p147-151.
14. Krishan Kumar. Op. Cit. p96.
15. Nicholas, David. Assessing information needs. London: Aslib, 2000. p132.
16. Goodall, D. Use of diaries in library and information research. *Library and Information Research News*, 18(59), 1994. p17-21.
17. Crawford, John. Op. Cit. p60-62.
18. Busha, Charles H. Op. Cit. p151-154.

Appendix I

Public Library

National Standard User Survey

This survey is collecting information to measure the quality of library services. After you have used the library, *please will you complete this form and return it as you leave.*

1. Tick all those boxes, which show what you did during todays visit to this library

   * Borrow/return*book(s)* or renew
   * Borrow/return compact disc(s)
   * Read newspaper(s)/magazine(s)
   * Borrow/return cassette(s)
   * Borrow/return video(s)
   * Seek information/find something out
   * Use the photocopier
   * Sit to study or work
   * Browse
   * See exhibition or event
   * Something else ... Please say what ....

If you did not come to the library today to borrow a book please go straight to Q5.

2. How many books did you borrow from the library today? ....

3. If you were seeking a particular book(s) during today's visit, please write either the TITLE or AUTHOR of up to 3, and show if you were able to obtain them: (see examples below)

	Yes	No	No, but did Reserve a book
....	☐	☐	☐
....	☐	☐	☐
....	☐	☐	☐

Examples: TITLE: Gone with the Wind, SUBJECT: Gardening, AUTHOR: Dick Francis

4. *If you came* to the library today *without a particular book in mind,* did you find one to borrow?

Yes	No
☐	☐

5. *If you came* to the library *to seek information*

	Yes	Partially	No
	☐	☐	☐

i. did you get the information you needed?

ii. did you consult a member of staff?

6. *If you came for* a Cassette(s), CD(s), or Video(s), did you borrow any?

Only tick a box if you intended to borrow such an item.

	Yes	No	No, but did Reserve an item
Music cassette(s)	☐	☐	☐
Talking Book(s) incl. Language courses	☐	☐	☐
Compact disc(s)	☐	☐	☐
Video(s)	☐	☐	☐

Appendix II

Academic Library

LibUAL+TM Questionnaire

Please rate the following statements by selecting your choices from the pull-down menus to indicate:

When it comes to...		My Minimum Service Level is Low High	My Desired Service Level is Low High	**Perceived Service Performance is** Low High	**N/A**
1.	Willingness to help users	1 2 3 4 5 6 7 8 9	1 2 3 4 5 6 7 8 9	1 2 3 4 5 6 7 8 9	N/A
2.	Space that facilitates quiet study	1 2 3 4 5 6 7 8 9	1 2 3 4 5 6 7 8 9	1 2 3 4 5 6 7 8 9	N/A
3.	Complete runs of journal titles	1 2 3 4 5 6 7 8 9	1 2 3 4 5 6 7 8 9	1 2 3 4 5 6 7 8 9	N/A
4.	Employees who are consistently courteous	1 2 3 4 5 6 7 8 9	1 2 3 4 5 6 7 8 9	1 2 3 4 5 6 7 8 9	N/A
5.	Making electronic resources accessible from my home or office	1 2 3 4 5 6 7 8 9	1 2 3 4 5 6 7 8 9	1 2 3 4 5 6 7 8 9	N/A
6.	Modern equipment that lets me easily access the information I need	1 2 3 4 5 6 7 8 9	1 2 3 4 5 6 7 8 9	1 2 3 4 5 6 7 8 9	N/A
7.	A library website enabling me to locate information on my own	1 2 3 4 5 6 7 8 9	1 2 3 4 5 6 7 8 9	1 2 3 4 5 6 7 8 9	N/A
8.	Timely document delivery/inter library loan	1 2 3 4 5 6 7 8 9	1 2 3 4 5 6 7 8 9	1 2 3 4 5 6 7 8 9	N/A
9.	Interdisciplinary library needs being	1 2 3 4 5 6 7 8 9	1 2 3 4 5 6 7 8 9	1 2 3 4 5 6 7 8 9	N/A

	addressed				
10.	A haven for quiet and solitude	1 2 3 4 5 6 7 8 9	1 2 3 4 5 6 7 8 9	1 2 3 4 5 6 7 8 9	N/A
11.	Dependability in handling users' service problems	1 2 3 4 5 6 7 8 9	1 2 3 4 5 6 7 8 9	1 2 3 4 5 6 7 8 9	N/A
12.	Easy-to-use access tools that allow me to find things on my own	1 2 3 4 5 6 7 8 9	1 2 3 4 5 6 7 8 9	1 2 3 4 5 6 7 8 9	N/A
13.	A place for reflection and creativity	1 2 3 4 5 6 7 8 9	1 2 3 4 5 6 7 8 9	1 2 3 4 5 6 7 8 9	N/A
14.	Giving users individual attention	1 2 3 4 5 6 7 8 9	1 2 3 4 5 6 7 8 9	1 2 3 4 5 6 7 8 9	N/A
15.	Employees who deal with users in a caring fashion	1 2 3 4 5 6 7 8 9	1 2 3 4 5 6 7 8 9	1 2 3 4 5 6 7 8 9	N/A
16.	Making information easily accessible for independent use	1 2 3 4 5 6 7 8 9	1 2 3 4 5 6 7 8 9	1 2 3 4 5 6 7 8 9	N/A
17.	Employees who have the knowledge to answer user questions	1 2 3 4 5 6 7 8 9	1 2 3 4 5 6 7 8 9	1 2 3 4 5 6 7 8 9	N/A
18.	Readiness to respond to users questions	1 2 3 4 5 6 7 8 9	1 2 3 4 5 6 7 8 9	1 2 3 4 5 6 7 8 9	N/A
19.	Convenient business hours	1 2 3 4 5 6 7 8 9	1 2 3 4 5 6 7 8 9	1 2 3 4 5 6 7 8 9	N/A
20.	Employees who	1 2 3 4 5 6 7 8 9	1 2 3 4 5 6 7 8 9	1 2 3 4 5 6 7 8 9	N/A

	instill confidence in users				
21.	A comfortable and inviting location	1 2 3 4 5 6 7 8 9	1 2 3 4 5 6 7 8 9	1 2 3 4 5 6 7 8 9	N/A
22.	Comprehensive print collections	1 2 3 4 5 6 7 8 9	1 2 3 4 5 6 7 8 9	1 2 3 4 5 6 7 8 9	N/A
23.	A contemplative environment	1 2 3 4 5 6 7 8 9	1 2 3 4 5 6 7 8 9	1 2 3 4 5 6 7 8 9	N/A
24.	Employees who understand the needs of their users	1 2 3 4 5 6 7 8 9	1 2 3 4 5 6 7 8 9	1 2 3 4 5 6 7 8 9	N/A
25.	Convenient access to library collection	1 2 3 4 5 6 7 8 9	1 2 3 4 5 6 7 8 9	1 2 3 4 5 6 7 8 9	N/A

Please indicate the degree to which you agree with the following statements:		
1.	In general, I am satisfied with the way in which I am treated at the libraries	1 2 3 4 5 6 7 8 9 Strongly Disagree Strongly Agree
2.	In general, I am satisfied with library support for my learning, research and/or teaching needs.	1 2 3 4 5 6 7 8 9 Strongly Disagree Strongly Agree
3.	How would you rate the overall quality of the service provided by the library?	1 2 3 4 5 6 7 8 9 Extremely Poor Extremely Good

* **Minimum** – the number that represents the *minimum* level of service that you would find acceptable.

* **Desired** – the number tat represents the level of service that *you personally want.*

* **Perceived** – the number that represents the level of service that you believe our library currently provides.

You must EITHER rate all three columns OR identify the item as N/A

Please indicate your library usage patterns:

How often do you use resources on library premises?

* Daily
* Weekly
* Monthly
* Quarterly
* Never

How often do you use electronic library services remotely?

* Daily
* Weekly
* Monthly
* Quarterly
* Never

Please enter any comments about library services below.

9
Methods for Analysis of Data

The quantitative and qualitative data collected through employing suitable methods of data collection has to be analyzed properly using appropriate methods of analysis. There are several methods for analyzing the data, significant among them are:

* Mathematical ratios like Recall ratio, Precision ratio, Scattering ratio, Exhaustivity ratio, etc.
* Statistical methods like Frequency distribution, Measures of Central Tendencies, Measures of Dispersions, Cause and Effect analysis methods like Correlation, Regression, etc. Histograms, Scatter diagrams, Fishbone diagrams, etc.
* Statistical Process Control methods like, Control charts, Pareto charts, etc.
* System methods like, System analysis, Time and Motion study, Flow charting, etc.
* Specialized management techniques like Benchmarking, SERVQUAL, SERVPERF, PCP model, WebQUAL, LibQUAL etc.

Mathematical Ratios

Numerical data collected can be mathematically analyzed to get needed results. All arithmetical operations like addition, subtraction, multiplication, division etc can be used for analysis. The mathematical ratios are generally used for assessing an indexing or information storage and retrieval system in the library. It can also be used to assess the document retrieval process in libraries. These ratios are Recall ratio, Precision ratio, Scattering ratio, and Exhaustivity ratio[1].

Recall Ratio

It is a method used to measure the efficiency of indexing systems. It can also be used to evaluate the quality of library services. Recall ratio is the ratio between the number of relevant documents retrieved and the total number of relevant documents available in the library collection. It is calculated by a simple formula.

$$\frac{A \times 100}{(A+B)}$$

Where $A =$ Number of relevant documents retrieved, and

$B =$ Number of relevant documents not retrieved

For example, there are 60 relevant documents needed for a user, of which the library is able to retrieve on demand 15 documents, then the recall ratio will be

$$\frac{15 \times 100}{(15+45)} = \frac{1500}{60} = 25\%$$

Which indicates that the quality of the document retrieval service is very poor. The ideal quality service expects 100% retrieval. This method can be heavily used in the assessment of the quality of electronic, digital, and online information retrieval services offered in modern libraries today.

Precision Ratio

It is another method used to measure the efficiency of indexing systems, which can also be used for measuring the quality of information services. The precision ratio measures the precision in the retrieval of documents relevant to the needs of the users. This ratio can be calculated with the help of the following formula.

$$\frac{A \times 100}{(A+C)}$$

Where A = Number of relevant documents retrieved

C = Number of non-relevant documents retrieved.

For example, there are 60 relevant documents of a user, of which the library is able to retrieve 15 documents, then the precision ratio will be:

$$\frac{15 \times 100}{(15+45)} = \frac{1500}{60} = 25\%$$

Which indicates low precision quality. If the precision quality of the service is very good, then the ratio should be 100%.

Scattering Ratio

This is used to understand the scattering of documents in subjects/ topics, which may affect the quality of document-based services in libraries. The scattering ratio can be found out with the following formula.

$$\frac{S \times 100}{(A+S)}$$

Where S = Number of documents in a subject

A = Number of the subject documents scattered in other subjects.

For example, if there are 20 documents in one topic, of which 16 are classed in the mother subject and the rest in other subjects, then the scattering ratio will be:

$$\frac{4 \times 100}{(16+4)} = \frac{400}{20} = 20\%$$

It indicates that 20% of the documents in the topic will not be available to the majority of the users, leading to low quality of document and information retrieval service. The ideal ratio should be zero.

Exhaustivity Ratio

Libraries are not able to develop exhaustive collections even in specific subjects and topics due to many reasons. The quality of the document and information service is based on the exhaustiveness of the collection available in the library. The capability of a library to meet the user requirements can be assessed with the help of the following formula.

$$\frac{B \times 100}{A}$$

Where B = Total number of documents supplied to the user

A = Total number of document demanded by the user

For example, if the library has a user demand for 200 documents in a time period and if the library is able to supply 180 documents to the users during this period, then the capability ratio of the library will be:

$$\frac{180 \times 100}{200} = \frac{18000}{200} = 90\%$$

Which indicates that the library is capable of meeting 90% of the document requirements of users, showing a good condition of the library. The document and information resources are very large due to the access to databases, other libraries and information networks, and online information resources and services.

Statistical Methods

The statistical methods are useful for the library and

information professionals to analyze and present the library statistical data, the facts and figures relating to the information sources, users, acquisition, technical processing, services provided, works done by the staff etc. in a library or information center. The statistical methods enable the librarians[2] to:

1. Present facts in a definite form
2. Simplify unwieldy and complex data
3. Help in classification of data
4. Facilitate comparison
5. Helps to study relationships and associations between different phenomenon
6. Enlarge individual experiences
7. Helps to formulate plans
8. Test hypothesis
9. Interpret the data

The data collected has to be classified and tabulated first for analysis. The classification of data is necessary to condense and simplify the data to make it ready for tabulation. There are four types of classification possible, namely numerical, chronological, geographical and qualitative. The classified data can be recorded in a table showing the frequency distribution of the data, which shows distinct values of the variable with their corresponding frequencies side by side.

Once the classification of data is over, these data can be tabulated easily. Tabulation is the process of recording the classified data in tables. A table is a systematic arrangement of statistical data in columns and rows. It is a good medium of communication with great economy in space and clear presentation, and easy analysis.

The tabulated data can be presented in the form of tables, graphs, and diagrams. The graphs and diagrams will give bird's eye view and impressing view of the data, make the complex data simple and easily understandable, makes the comparison of data very simple and facilitate selection of suitable statistical measures for analysis. There are mainly four types of diagrams, namely, 1. One-dimensional diagrams like bar diagrams, 2. Two-dimensional diagrams like rectangles and squares, 3. Three-dimensional diagrams like cubes and cylinders, and 4. Pictograms and cartograms.

According to Sardhana[3], the statistical tools, techniques and methods that can be used for the analysis of data to assess the quality of library services are:

1. Frequency distribution
2. Graphical presentation
3. Measures of Central tendency like Mean, Median, and Mode
4. Measures of Deviation like Standard Deviation
5. Sampling methods and techniques
6. Probability distributions like Binomial, Poisson, Normal distributions etc
7. Tests of significance
8. Cause and Effect analysis like Correlation, Regression, etc.

The data may be analyzed and measured according to its central tendency, dispersion, correlation, regression etc. The measure of central tendency or average is the most representative figure in a group of data. It is the single value that describes the salient features of a mass of complex data. It facilitates comparison, traces mathematical relationships, helps in decision-making, and assist to know the universe of data. The measures of central tendencies include mean, median and mode.

The measure of dispersion is the measurement of the variation or dispersion of data around the average figure derived. It is the technique used to study the variability of data from its average, which in turn may help to control unnecessary variation. It can be used to judge the reliability of the measures of central tendency derived. It can also be used to facilitate the use of other statistical measures. There are two types of measure of dispersion, one to measure distance and the other to measure the average deviation from the measure of central tendency. It includes range, quartile deviation, mean deviation, and standard deviation.

Correlation analysis is the analysis made to discover the relationships between different sets of data. It measures the direction as well as the degree of relationship existing between two variables. The relation identified can be verified and tested to measure the significance of the correlation. The degree of correlation is measured by the coefficient of correlation. The coefficient of correlation is the ratio to which the changes in one variable are accompanied by the changes in related variable. The correlation may be either negative or positive, simple or multiple, linear or non-linear, and partial or total. Regression analysis is the analysis made to identify the extend to which one variable varies in response to a given change in the related variable. It reveals the nature of relationship between the two variables and determines the average probable change in one variable when there is a known change in the other.

Histograms

Histogram is a vertical bar graph displaying numerical information about the frequency of distribution of continuous data. It is a direct way of showing frequencies of occurrences. It is very useful for determining the distribution of the data.

For preparing a histogram, data related to the problem is collected through check sheets. Then create a range for the data by taking least and most figure into consideration.

Then decide the intervals needed in the data. Mark the data collected in these intervals. After that, mark the data on the Y-axis, and draw the histogram. Calculate mean or median or mode and add this to the histogram. If most of the bars are in center of the graph, there is a small variation in quality, if the bars are spread out along the x axis, there is a large variation, if most of the bars are left sided, there is a positive skew to the diagram, if the bars are right sided, there is a negative skew to the diagram and if there is a peak in the histogram, there is great variation and it must be investigated immediately.

Histogram can be used to represent various data related to the library operations and services, users' satisfaction, etc. in more informative and comparative manner. It helps the librarian to present the data in an easily understandable and attractive manner, which will enable the library management what the data says about the problem in question. As the histogram helps to draw frequency curves correctly, it will help the librarian to decide data model (normal and non-normal) for selecting suitable methods for further analysis of the data.

Scatter Diagrams

Scatter Diagrams are used to study the potential relationship between two variables. It is related to the correlation and regression statistical analysis. It is a useful tool to establish a possible relationship between two variables. Once a relationship between two variables is identified, the scatter diagram can be used to see areas for control. If a relationship exists, there will be a change in one variable as soon as there is a change in the other variable.

For creating such a diagram, decide the variable to be marked on x-axis and y-axis. Then collect data and plot each data point. View the diagram and see how the points cluster or scatter in the graph. A positive relationship occurs when y increases as x increases. A negative relationship occurs when x decreases as y increases. A non-relationship occurs when dots are scattered all over the graph. An understanding of the type of relation is necessary for the selection of adequate tools for further analysis.

Libraries can use it to test the relationship between two variables that are found correlated. For example, working hours and number of users visited the library or documents issued can be studied using scatter diagrams.

Fishbone Diagram /Cause and Effect Diagram / Ishikawa Diagram

Fishbone Diagram is another problem solving technique used to separate causes from effects. It is very important in quality management as a great deal of effort can be used to correct the effects by removing its causes. It is a line graph, which contains data points over a specified period of time. A straight line indicating the average data can be included in the graph, which will help to understand the strength or the cause for poor performance.

In this technique, the problem identified is written on the right-hand side of the diagram. Major causes are at the end of each branch and the individual causes are written as sub-branches. Standard set of headings like people, place, price, promotion, product or methods, machines, material, maintenance, manpower is used to indicate major causes. Cause and Effective Diagram takes a final effect and tries to determine causes by breaking them into various categories such as manpower, machines, materials and methods or processes. Each of these categories is placed on a spine so that the entire diagram looks like the skeleton of a fish, so it is also called fishbone diagram. Each of the major cause may have so many minor causes, which can also be marked on the diagram. This diagram will help to understand the major area, which causes for the poor service delivered.

Figure 9.1 illustrates[4] the problems in using a library effectively.

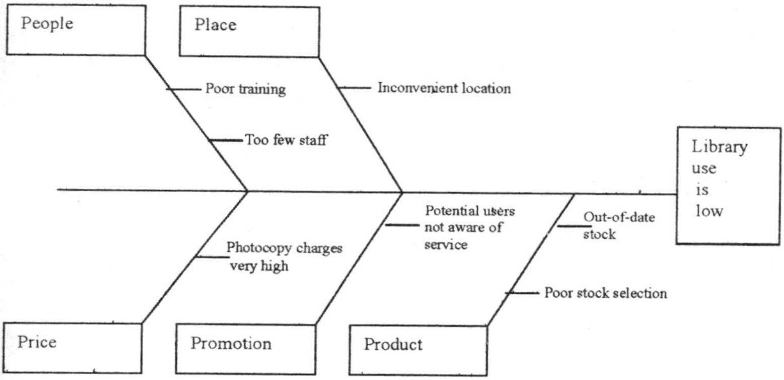

Figure 9.1. Fish-bone Diagram showing the problems in using a Library

The above figure shows that there are certain reasons for the low use of information resources and services in a library. These reasons are related to the people, place, price, promotion, and products in the library. Inadequate number of staff and their un-trained condition is identified as the people oriented reasons for the low use of a library. Similarly, inconvenient location (related to place), very high charges of photocopies (related to price), lack of knowledge about services (related to promotion), and poor document selection method and old stock (related to product) are the other reasons for the non-use or low use of a library. So, the reasons and its effect on the library work, service or the attainment of objective can be properly represented with the help of these fishbone diagrams.

Statistical Process Control Methods

There are some statistical devices used for particular purposes, called Statistical Process Control Device. It is a group of statistical techniques, which can be applied to processes in order to monitor variability and to get information on which to base quality improvement activities. It can be applied to any process, including service processes. It measures common and special variability and the aim is to eliminate special variability, which arises from specific events. The management is responsible for special variability. The techniques include Control charts, and Pareto diagram.

Control Charts

Control Chart is a quality control tool aimed to study the behaviour of variations on important quality characteristics and help to reduce the variation for process improvements. It is a powerful tool for identifying when and where problems, due to special variability, are occurring and thereby enable the management to concentrate on it very seriously. The data, averages, ranges, standard deviations, etc. obtained by testing a product or service for its quality characteristics can be examined by viewing a graph (control chart) of the measurements in the order in which the units were measured.

Control chart is a useful tool for studying variations. The control limits shown in the chart enable the researcher to determine whether a process can be considered stable and predictable or unstable and unpredictable. Such information about an important quality characteristic enables one to continue the control in stable cases and gain control in unstable cases.

A control chart is a graphic representation of the variation in the computed statistics being produced by the process. It has an added advantage over to the frequency distribution method of presentation of data. It shows how the variation of a particular set of data, representing process characteristics was produced. Compared to histogram, the control charts show the control limits. It shows the amount and nature of variation by time, indicates statistical control or lack of it, and enables pattern interpretations and detection of changes in the process under study.

The control charts do not require statistical calculation and so, it can be applied quickly by the responsible staff to track the processes. As the chart contains upper control limit, lower control limit and the average control limit, the data marked on the chart, shows whether it is within or beyond the control limit, which helps the management to take correct decisions.

In libraries, it will help the librarian to identify whether the process is in control or not. It can be used to measure the processing and service delivery time used. For example, the library can use a control chart to reveal the unexpected variations in the processing and delivery of the document newly acquired in the library.

Pareto Charts

Pareto Chart is a vertical bar graph used to organize data to help focus action on the primary causes of the problems. It is a tool for data summary and evaluation for assisting the identification of the principal causes of problems. It helps the management to identify problems in quality and customer dissatisfaction by the frequency of their occurrence. It is based on data collected through check sheet, frequency distribution or observation.

To construct a chart, first identify the problems to be studied and then decide unit of measurement. After that collect data over a specific period, and then draw the results on a graph in priority order with the most frequent one first. It will show how a small percent of activities causes a large percentage of quality problems.

Pareto Analysis, developed by Vilfredo Pareto, shows that 20 percent of service is used by 80 percent of its customers and 80 percent of the services are used by 20 percent of the customers. This principle can be represented graphically by plotting the activity or service along the horizontal axis. It can help to identify where action might best be concentrated.

In libraries, it helps the librarian to identify the causes for a defect in the library process affecting the quality library services. In addition to that, it enable the librarian to find out the most important causes for the defect. The major causes for the defect can be further studied with the help of control charts and see whether the cause and defect is in control or not. For example, the library can use it to identify the peak hours of working, most useful documents, most needed processes, and facilities, most important users etc. Figure 9.2 shows[5] the reasons for the non-availability of documents in a library. Histograms of problem areas can be used to identify the key areas for attention.

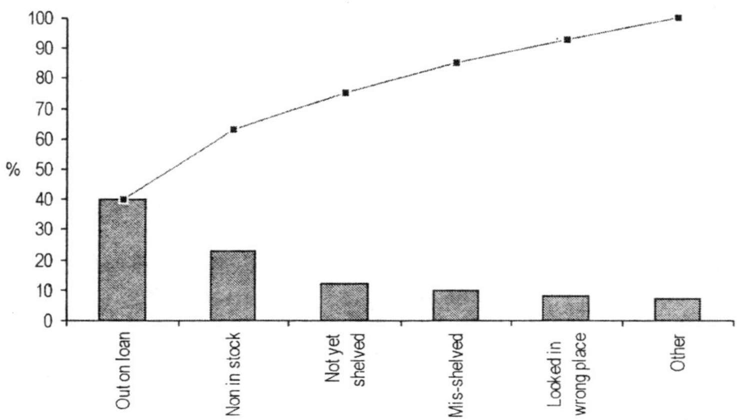

Figure 9.2. The non-availability of documents in Libraries

It is found that the reasons for the non-availability of documents from a library are: out on loan, non-availability in the stock, non-timely re-shelving, mis-shelving, search in wrong places, etc. Among these, 'out on loan' becomes the major reason for the non-availability of documents to the users. It indicates that the problem of non-availability of documents in a library is mainly due to loan service, and the non-availability in the stock, which can be reduced to the maximum by having sufficient number of copies of documents or reducing the loan period and acquiring new documents needed to the users. The histogram given shows the major reasons for the non-availability of documents to the users.

System Methods

System is an organized relationship among functioning units or components. It is designed to achieve one or more objectives. Every organization is a system consisting of interrelated departments (subsystems) such as production, sales, personnel, and an information system. Each of the subsystems has its own objectives and works, but it cannot be seen as a separate system. The organization becomes successful when it coordinates these subsystems properly to attain its objectives. All the subsystems are interrelated and work for a common goal.

Library and information center is treated as a system, which contains subsystems like collection development section, technical section, circulation section, reference and information service section, staff management section etc. All these sections have its own objectives and works towards the attainment of the unified library objective of meeting all the information requirements of users.

A library system can be analyzed with the help of the principles of system analysis, time and motion study, flow charting etc:

Systems Analysis

General system theory is a research paradigm, which attempts to facilitate the generalization of behavioral principles across a wide range of organizations. The system theory suggests that an organization, including service organization, consists of an arrangement of smaller subsystems and acts within a large system. The central themes of the systems theory are the interaction of subunits within a system and the interaction of the system with its environment.

In production theory, system theory explains how inputs are acquired from the environment, fed in to the manufacturing cycle, transformed to a finished product, and marketed to customers as output of the organization. Inputs, processes and outputs play important roles in the successful operation of the firm. Systems approach is suitable to study of services and service quality.

In evaluating the quality of products, customers are concerned primarily with the output. In services, customers are exposed to and affected by the inputs, processes and outputs of the service organization. A measure of service quality will include judgments of all dimensions of the service, inputs, processes and outputs. The input quality includes the quality of the equipment, surroundings, resources, cleanliness, furniture, lighting and ventilation, service providers, etc. The process quality indicates the quality of the interaction between the service provider and the customer, service production and consumption, service accessibility and availability. Output quality is a measure of what is produced as a result of providing the service. It includes intangible benefits and tangible outputs of the service.

It is reported that the processing and feedback stages, input and output stages are crucial in the evaluation of services. The relationship between service provider and service performance, and lack of expertise for evaluating outputs to customers will affect input quality measurement.

It is found that the service dimensions, as envisaged through SERVQUAL method of measurement of quality, demonstrate system theory as material quality, tangibles, corporate image, technical quality, and physical support as part f input quality. At the same time, interactive quality, staff-customer interaction, functional quality, assurance and responsiveness are related to process quality, and outcome and reliability are part of output quality.

There are certain benefits[6] of using system analysis in service organizations:

1. System approach frees the manager from taking a narrow functional viewpoint of a task and helps to identify subsystems that cut across functional areas.
2. It permits the manager to relate his/her goals to the goals of the organization.
3. It permits the organization to structure the different subsystems in a manner consistent with the system goals
4. It allows for evaluation of both the subsystems and the system as a whole.
5. It can be used to address subsystems like employee training system, complaint resolution system, etc.
6. Measuring the customer perception of input quality helps to understand how much investment is needed in the service environment.
7. Measuring the process quality of a service system enable the management to determine how much investment is needed to maintain or improve the service experience
8. Measuring the output quality of the service program helps to determine what has been the return from the investments made in service production.

Time and Motion Study

Time and motion study is used to understand the time and movements involved in the library processes and services carried out in a library. It is aimed to increase the productivity of a library through the systematic analysis of existing operations, processes and work methods with a view to increase their efficiency. Motion study helps to simplify the job and develop more economical methods of doing it and time study helps to determine how long it should take to carry out the work.

Time study is the application of techniques designed to establish the time for a qualified worker to carry out a specified job at a defined level of performance. On the other hand, motion study is the systematic recording and critical examination of existing and proposed ways of doing work as a means of developing and applying easier and more effective methods and recording costs. Therefore, time study and motion study are closely linked. Time study is mostly concerned with the investigation and reduction of any ineffective time associated with it, and with the subsequent establishment of time standards for the operation when carried out in the improved fashion, as determined by motion study.

The main objectives of motion study[7] are:

1. Improvement of processes and procedures
2. Improvement of the physical layout
3. Economy in human effort and reduction of unnecessary fatigue
4. Improvement in the use of materials, machines and manpower
5. Development of better physical working environment

Time and Motion study comprises the following eight stages[8]:

1. Select the work to be studied
2. Record all the relevant factors about the present method by direct observation
3. Examine those facts critically and in ordered sequence, using the technique best suited to the purpose

4. Develop the most practical, economic and effective method
5. Measure the effectiveness of the method
6. Define the new method so that it can be identified
7. Install the method as a standard practice
8. Maintain that practice by regular routine checking

Flow Chart

Flow chart is a graphic method of displaying a system's operations and sequence. It is a tool to show the various steps involved in a process. It serves as an instruction for process and its control. The workflow of a process in a system can be understood very easily from flow chart prepared.

Flow chart is the graphic representation of the process showing all its works and stages involved. It is a method of graphically depicting and describing a process. It helps to break a process down step by step to determine what is done when, where and by whom and how each action occurs. It helps to identify gaps in quality service efforts.

It uses six basic symbols to denote a particular step or action in a process. 'Circle' for operation, 'square' for inspection, 'arrow' for transport, 'diamond' for decision, D for delay and Triangle, for storage/filing. A flow chart will help to determine how the quality of service can be improved well.

Preparing the flow chart describing the actual process that is being used is considered as the good first step for quality improvement programmes. Some times, the flow-charting itself leads to a major improvement of the process. A study of flow chart will enable the management to find out the areas that can be improved easily.

In libraries, it can be used very well to show the stages through which each library processes and services are completed. It will enable the librarian to identify the delay areas, problem areas, unnecessary stages in the processes and services carried out in the library. Based on that, the librarian can restructure the processes and services to improve them in time. As a system, library can use it for analyzing the library as a whole system or part-by-part subsystems.

A typical flow chart for the processes of issue of documents carried out in a library is shown in Figure 9.3.

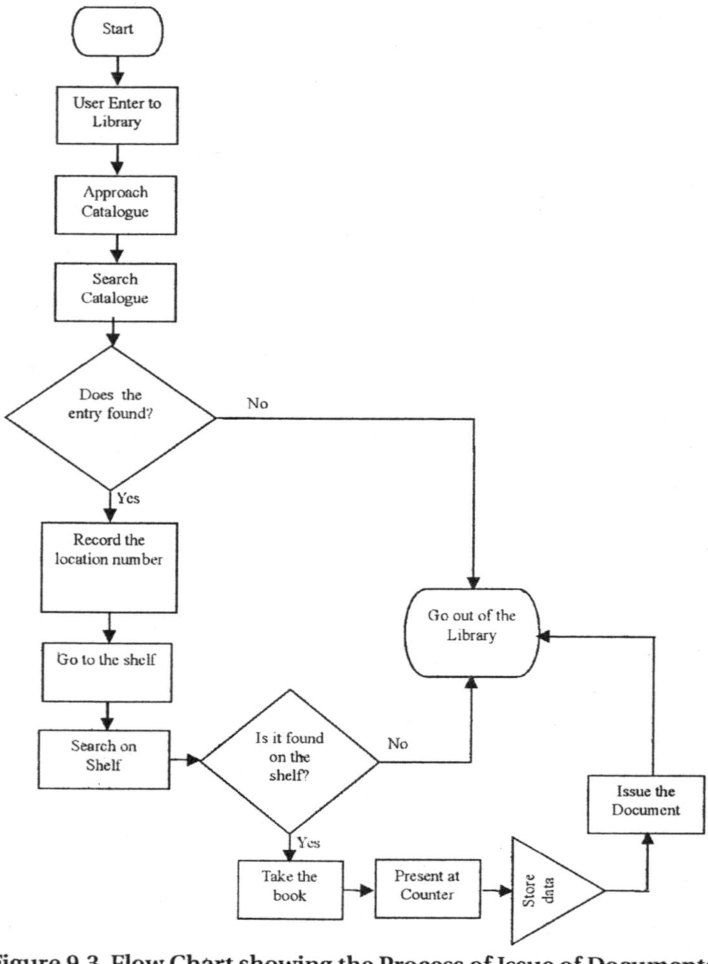

Figure 9.3. Flow Chart showing the Process of Issue of Documents

The flow chart shows that, the issue process in a library begins with the entry of the user who first go to the library catalogue and search to see whether the needed document is available in the library or not. If it is not available, the user go out of the library, otherwise he makes note of the location number of the document needed and moves to the shelf where the document is suppose to be found. Then he searches on the shelf for the document and if it is not found, the user go out of the library. If the document is found on the shelf, he takes it and presents it in the issue counter for issuing it. The issue counter record the details of the document and the user and after that the counter staff gives the document to the user and the process ends with the exiting of the user from the library.

Such flow charts will help the librarian to analyse the stages involved in each activity carried out in the library, assess the time and staff involvement, and improve the activities and services by eliminating unnecessary bottlenecks.

Specialized Management Methods

Specialized management methods like Benchmarking, SERVQUAL, SERVPERF, PCP model, WebQUAL, and LibQUAL are now very extensively used to measure the performance quality of library products and services.

Benchmarking

Benchmarking is the process of comparing an organization or its services with others. It is the process of identifying, understanding and adapting outstanding practices from organizations any where in the world to help the organization to improve its performance. It is a highly used practice in the business world, which looks out best practices and high performance measure the actual business with that of others. It helps the organization to find out how well the competitor performance its process and what practices are to be adapted to organization. It also enable to shortlist the competitors in the order of performance or best practices.

Benchmarking can be conducted in different ways. The organizations to benchmark against should be either the direct competitors in the same country or foreign country, indirect competitors, or other successful organizations. Comparing an organization with other is difficult when organization has a monopoly on its service or product, when the competitor uses a worse standard. It is necessary to find out the patterns which can be compared and get new ideas.

Benchmarking is a time bound process. Based on the subject and the information available, a benchmarking exercise may take three months to one-year time. It is necessary to repeat the process later and monitor the impacts of the benchmarking already done. It is good to employ a consultant who interacts and monitors the process.

It is considered as the process of determining standards for a service, based on service rather than aimed at excellence. It is the process of studying and evaluating similar services in order to establish best practices. It is aimed to identify areas for improvement and to stimulate changes by competitive analysis, best practice, performance comparison or standard setting.

The bench marking process comprises five stages, namely planning, collection of data, analysis of results, implementation of changes, and evaluation of the progress. The planning stage involves the decision about what is to be bench marked, focusing on those areas, which are more important and deliver greatest returns. Once the planning process is over, then the necessary data are collected from the administrators and managers, workers, providers and users. Needed results are derived on the basis of analysis, and the required changes in the organization are planned and executed. Finally the changes made are reviewed and corrective actions are taken to improve the situation

SERVQUAL

Parasuraman and others (1988)[9] have developed an instrument called SERVQUAL in the form of a questionnaire, which contains 22 statements addressing expectations about service that should be offered followed by 22 statements addressing perceptions about actual service received. The formula for quality is Q = P – E Where Q represents perceived quality, P represents ratings on perception and E represents ratings on expectation statements. It is a management technique to assess the expectations and perceptions of users through questionnaires and the dimensions of service quality are measured with the help of user perceptions and expectations based on gap theory.

A modified SERVQUAL instrument can be used to understand the nature of the user expectations and perceptions of library products and services, and to measure the library service quality.

SERVQUAL method is discussed in detail in a separate chapter

SERVPERF

Cronin and Taylor[10] have developed SERVPERF model for measuring service quality through service performance measures. The two types of performance measures that can be obtained are internal measures and customer measures. Internal measures are designed to provide objective measures of the organization's performance and customer measures are designed to measure attitudes and opinions of customers. Internal measures help to locate weak areas and to identify areas of expertise. At the same time customer measure helps to get information about how customers feel about services. It also helps to get information on customer needs. The major disadvantages of internal measures are:

1. It lacks customer perspective;
2. It may not be important to customers; and
3. It does not measure behavioral side of service.

And the major disadvantages of customer measures are:

1. It does not reflect opinions of non-customers;
2. It does not provide comparative information; and
3. It is difficult to get unbiased information.

Customer complaints can be treated as internal measure of service quality, but customers who are totally dissatisfied with the service may not complain to the organization about it.

P-C-P Model

Pivotal-Core-Peripheral (P-C-P)[11] model is a ranked structure based on three main classes of attributes, namely Pivotal, Core and Peripheral. There is a growing need to explore and develop specific attributes of service sector. Accordingly, P-C-P bases on three ranked levels of inputs, processes, and outputs of a service organization. Pivotal represents outputs, and the core and peripheral attributes together represent inputs and processes in a service.

According to the P-C-P model, every service consists of three areas, which will include majority of the dimensions and concepts used to define service quality. These areas can be defined as inputs, processes, and outputs of a service organization. This model is similar to the system model of an organization.

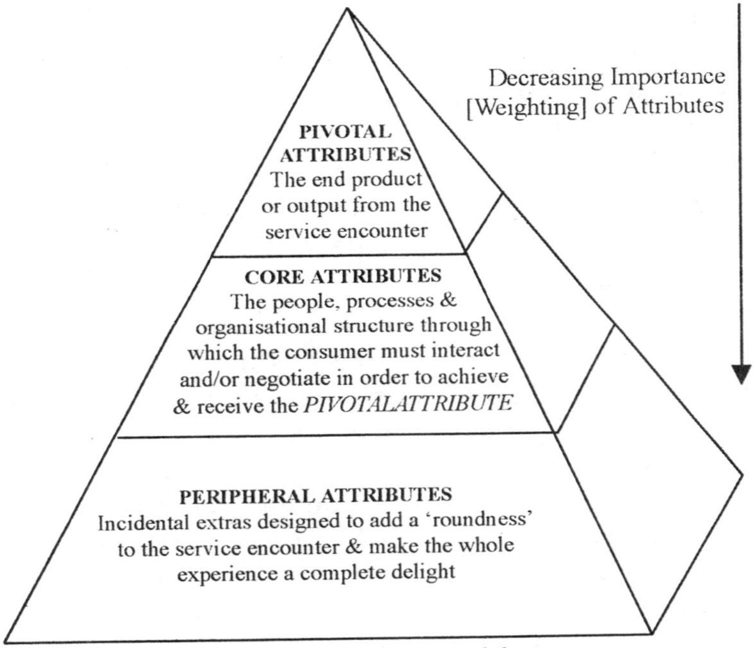

Figure 9.4. P-C-P Model

Pivotal attributes are the end product or output from the service encounter, i.e. what the customer expects to achieve and take away from the service process. Core attributes are the people, processes and organizational structure through which the customer must interact and/ or negotiate in order to achieve and receive the pivotal attribute. The peripheral attributes are the incidental extras designed to add a roundness or completeness to the encounter and make the whole experience a complete delight.

Pivotal attributes are considered as the most determining influence on why the customer decided to approach a particular service organization in the first place. These attributes focus on the outcomes of the interactions between the service providers and the customer.

Core attributes are centered on the pivotal attributes

and have a serious role in the successful delivery of the service encounter. It is the amalgamation of all the people and the organizational processes and the hierarchy through which a customer must interact or negotiate to achieve pivotal attribute.

Peripheral attributes may include the attributes added to make the service delivery complete, like tangibles, access and other facilities.

Pivotal attribute is what the customer expects to achieve and receive, and take away when service process is completed. During service encounter, the customer comes into contact with anyone or anything in the service organization is considered as core attributes. When a customer makes an evaluation about a service encounter, he/she attaches more importance to the achievement of the pivotal attributes. If the service is experienced only once and all the items embodied in the pivotal attributes are achieved with a lower degree of achievement of core and peripheral attribut, then the customer is expected to be reasonably satisfied. It is found that the more the service is used, the core and peripheral attributes may get greater importance. If pivotal attributes are in good standard, then the customer consider other attributes very seriously. The customer satisfaction level may depend more on pivotal attributes and less on the others. Therefore, it is necessary to make the customers delight in all the three areas.

The model suggests that the personnel and organizational structure are only in place to allow the service to be delivered and whether the service is satisfactorily achieved or whether the customer receives the required output. While evaluating a service, the customer gives more credence to the successful achievement of the output in preference to core and peripheral attributes.

The organizations plan to adopt the P-C-P model should consider the following[12]:

1. The outputs or deliverables from the service to the customers. It is to be decided first as it will help to identify the pivotal attributes that are relevant to the service operation.
2. Their personnel involved and the organizational structure used in the delivery of the service. It is to be decided prior to the adoption of the model, as it will enable the organization to recognize and isolate the core and peripheral attributes. The courtesy, empathy and the reliability of the employees will be reflected in the evaluation and the satisfaction of customers.
3. Customers' changing expectations due to repeated experience of the same service. A customer experiencing the service for the first time may have more delight to the pivotal attributes, than a customer who frequently uses the same service.

In libraries, the P-C-P model of study enable the librarian what are the issues most important and not important to the users relating to the quality of the library and information services offered to the users. It will help the librarian to focus on such issues and improve the library service quality.

WebQUAL

WebQUAL[13] is a tool for examining the quality of information produced and transmitted within an information system, or transmitted by the sender. There are nine items pertaining to information quality. They are: Accuracy; Precision; Currency; Timeliness; Reliability; Completeness; Volume; Format; and Relevance

Besides, there are some other items to be included while considering the quality of information in the websites. They are: Confidence/Security of data; Convenience of access; Language; Understanding; Utility; and Integration

WebQUAL is an instrument developed to measure the

general perceptions and expectations of users' about a website and its quality. In WebQUAL, users are asked to rate target sites against each of a range of qualities using a 5-point scale. The users are also asked to rate each of the qualities for importance using a 5-point scale, which helps to understand about which qualities are considered by the users most important in any given situation. The collected data is analyzed using quantitative techniques, to conduct tests of the reliability of the instrument. The WebQUAL instrument uses Website perceptions and importance to customer ratings in equivalent to a two-column format. It is developed on the basis of tried and tested ideas about service quality and its measurement on websites.

The WebQUAL questionnaire used to assess the quality of an information/News website like BBC[14] contain the following questions:

1. Website has an appropriate appearance
2. Website provides accurate information
3. Website provides up to date information
4. Website provides relevant information
5. Website provides information which is easy to understand
6. Website provides the right level of details
7. Website provides fast navigation to what I intend to find
8. Website provides navigation which is free from errors
9. It is easy to find my way around and return to
10. It has content designed and selected for mobility
11. It has content which creates a sense of user community
12. It has interesting content.

These statements are grouped into 3 quality determinants, namely information quality, site quality and user quality. The information quality includes aspects of hard aspect of quality such as accuracy and currency and soft aspects of quality such as relevance, ease of understanding and level of detail. The site quality includes aspects of the design of the website, such as format and style of appearance, quality of navigation, easiness to find right information and its retrieval. The user quality includes suitability of content, ability to meet user needs, user group based services etc.

From the study it has been identified that the major determinants of an information/news website are: Hard information; Soft information; Site appearance; Site Navigation; User empathy; and User mobility

The questions in the WebQUAL instrument used for assessing the Websites of four business schools in UK[15] are the following:

1. The website is easy to use
2. The website has things where I expect to find them
3. The website is easy to find my way around
4. The website has fast navigation to pages
5. The website has useful links to other sites
6. The website is easy to find
7. The website facilitates return visits
8. The website has an attractive appearance
9. The website has an appropriate style of design for site type.
10. The website provides quick and easy access to find information
11. The website provides relevant information
12. The website provides information at an appropriate level of detail
13. The website provides information content that is easy to read
14. The website communicates information in an appropriate format

15. The website provides information content that is easy to understand
16. The website has information that is updated regularly
17. The website has reliable information
18. The website has a reasonable loading time
19. The website creates an experience
20. The website conveys a sense of community
21. The website keeps the users attention
22. The website is a site that feels secure
23. The website makes it easy to feedback
24. The website makes it easy to contact the organization.

The items to be included in the WebQUAL questionnaire can be developed through focus group discussions, in which a list of website qualities can be formulated, tested and finalized. Finally the qualities are developed in to an Internet based questionnaire to evaluate the website quality in question. The number of questions, its style and nature depends upon the study purpose. The users may give high priority to easy access and get good information. The questions/quality statements so derived can be grouped in to quality determinants/ dimensions for easy analysis, and understanding of the results. The possible dimensions are:

1. **Ease of use:** is related to the ability to get around the site and find needed products/services. It includes simple, intuitive and consistent navigation possible.
2. **Experience:** is related to the visual and personal experience of visiting the website. It includes the aspects like design, use of colors and style and its ability to develop interest and a sense of community.
3. **Information:** is related to the access to good quality information content. It may include aspects like

easiness to read and understand, relevance, currency, reliability, the details given and the format used.

4. **Communication and Integration:** is related to how the site is integrated with the external environment and communicates with the user. It may include aspects like ability to find and return to a site, links with other sites, speed and security of communication, provision for feedback and other contacts.

LibQUAL+

LibQUAL+[16] is a library service quality measurement tool based on the SERVQUAL model of assessing service quality in marketing research. It is a standardized survey instrument used in many libraries. It is a web-based survey for measuring library users perceptions of service quality and identifies gaps between desired, perceived and minimum expectations of service. The questionnaire contains 25 items grouped under four library quality dimensions, namely access to information, affect of service, library as place, and personal control.

LibQUAL instrument is discussed in detail in a separate chapter.

References

1. Chowdhury, G.G. Information Retraieval Systems. Calcutta: IASLIC, 1994. p38-44.
2. Sardana, J.L. and Sehgal, R.L. Statistical methods for librarians. New Delhi: Ess.Ess, 1996. p6-7.
3. Sardana, J.L. Statistical methods and quality in Library services and products. In C. P. Vashishth, Ed. Quality in Libraries. New Delhi: ILA, 1986. p124-126.
4. Brophy, Peter and Coulling, Kate. Quality Management for Information and Library Managers. Aldershot: Aslib Gower, 1996. p95.
5. Brophy, Peter and Coulling, Kate. Op. Cit.. p91.
6. Johnson, R.L et.al. Measuring service quality: systems approach. *Journal of Service Marketing*, 9(5), 1995. p6-19.

7. Raj, Janak. Method study of acquisition and technical sections of Kurukshetra University Library. In C. P. Vashishth, Ed. Quality in Libraries. New Delhi: ILA, 1986. p79-102.

8. Ibid.

9. Parasuraman, A et al. SERVQUAL: A multiple item scale for measuring consumer perceptions of service quality. Journal of Retailing. 64 (1) 1988. pp 12-40.

10. Cronin, J.J and Taylor, S.A, 'Measuring service quality: a reexamination and extension', Journal of Marketing, 56, 1992, p55-68.

11. Philip, George and Hazlett, Shirley-Ann. Evaluating the service quality of information services using P-C-P attributes model. *International Journal of Quality and Reliability Management*, 18(9), 2001. p900-916.

12. Philip, George and Hazlett, Shirley-Ann. The measurement of service quality: a new P-C-P attributes model. *International Journal of Quality and Reliability Management*, 14(3), 1997. p260-286.

13. *www.webqual.co.uk*

14. Barnes, Stuart J and Vidgen, Richard T. 'Assessing the Quality of WAP News Sites: The WebQual/M Method'. *Vision* (Special Issue), 2001. p81-91.

15. Barnes, S and Vigden, R. 'WebQual : An Exploration of Web Site Quality'. In *Proceedings of the Eighth European Conference on Information Systems*, 2000.

16. *http://www.libqual.org/*

10
SERVQUAL, A Scale for Measuring Service Quality

SERVQUAL is a multiple item scale for measuring customer perceptions of service quality and not a tool for improving the service quality. It is based on the premise that service quality is the difference between customers' expectations and their evaluation of the service received. It was developed by Parasuraman et.al[1] in 1985 and further modified in 1988[2], 1991[3] and in 1994[4].

It enables an organization to compare expectations and perceptions of customers' overtime. The SERVQUAL scores can be compared with the scores of competitors and understand the service quality of the organization with other similar organizations. It can be used to understand the category of customers who are regular customers for a long period. It can also be used to measure the quality perceptions of internal customers, employees in different departments, in the organization.

Genesis of SERVQUAL

In 1985 Parasuraman identified 5 service quality gaps. This is recognized as a major contribution to the field of marketing and it laid the foundation for service quality research later. These five gaps are:

Gap 1: Difference between customer expectation and management perception of customer expectation.

Gap 2: Difference between management perception of customer expectation and service quality specification.

Gap 3: Difference between service quality specifications and the service actually delivered.

Gap 4: Difference between service delivery and what is communicated about the service to customers.

Gap 5: Difference between customer expectation and perceptions.

In 1988, Parasuraman et.al[5] developed the famous equation: '$Q = P - E$'

Where Q = quality,

P = perception of customer about the service, and

E = customer expectations about the service.

They also identified five quality perceptual dimensions, namely

Tangibles = physical facilities and appearance of personnel.

Reliability = ability to perform the promised service dependably and accurately

Responsiveness = willingness to help customer and provide prompt service.

Assurance = knowledge and courtesy of employees and their confidence.

Empathy = caring, individualized attention the firm provides to its customers.

In 1988, Zeithaml et.al identified a variety of factors, internal to an organization that affects the level of service quality delivered to the customers. Based on that, they offered an extended model of service quality. The internal factors[6] related to the service quality gaps are shown in the Figure 10.1.

Gap 1 = Difference between customer expectations and management perception of customer expectations

The extend, nature and quality of marketing research

conducted by the organization can widen or narrow down the differences between customer expectations and management perceptions of customer expectations. The upward communication of customer expectations and perceptions by contact personnel to top management can also widen or reduce this gap. The number of layers of management between customer contact people and the management will also affect the gap. The layers of management may place barriers between customer contact personnel and the top management.

Gap 2 = Management perception – service quality specification gap

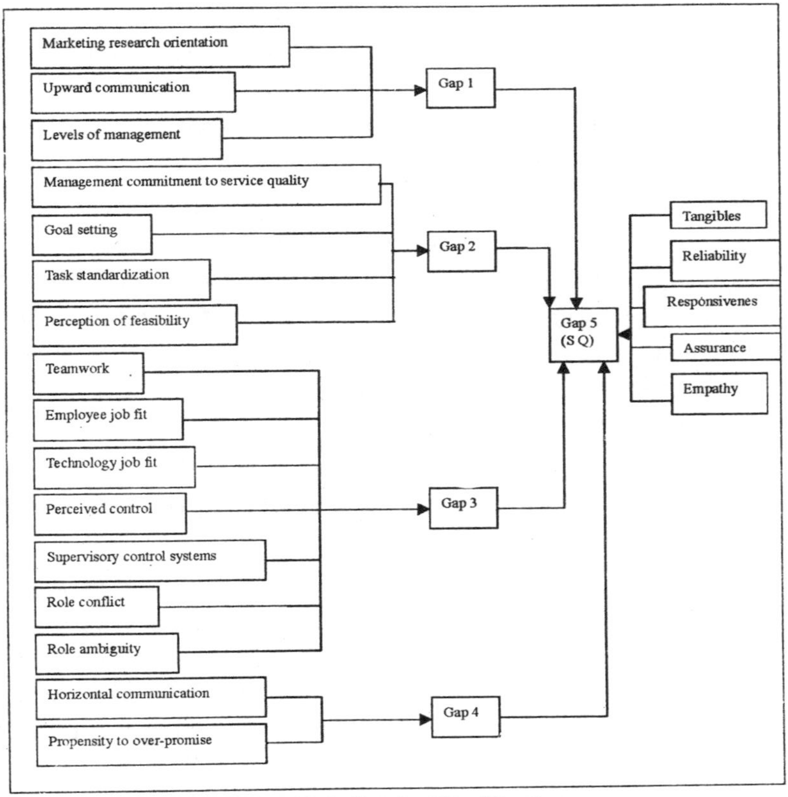

Figure 10.1. Service Quality Gaps

If the management is not truly committed to service quality, there will be a gap between the management perception and service quality specification. Goal setting is necessary for an organization to be successful in delivering good quality services to its customers. It will standardize what service is and how the organization will deliver quality service to the customers. Standardization of tasks related to service delivery can significantly affect this gap. The more the tasks are standardized the gap will be smaller.

Gap 3 = Service quality specification – service delivery gap

Service performance gap occurs when employees are unable or unwilling to perform the service at the desired level. The gap is affected due to teamwork, employee – job – fit, technology – job – fit, perceived control, supervisory control systems, role conflict and role ambiguity.

Gap 4 = Difference between service delivery and external communications

The communication within and between departments in an organization (horizontal communication) will affect the service quality. If top management decides and communicates customers about the provision of good services without informing the working employees properly will result in this gap.

Gap 5 = The actual gap between the customer expectation and perceptions. It includes all the four gaps mentioned above.

In 1993, Parasuraman et.al[7] developed the 'Zone of Tolerance' concept as part of their conceptual model of service quality. Zone of tolerance is the area between a customers' adequate service level and the desired service level. There are a number of factors that affect zone of tolerance, which includes situational factors, past experience and explicit business promises. Based on zone of tolerance, Parasuraman et.al have developed a new model of service quality which is based on two propositions:

Customer assesses service performance based on two standards:

1. What they desire and what they deem acceptable, and
2. A zone of tolerance separates desired service from adequate service

The nature and determinants[8] of customer expectations of a service is shown in the Figure10.2.

In 1994, Parasuraman et.al[9] further tested and improved the operational definition of the zone of tolerance concept. They devised a three-column format to calculate zone of tolerance. It includes minimum service level, desired service level and perception level of service.

In 1996, Zeithaml et.al[10] reported about the impact of service quality on customer behavioural intentions. There are significant associations among service quality, marketing variable and profitability. Based on this relationship, Zeithaml et.al have developed a conceptual framework of the behavioural and financial consequences of service quality. The behavioural intention measures include:

Loyalty = the strength of the relationship between the customer and service provider

Switch = the extend to which a customer might change to the competitor

Pay More = the extend to which a customer purchase service on a higher charge.

External Response = the likelihood a customer would complain others and switch to competitor.

Internal Response = the propensity a customer would complain to employees about service problems.

It is said that, improving service quality will positively impact behavioural intentions.

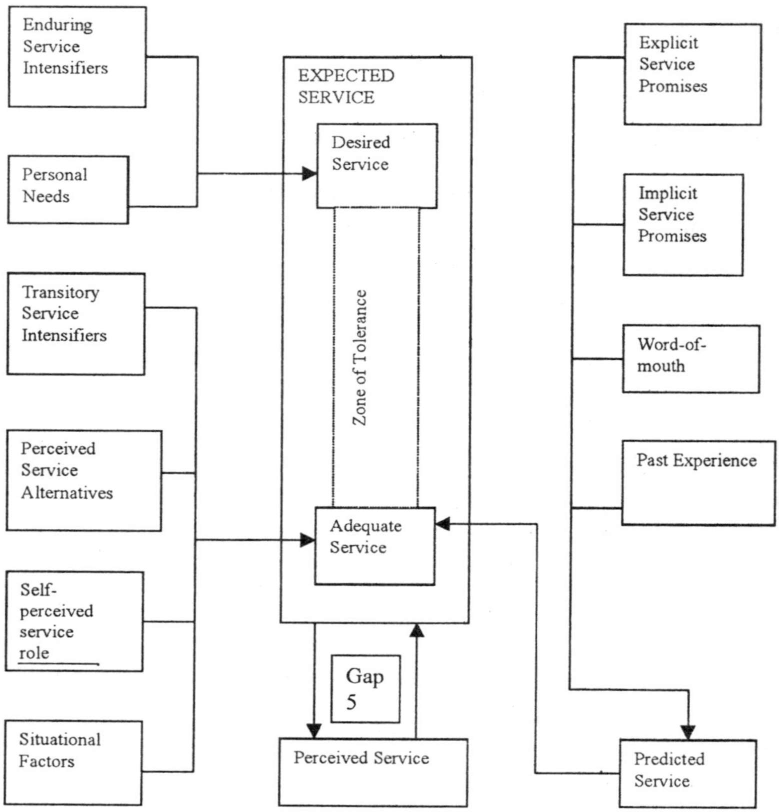

Figure 10.2. Nature and Determinants of Customer Expectations of a Service

In 1997, Berry and Parasuraman[11] put forward a 'multiple-method listening' as a service quality information system, to encourage all organizations to measure the quality of their customer service. It directs the management to incorporate a dynamic service quality system that measures service quality from multiple perspectives and from multiple points of view. An effective service quality information system can survey customers, competitors and employees periodically. Transactional surveys, customer complaint capture, total market survey and employee survey can be used for the purpose. In addition to that, focus groups and customer advisory panels can also be used wherever necessary.

The following guidelines will ensure a good and effective service quality information system:

1. Measure desired service, adequate service and perceived service
2. Generate relevant, precise, useful, credible, understandable and timely information of service quality
3. Include customers' own comments in report on service quality
4. Link service performance to the business results to make the investment more credible and fact-based.
5. Give information on service quality and the feed back on their performance in the delivery of service to the staff

The major benefits of a service quality information system are:

1. It encourages and enables management to incorporate the voice of the customer in to decision making
2. It reveals customers' service priorities
3. It identifies service improvement priorities and guides resource allocation decisions.
4. It allows the repacking of company and competitor service performance overtime.
5. It discloses the impact of service quality initiatives and investments
6. It offers performance-based data to reward excellent service and correct poor service.

Delivering superior service quality appears to be a prerequisite for the success of business and service organizations. The quality of a product can be measured objectively with the help of indicators like durability, number of defects etc. But the quality of a service cannot be measured objectively because of the three features unique to services, namely intangibility, heterogeneity and inseparability of production and consumption. There are no quantitative yard stick available for assessing the quality of service. The search for a quantitative tool for measuring the service quality led to the development of SERVQUAL, a multiple item scale for measuring consumer perceptions of service quality.

Steps for the Construction of SERVQUAL Scale

The basic steps involved in the construction of the SERVQUAL scale[12] are given in Figure 10.3.

Step 1. Definition of service quality. Parasuraman et al. has defined service quality as "the discrepancy between consumers' perception of services offered by a particular firm and their expectations about firms offering such services.

Step 2. Identification of Dimensions. As part of the scale development, ten dimensions, namely *Reliability, Access, Security, Credibility, Understanding, Responsiveness, Competence, Courtesy, Tangibles, and Communication,* which make the domain of service quality are identified.

Step 3. Generation of items – Initially 97 items representing the 10 dimensions have generated for the purpose of use in the scale.

Step 4. Pilot study: In order to assess the suitability of the 97 items and the 10 dimensions of service quality, a pilot study is conducted. The expectation and perceptions data from a sample of 200 respondents, who were the current or recent user of a commercial service, were collected.

Step 5. Scale purification: Based on the data collected and analyses made, the proposed scale is purified through an iterative sequence. This sequence include :

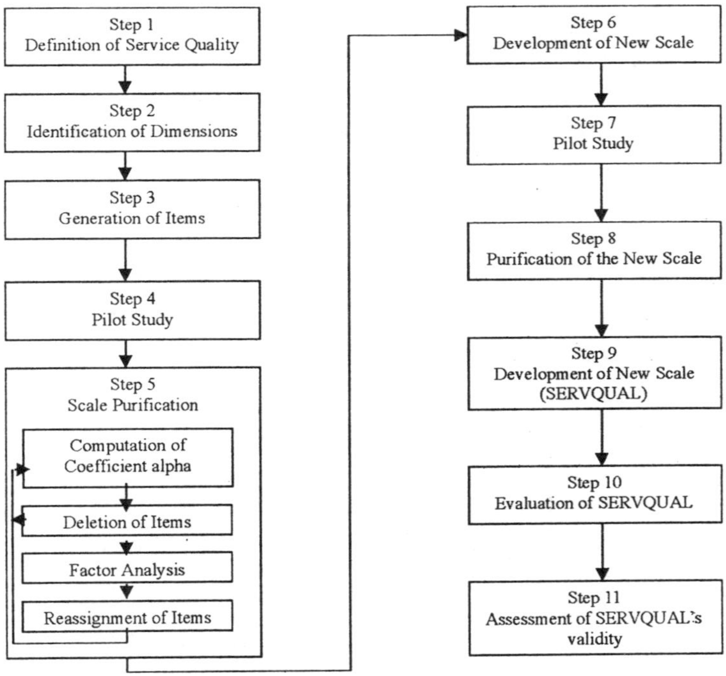

Figure 10.3. Steps for the Construction of SERVQUAL Scale

1. Computation of coefficient alpha and item-to-total correlations for each dimensions.
2. Deletion of items whose item-to total correlations were low and whose removal increased coefficient alpha
3. Factor analysis to verify the dimensionality of the overall scale.
4. Reassignment of items and re-structuring of dimensions wherever necessary
5. Repetition of the above 4 steps till the scale purification is complete.

Step 6. Development of purified scale: As a result of the purification process of the 97 items and the 10 dimensions of service quality, a modified scale containing 34 items and 7 dimensions are identified.

Step 7. Pilot study: For assessing the suitability of the 34 items and 7 dimensions of service quality, another pilot study is conducted. The expectation and perceptions data from four independent samples of 200 respondents, who were current or recent customers of service firms were collected.

Step 8. Purification of the scale: With the help of the pilot study, the 34 items and 7 dimensions of service quality are further evaluated and purified through the same iterative sequence mentioned in step 5.

Step 9. Development of the new scale: The purification process of the 34 items and 7 dimensions of service quality identified a new scale, which contains 22 items representing 5 dimensions of service quality, called SERVQUAL

Step 10. Evaluation of SERVQUAL. Before to the finalisation of the scale, evaluation of the reliability and factor structure of the scale is done. An analysis of data collected in step 4 is done to prove the SERVQUAL's reliability and factor structure.

Step 11. Assessment of SERVQUAL's validity. Research to assess the validity and applicability of the SERVQUAL instrument in different service environments.

The conceptual foundation for the SERVQUAL scale was derived from the works of researchers who examined the meaning of service quality and from a comprehensive qualitative research study that defined service quality precisely and identified the dimensions along which the customers perceive and evaluate service quality.

SERVQUAL scale measure perceived quality of a service firm or a specific service. Perceived quality is the consumers judgment about an entity's overall excellence or superiority. It is a form of attitude, related but no equivalent to satisfaction, results from the comparison of expectations with perceptions of performance.

SERVQUAL instrument uses 22 pairs of 7-point Likert scale statements to measure the five dimensions of service quality, namely Tangibles, Reliability, Responsiveness, Assurance and Empathy. The first 22 statements are designed to measure customer expectations while the remaining 22 are intended to measure the perceive level of service provided by a particular service firm. The level of service quality is determined by subtracting the perceived service score from the customers' expectation score for each of the statement. This method of determining service quality is called the GAP theory.

The SERVQUAL questionnaire is given as Appendix to this chapter.

Initially, the SERVQUAL study identified the criteria used by customers in assessing, service quality, called dimensions. These 10 dimensions identified are: tangibles, reliability, responsiveness, communication, credibility, security, competence, courtesy, understanding/knowing the customer and access. These 10 dimensions and their descriptions served as the basis of SERVQUAL scale. Then items representing these dimensions were generated. Accordingly 97 items were identified. Each of these item are recasted into two statements, one to measure expectations and the other to measure the perceptions of service quality. A seven point scale ranging form 'strongly agree' (7) to strongly disagree (1), with no verbal labels for scale points 2 through 6. The first half of the SERVQUAL instrument contains statements on expectations and the other contains statements on perceptions. The perceived service quality is derived on the basis of the principle 'Q = P - E' where Q = Perceived service quality, P = Perceptions and E = Expectations.

The reliability and factor structure of the SERVQUAL scale was evaluated and found that the reliabilities and factor structures are consistently high. The total-scale reliability was also found very high. The reliabilities and factor structures indicates that the final scale and its five dimensions have sound and stable psychometric properties. Therefore, SERVQUAL can be used in its original form to assess and compare service quality across a wide variety of service firms or units within a firm, or a particular service. Appropriate adaptation of the instrument for specific services or service firms is desirable. Items under each of the five dimensions can be suitably reworded or augment to the context in which the instrument is to be used.

As part of the assessment of SERQUAL's validity, the content validity and scale's validity (does the scale appear to measure what it is supposed to? and do the scale items capture key facets of the unobservable construct being measured?), are evaluated and found that it possess both content validity and scale's validity very well. Its validity was further assessed by examining whether the construct measured by it was empirically associated with measures of other conceptually related variables.

The instrument has been designed to be applicable across a broad spectrum of services. It provides a basic skeleton through its expectations/perceptions format encompassing statements for each of the five service quality dimensions. The skeleton can be adapted or supplemented to fit the characteristics or needs of a particular organization.

Applications of SERVQUAL are:

1. Understand the service expectations and perceptions of customers.
2. Understand service quality trends periodically
3. Assess firms quality along each of the five service dimensions

4. Assess firm's overall service quality
5. Determine the relative importance of the five dimensions in influencing customers' overall quality perceptions.
6. Categorise firm's customers into several perceived-quality segments, as high, medium and low, on the basis of their individual SERVQUAL scores.
7. Help in pin-pointing areas regarding managerial attention and action to improve service quality.

Application of SERVQUAL in Libraries

Understanding the expectations of library users begins with the classification of service expectations into seven service determinants. The dimensions of service quality and its constituent items in a library are as follows.

1. Reliability

It involves delivery of the promised library service dependably and accurately. It means that the public services performed by staff members are for the first time and the library collections contain information appropriate to the needs of the users. It involves:

* Giving correct information asked
* Making relevant information available
* Keeping records consistent with actual holdings
* Keeping databases up and running
* Making sure that overdue notices and fine notices are accurate

2. Responsiveness

It indicates the readiness of library staff to provide services timely. It involves:

* Making new information available
* Checking in new journals and newspapers promptly

* Contacting a user immediately once the requested document or information is received in the library
* Re-shelving books quickly
* Minimizing the time needed for processing a document before its release to the user

3. Assurance

It refers to the knowledge and courtesy of the library staff and their ability to convey confidence. It involves politeness, friendliness, skill to provide information about library collection and services. It involves:

* Valuing all requests for information equally and convey worthiness of the inquiry to the users;
* Clean and neat appearance of staff;
* Thorough understanding of the collection by the staff;
* Familiarity with working of equipments and technology;
* Learning the user's requirements;
* Providing individual attention to users; and
* Recognizing the regular users.

4. Access

It means that there are adequate staff and equipments as well as hours of operation. It involves:

* Waiting time in circulation check out line is minimal
* Provision of sufficient computer terminals and OPAC
* Library hours; and
* Location of the library is central and convenient.

5. Communications

It means keeping the customers informed in language they can understand and also listening to them. It demands the use of language understandable to different category of users. It involves:

* Avoiding unnecessary library jargons;
* Understanding the user's needs precisely;
* Using precise and clear instructions;
* Provision of user education, teaching library skills to users; and
* Assuring users that their problems will be handled properly.

6. Security

It means freedom from danger, risk or doubt. It involves:

* Physical safety within the library; and
* Keeping library dealings confidential.

7. Tangibles

It includes maintenance of physical facilities and serviceability of equipments. It involves:

* Physical conditions of library buildings like heat, light, ventilation, etc.;
* Conditions of equipments like microfilm reader, copiers, computers etc.
* Impact of other users in the library.

In this method, the comments of users are classified and categorized in to one of the seven service quality categories or determinants. Then each of these comments is assessed for its positive or negative attribute. The comments of each user will be given in 5 score scale. That is, the questionnaire will contain quantifiable 5 score scaled questions. So the survey results become a good basis for defining quality library services.

The user expectations of library services can be met in a library by

* Defining the service role;
* Hiring service oriented employees;

* Providing an accommodating environment to users; and
* Reliability, i.e., Doing it first time.

The survey should cover not only the regular users but the potential users also. It is necessary to the growth of library services and improving the service quality. The knowledge of user expectations will help to decide the service priorities to be followed in the library. It will help to develop service standards and have a basis for measuring staff performance.

However, there are theoretical and operational criticisms leveled against the SERVQUAL instrument developed by Parasuraman et al. in 1985.

Criticism Against SERVQUAL

The theoretical criticisms against this instrument are:

1. SERVQUAL is based on a disconfirmation paradigm rather than an attitudinal paradigm and it fails to draw on established economic, statistical and psychological theory. Cronin and Taylor (1992, 1994)[13, 14] observed that SERVQUAL is based on the disconfirmation model adopted in customer satisfaction literature. In this literature, customer satisfaction is measured in terms of the relationship between expectations and outcomes. If expectation matches outcomes, (expectation = outcome), it is predicted that the customer is satisfied, if expectation exceeds outcome (expectation>outcome), customer is said to be dissatisfied and if expectation is lower to the outcome (expectation < outcome), the customer is said to be delighted. According to Cronin and Taylor (1992, 1994), SERVQUAL is paradigmatically flawed because of its ill-judged adoption of the disconfirmation model of perceived quality. Perceived quality is generally conceptualized as an attitude.

Iacobucci et al (1994)[15] commented that service quality and customer satisfaction have not been consistently differentiated from each other. Though Parasuraman et al

(1985) had described satisfaction as more situation/ encounter-specific and quality as more holistic without necessary empirical evidences to support their view. Oliver (1980)[16] had observed that service quality and customer satisfaction are distinct constructs, but are related to each other. Satisfaction mediates the effect of prior period perceptions of service quality and causes revised service quality perceptions to be formed.

Cronin and Taylor (1994)[17] commented that the original SERVQUAL scale measure neither service quality nor customer satisfaction, but is only one of the many forms of expectancy-disconfirmation. Similarly Anderson (1992)[18] viewed that:

* It does not consider the cost of improving service quality. It is found that marginal revenue of service quality improvement does not always exceed the marginal cost of service quality improvement.
* Ordinal scale methods (Likert scale) is used to collect data, but methods like factor analysis, are used to analyse this data.
* Limited level of statistical methods are used for analysis and ordinal scales do not allow for correct correlation measurements and so the elasticity among quality dimensions and customer value of improvements cannot be measured precisely.
* It failed to draw on psychology of perception.

2. There is little evidence that customers assess service quality in terms of perception-expectation gaps. The value and meaning of gaps identified in the SERVQUAL model was criticized heavily. Babakus and Boller (1992)[19] observed that the difference scores between customer perceptions and expectations do not provide any additional information beyond the score of perceptions component of the scale. It is reported that prominent score in the gap score is

perception score as expectation scores are generally rated high.

According to Iacobucci et al (1994)[20] expectations may not be enough to serve as a standard for evaluation of a service experience, as expectations may be formed simultaneously with service consumption. Kahniman and Miller (1986)[21] viewed that customers use experience based norms to form their expectations.

Teas (1993a, 1993b, 1994)[22,23,24] was doubtful about the expectation ratings across the items and dimensions included, as there are six ways of getting the P-E gap as –1 (minus one), i.e. when P=1 and E=2, P=2 and E=3, P=3 and E=4, P=4 and E=5, or P=6 and E=7 and these does not represent equal perceived service quality.

Customers learn from experiences. Good experiences influence in their expectations and go down when there is a bad experience to them. But SERVQUAL had failed to consider the dynamics of changing expectations. Therefore Gronroos (1993)[25] and Wotruba and Tyagi (1991)[26] reported that serious studies on the dynamics of service quality evaluation, and on expectation and its formations and changes were very important. Hardie et al. (1992)[27] argue that failure to meet expectation is more significant than to the case of success in meeting or exceeding expectations. customers always prefer to comment on a poor service performance more than to praise good performance of a service. Recently Cronin and Taylor (1992)[28] tested a performance-based measure of service quality, called SERVPERF, and found that it is more good than the SERVQUAL.

3. SERVQUAL is focused on process of service delivery instead of outcomes of the service encounter. The critics, like Cronin and Taylor (1992)[29], Mangold and Babakus (1991)[30], and Richard and Allaway (1993)[31], argued that SERVQUAL has lost outcome quality from its purview.

4. SERVQUAL'S five dimensions are not universal, as the number and style of items and dimensions changes according to a change in service environment. Instead of the RATER dimensions, Gronroos (1984)[32] identified three dimensions of service quality, namely technical, functional and reputational quality. Similarly Lehtinen and Lehtinen (1982)[33] had also identified three components of service quality, namely inter-active, physical and corporate quality. Hedvall and Paltschik (1989)[34] identified two dimensions of service quality, namely willingness and ability to serve, and physical and psychological access. Leblanc and Nguyen (1988)[35] identified five components of service quality, namely corporate image, internal organization, physical support of the service producing system, staff/customer interaction and the level of customer satisfaction. Against to this criticisms against dimensions Parasuraman et al (1988) argued that SERVQUAL is a skeleton which can be adapted or supplemented to fit the specific environment or characteristics of a service firm. As a result, the number of dimensions, items and its wordings are different in different service environments.

5. The relationship between the dimensions and its items are not strong in SERVQUAL. Carman (1990)[36] observed that the items have not loaded on the dimension to which they were expected to belong. It is found that two items in Empathy dimension in SERVQUAL instrument has heavily loaded on the Tangible dimension. The item loading changes differently in different service environments.

Similarly the convergent validity and discriminant validity of items in the SERVQUAL tools are also questioned. Convergent Validity indicates the high level of inter-correlations between the items to measure a dimension and discriminant indicates the independent nature of each item and the dimension. Babakus and Boller (1992)[37] noted that the rules for convergence and discrimination do not indicate the existence of the five dimensions.

There are also criticisms against operational part of the SERVQUAL instrument.

6. There is a strong criticism that expectations play no significant role in the conceptualization of service quality. Teas (1993)[38] has tested the validity of expectations in the instrument and observed that the customers use any one of the six interpretations given below to rate their expectations:

* Service attribute importance [expectations statements according to the importance]
* Forecasted performance [performance they would expect]
* Ideal performance [optimal performance]
* Deserved performance [what the performance should be]
* Equitable performance [level of performance ought to receive]
* Minimum tolerable performance [what performance must be]

Zeithaml et al. (1991)[39] themselves have identified two comparison norms for service quality assessment, namely desired service (the level of service a customer believes can and should be delivered) and adequate service (the level of service the customer considers acceptable).

7. The number of items included in each dimensions are questioned as some argue that four or five items in SERVQUAL scale are inadequate to capture the variance within a dimension. Therefore, Bouman and Vander Wiele (1992)[40] used 48 items, Carman (1990)[41] used 40 items, Saleh and Ryan (1992)[42] used 33 items, Fort (1993)[43] used 31 items to assess service quality of different firms.

8. SERVQUAL as the global construct is criticized heavily as several services are delivered over several

moments of truth or encounter between service staff and customer. The items are loaded to a dimension according to the context in which it is applied. Carman (1990)[44] observed that customers evaluate service quality with reference to multiple encounters.

9. The negatively worded and positively worded items in the SERVQUAL instrument is criticized on the ground that the negative items belongs to Responsiveness and Empathy dimensions (9 items) and the other (13 items) belongs to the other three dimensions. Babakus and Boller (1992)[45] argued that negatively worded items are loaded heavily to one dimension, while the positively worded items are loaded to another. Not only that there is a significant difference between the scores of positively worded and negatively worded items.

10. The seven-point Likert scale used in the instrument is criticized on several grounds. Lewis (1993)[46] criticized the scale for its non-verbal labeling for points two to six. Babakus and Mangold (1992)[47] suggested to use five-point scale, as it will reduce the frustration level of respondents, increase the response rate and its quality.

In the initial stage, Parasuraman et.al had used a seven-point Likert scale to measure expectations and perceptions, but later they have extended it to nine-point scale to offer a wide range of choices. At this context the number of points to be used in the scale is questioned and some argued that the reliability is maximized in seven-points, five-points, four points or three points. The verbal tags used for some points in the scale is also a matter for discussion and say that using verbal label to all points in the scale will help customers understand the meaning much more accurately than the other.

11. Bouman and Vander Wiele (1992)[48] has criticized the two level administration of SERVQUAL instrument (One

for assessing Expectations and the other for Perceptions). Carman (1990)[49] criticized the timing of the two administrations. SERVQUAL insist the customers to complete the two parts of the instrument in single sitting. Carman has suggested to use a single question at a single administration which contain expectation-perception difference.

Besides, there are some other criticisms leveled against the SERVQUAL instrument:

12. It is found that the timings of expectation measurements are of crucial importance. The SERVQUAL instrument implies that respondents must rate their expectations on a scale of 1 = strongly disagree to 7 = strongly agree and also their perceptions of the service in the same scale. The expectations must be measured before the service availed and the perceptions on that service are to be measured after the use of the service. In practice this may be impossible and so the respondents are interviewed only once (usually after experiencing the service) and take the measurement of both expectations and perceptions at that time.

13. It is argued that increasing perceptions minus expectations scores do not reflect continually increasing levels of perceived quality. That is, a higher P - E score does not necessarily imply higher quality. For example, if a customer rate both at 6, then the P - E score is 0 and if another rate E = 1 and P = 2, then P - E score here is 1 and it indicates that there is a higher perceived quality than the first case. This is not true and correct. There is a complaint that the 5 dimensions used in the instrument are treated as equally important which is not correct, as determinants of service quality may differ in their importance to individual customers and in different service environments.

Parasuraman et.al have suggested that the SERVQUAL instrument can be modified to suit the specific service environment of an organisation. Accordingly, Association of Research Libraries (ARL), New York has modified SERVQUAL instrument to measure the library service quality, and to understand the nature of their user expectations and perceptions of library products and services. This modified version of the SERVQUAL instrument is called LibQUAL[50].

References

1. Parasuraman, A. et al. A conceptual model of service quality and its implications for future research. *Journal of Marketing*. 49, 1985. pp45-48
2. Parasuraman, A et al. SERVQUAL: A multiple item scale for measuring consumer perceptions of service quality. *Journal of Retailing*. 64 (1) 1988. pp 12-40
3. Parasuraman, A et.al, 'Refinement and reassessment of the SERVQUAL scale', *Journal of Retailing*, 67, (4), Winter 1991, 420-450
4. Parasuraman, A et.al, Alternative scales for measuring service quality: a comparative assessment based on psychometric and diagnostic criteria', *Journal of Retailing*, 70, (3), 1994, pp201-230
5. Parasuraman, A et al.(1988). Op. Cit
6. Zeithaml, *V.A et.al.* Consumer perceptions of price, quality and value. *Journal of Marketing*. 52, 1988. pp22-28.
7. Parasuraman, A et.al. The nature and determinants of customer expectations of service. *Journal of the Academy of Marketing Science*, 1993. pp1-12.
8. Parasuraman, A et.al (1993) Op. Cit.
9. Parasuraman, A et.al. (1994). Op. Cit.
10. Zeithamal et.al. The behavioural consequences of service quality. *Journal of Marketing*, 1996. pp31-46.
11. Berry and Parasuraman, A. Multiple method listening. *Sloan Management Review*, 1997. pp65-76.
12. Parasurman, A. et.al. (1988). Op. Cit.
13. Cronin, J.J and Taylor, S.A, 'Measuring service quality: a reexamination and extension', *Journal of Marketing*, 56, 1992, pp55-68

14. Cronin, J.J and Taylor, S.A. SERVPERF and SERVQUAL: Reconciling performance based and perception minus expectations measurement of service quality. *Journal of Marketing*, 58, 1994. pp 125-131.

15. Iacobucci, D et.al. The calculus of service quality and customer satisfaction. *Advances in Service Marketing and Management*, 3, 1994. pp1-68.

16. Oliver, R.L. A cognitive model of the antecedents and consequences of satisfactin decisions. *Journal of Marketing Research*, 17, 1980. p460-469.

17. Cronin, J.J and Taylor, S.A (1994). Op. Cit.

18. Anderson, T.D. Another model of service quality. In Quality Management in Service. Ed by Kunst, P and Lemmink, J. The Netherlands: Van Gorcum, 1992. pp41-58.

19. Babakus, E and Boller, G.W. An empirical assessment of SERVQUAL Scale. *Journal of Business Research*, 24, 1992. pp253-268.

20. Iacobucci, D et.al. Op. Cit.

21. Kahneman, D and Miller, D.T. Norm theory: Comparing reality to its alternatives. *Psychological Review*, 93, 1986. pp136-153.

22. Teas, K.R. Expectations, performance evaluation and consumers' perceptions of quality. *Journal of Marketing*, 57, 1993.pp18-24.

23. Teas, K.R. Consumer expectations and the measurement of perceived service quality. *Journal of Professional Services Marketing*, 8, 1993. pp33-53.

24. Teas, K.R. Expectations as a comparison standard in measuring service quality. *Journal of Marketing*, 58, 1994. pp132-139.

25. Gronroos, C. Towards a third phase in service quality research. *Advances in Services Marketing Research*, 2, 1994.pp49-64.

26. Wotruba, T.R and Tyagi, P.K. Met expectations and turnover in direct selling. *Journal of Marketing*, 55, 1991.pp24-35.

27. Hardie, B.G.S, et.al. Modeling loss aversion and reference dependence effects on brand choice. University of Pennsylvania, 1992 (working report)

28. Cronin, J.J and Taylor, S.A (1992). Op. Cit.

29. Cronin, J.J and Taylor, S.A (1992). Op. Cit.

30. Mangold, G.W and Babakus, E. Service Quality: the front stage perceptive vs the back stage perceptive. *Journal of Service Marketing*, 5 (4), 1991. pp59-70.

31. Richard, M.D and Allaway, A.W. Service quality attributes and

choice behaviour. *Journal of Service Marketing*, 7(1), 1993. pp59-68.

32. Gronroos, C. A service quality model and its marketing implications. *European Journal of Marketing*, 18, 1984. pp36-44.
33. Lehtinen, J.R. and Lehtinen, O. Service Quality: A study of quality dimensions. Helsinki: Management Institute, 1982.
34. Hedvall, M.B and Paltschik, M. An investigation in and generation of service quality concepts. In Marketing thought and practice in the 1990s. Ed by G.J. Avlonitis. Athens: European Marketing Academy, 1989. pp473-483.
35. Leblanc, G and Nguyen, N. Customers' perceptions of service quality in Financial institutions. *International Journal of Bank Marketing*, 6(4), 1988. pp7-18.
36. Carmen, J.M. Consumer perceptions of service quality: An assessment of SERVQUAL dimensions. *Journal of Retailing*, 66(1), 1990. pp33-35.
37. Babakus, E and Boller, G.W (1992). Op. Cit.
38. Teas, K.R (1993) Op. Cit.
39. Zeithaml, V.A et.al. The nature of determinants of customer expectations of service. Cambridge: Marketing Science Institute, 1991.pp91-113.
40. Bouman, M and Vander Wiele, T. Measuring service quality in the car service industry.*International Journal of Service Industry Management*,3(4),1992. pp4-16.
41. Carmen, J.M (1990). Op. Cit.
42. Saleh, F and Ryan, C. Analysing service quality in the Hospitality Industry using SERVQUAL model. *Service Industries Journal*, 11(3), 1992. pp324-343.
43. Fort, M. Customer defined attributes of service quality in the IBM Mid Range Computer Software Industry. Manchester: Manchester Business School, 1993. (MBA Dissertation).
44. Carmen, J.M. (1990). Op. Cit
45. Babakus, E and Boller, G.W (1992). Op. Cit.
46. Lewis, B.R. Service Quality measureament. *Marketing Intelligence and Planning*, 11(4), 1993.pp4-12.
47. Babakus, E and Mangold, W.G. Adapting the SERVQUAL Scale to Hospital services. *Health Services Research*, 26(2), 1992. pp767-786.
48. Bouman, M and Vander Wiele, T (1992). Op. Cit.
49. Carmen, J.M. (1990). Op. Cit.
50. http://www.libqual.org/

Appendix

THE SERVQUAL INSTRUMENT*

Directions: the survey deals with your opinions of .... services. Please show the extent to which you think firms offering .... services should possess the features described by each statement. Do this by picking one of the seven numbers next to each statement. If you strongly agree that these firms should possess a feature, circle the number 7. If you strongly disagree that these firms should possess a feature, circle 1. If your feelings are not strong, circle one of the numbers in the middle. There are no right or wrong answers .... All we are interested in is a number that best shows your expectations about firms offering .... services.

E1. They should have up-to-date equipment.

Strongly Agree 1 2 3 4 5 6 7 Strongly Disagree

E2. Their physical facilities should be visually appealing.

Strongly Agree 1 2 3 4 5 6 7 Strongly Disagree

E3. Their employees should be well dressed.

Strongly Agree 1 2 3 4 5 6 7 Strongly Disagree

E4. The appearance of the physical facilities of these firms should be in keeping with the type of services provided.

Strongly Agree 1 2 3 4 5 6 7 Strongly Disagree

E5. When these firms promise to do some thing by a certain time, they should do so.

Strongly Agree 1 2 3 4 5 6 7 Strongly Disagree

E6. When customers have problems, these firms should be sympathetic and reassuring.

Strongly Agree 1 2 3 4 5 6 7 Strongly Disagree

E7. These firms should be dependable.

Strongly Agree 1 2 3 4 5 6 7 Strongly Disagree

E8. They should provide their services at the time they promised to do.

Strongly Agree 1 2 3 4 5 6 7 Strongly Disagree

E9. They should keep their records accurately.

Strongly Agree 1 2 3 4 5 6 7 Strongly Disagree

E10. They shouldn't be expected to tell customers exactly when services would be performed.

Strongly Agree 1 2 3 4 5 6 7 Strongly Disagree

E11. It is not realistic for customers to expect prompt service from employees of these firms.

Strongly Agree 1 2 3 4 5 6 7 Strongly Disagree

E12. Their employees don't always have to be willing to help customers.

Strongly Agree 1 2 3 4 5 6 7 Strongly Disagree

E13. It is okay if they are too busy to respond to customer requests promptly.

Strongly Agree 1 2 3 4 5 6 7 Strongly Disagree

E14. Customers should be able to trust employees of these firms.

Strongly Agree 1 2 3 4 5 6 7 Strongly Disagree

E15. Customers should be able to feel safe in their transaction with these firms' employees.

Strongly Agree 1 2 3 4 5 6 7 Strongly Disagree

E16. Their employees should be polite.

Strongly Agree 1 2 3 4 5 6 7 Strongly Disagree

E17. Their employees should get adequate support from these firms to do their jobs well.

Strongly Agree 1 2 3 4 5 6 7 Strongly Disagree

E18. These firms should not be expected to give customers

individual attention.

Strongly Agree 1 2 3 4 5 6 7 Strongly Disagree

E19. Employees of these firms cannot be expected to give customers personal attention.

Strongly Agree 1 2 3 4 5 6 7 Strongly Disagree

E20. It is unrealistic to expect employees to know what the needs of their customers are,

Strongly Agree 1 2 3 4 5 6 7 Strongly Disagree

E21. Employees of these firms know what the best interests of their customers are.

Strongly Agree 1 2 3 4 5 6 7 Strongly Disagree

E22. They shouldn't be expected to have operating hours convenient to all their customers.

Strongly Agree 1 2 3 4 5 6 7 Strongly Disagree

Directions: The following set of statements relate to your feelings about XYZ. For each statement, please show the extent to which you believe XYZ has the features described by the statement. Once again, circling a 7 means that you strongly agree that XYZ has that feature, and circling 1 means that you strongly disagree. You may circle any of the numbers in the middle that show how strong your feelings are. There are no right or wrong answers, all we are interested in it is a number that best shows your perceptions about XYZ.

P1. XYZ has up-to-date equipment.

Strongly Agree 1 2 3 4 5 6 7 Strongly Disagree

P2. XYZ's physical facilities are visually appealing.

Strongly Agree 1 2 3 4 5 6 7 Strongly Disagree

P3. XYZ's employees are well dressed and appear neat.

Strongly Agree 1 2 3 4 5 6 7 Strongly Disagree

P4. The appearance of the physical facilities of XYZ is in keeping with the type of services provided.

Strongly Agree 1 2 3 4 5 6 7 Strongly Disagree

P5. When XYZ promises to do some thing by a certain time, it does so.

Strongly Agree 1 2 3 4 5 6 7 Strongly Disagree

P6. When you have problems, XYZ is sympathetic and reassuring.

Strongly Agree 1 2 3 4 5 6 7 Strongly Disagree

P7. XYZ is dependable.

Strongly Agree 1 2 3 4 5 6 7 Strongly Disagree

P8. XYZ provides its service at the time it promises to do so.

Strongly Agree 1 2 3 4 5 6 7 Strongly Disagree

P9. XYZ keeps its records accurately.

Strongly Agree 1 2 3 4 5 6 7 Strongly Disagree

P10. XYZ does not tell customers exactly when services will be performed.

Strongly Agree 1 2 3 4 5 6 7 Strongly Disagree

P11. You do not receive prompt service from XYZ's employees.

Strongly Agree 1 2 3 4 5 6 7 Strongly Disagree

P12. Employees of XYZ are not always willing to help customers.

Strongly Agree 1 2 3 4 5 6 7 Strongly Disagree

P13. Employees of XYZ are too busy to respond to customer requests promptly.

Strongly Agree 1 2 3 4 5 6 7 Strongly Disagree

P14. You can trust employees of XYZ.

Strongly Agree 1 2 3 4 5 6 7 Strongly Disagree

P15. You feel safe in your transactions with XYZ's employees.

Strongly Agree 1 2 3 4 5 6 7 Strongly Disagree

P16. Employees of XYZ are polite.

Strongly Agree 1 2 3 4 5 6 7 Strongly Disagree

P17. Employees get adequate support from XYZ to do their jobs well.

Strongly Agree 1 2 3 4 5 6 7 Strongly Disagree

P18. XYZ does not give you individual attention.

Strongly Agree 1 2 3 4 5 6 7 Strongly Disagree

P19. Employees of XYZ do not give you personal attention.

Strongly Agree 1 2 3 4 5 6 7 Strongly Disagree

P20. Employees of XYZ do not know what your needs are.

Strongly Agree 1 2 3 4 5 6 7 Strongly Disagree

P21. XYZ does not have your best interests at heart.

Strongly Agree 1 2 3 4 5 6 7 Strongly Disagree

P22. XYZ does not have operating hours convenient to all their customers.

Strongly Agree 1 2 3 4 5 6 7 Strongly Disagree

11

LibQUAL, An Instrument for Assessing the Quality of Libraries

The LibQUAL+ survey[1] is a research and development project undertaken to define and measure library service quality across institutions and to create useful quality assessment tools for local planning. It is a web-based survey piloted by Association of Research Libraries (ARL) in collaboration with Texas A&M University Libraries. The survey involved 169 participating libraries including University of Illinois at Urbana, Ohio State University, Penn State University and Northwestern University of Health Sciences. It is intended to provide a measure of the value of library service quality across multiple academic and research libraries. The LibQUAL+ instrument measures library users' perceptions of their libraries' service quality and identifies gaps between minimal, desired and perceived levels of service.

In 2000 Texas A&M University endorsed a pilot project proposal entitled the use of a protocol well grounded in marketing research, SERVQUAL, to assess the service quality in research libraries. This project had its origin in the gap theory of service quality developed by the marketing research team of Parasuraman et.al (1985)[2]. The gap theory assumes that, service quality can be measured by the gap between customers desired service levels and the perceived level of service delivery. Danuta Nitecki (1995)[3] had initially explored the study of its application to libraries.

The Texas A&M University research team had re-grounded and evaluated the SERVQUAL protocol within a research library environment that led to the development of LibQUAL+ protocol. The SERVQUAL was re-grounded for the research library environment through a series of interviews with faculty, and students at various universities in North America. These interviews helped to prepare the web-based questionnaire to measure, in the users' own words, their library service quality. Ascertaining library quality is a good step to develop an understanding of preferred and best services and to recognize standards of library quality.

The major goals[4] of the LibQUAL+ survey are:

1. Establish a library service quality assessment program at ARL;
2. Develop web-based tools for assessing library service quality;
3. Develop mechanisms and protocols for evaluating libraries; and
4. Identify best practices in providing library service.

Genesis of LibQUAL+ Instrument

The first iteration of the LibQUAL+ protocol[5] was developed in 2000. The initial phase of the study involved participation with Texas A&M University and twelve additional institutions, namely:

1. University of Arizona
2. University of California
3. University of Connecticut
4. University of Houston
5. University of Kansa
6. Michigan State University
7. University of Minnesota

8. University of Pittsburgh
9. University of Pennsylvania
10. Viginia Tech
11. University of Washington
12. York University.

In its first phase, the protocol used twenty-two items in the SERVQUAL instrument. But these items have not yielded the expected five-factor structure in the library setting. So in depth interviews were conducted with the users in all the thirteen institutions under study. Accordingly nineteen items were added to the items in SERVQUAL instrument, making a total of forty-one items for the pilot study. New items are continuing to evolve during the study. The qualitative and quantitative analysis will strengthen the process.

LibQUAL+ is grounded in the epistemological view that 'dynamic theory building' and construct measurement are joint boot step operations.

The reliability item analysis and factor analysis of the data collected in pilot study resulted in the identification of thirty-four items from the forty-one items of initial LibQUAL+ protocol. These items are[6]:

1. Convenient access collections
2. Providing services as promised
3. Keep users informed
4. A place for reflection
5. Service at promised time
6. Employees instill confidence
7. Resources added to collection
8. Employees understand needs
9. A contemplative environment
10. Users' best interests at heart

11. Comfortable and inviting location
12. Instruction in use when needed
13. Maintain error free records
14. Timely document delivery
15. Readiness to respond to users
16. Willingness to help users
17. Employees have knowledge
18. A secure and safe place
19. Center intellectual interaction
20. Deal with users in caring fashion
21. Full text delivered electronically
22. Comprehensive print collection
23. Performing services right
24. Space group/ individual study
25. A heaven for quiet and solitude
26. Library materials in the stacks
27. Employees are courteous
28. Modern equipment
29. Inter-disciplinary needs addressed
30. Complete runs of Journal titles
31. Employees have neat appearance
32. A meditative place
33. Space that facilitates quiet reading
34. Giving users individual attention.

These thirty-four items are related to four quality dimensions namely, Affect of Service (11 items), Library as place (9 items), Access to collection (7 items), and Reliability (7 items). The hierarchical LibQUAL+ factor model[7] is shown in Figure 11.1.

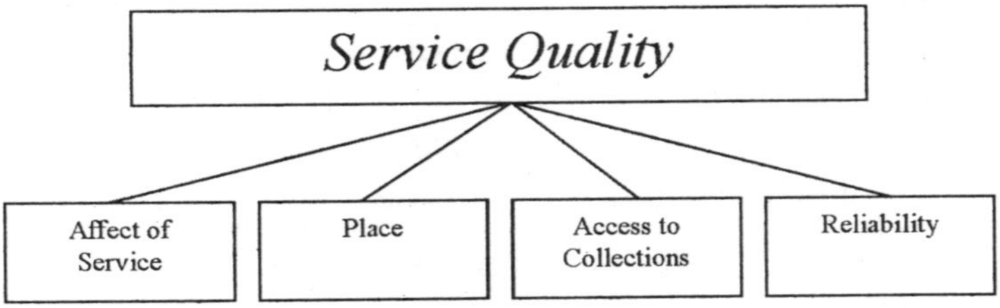

Figure 11.1. The hierarchical LibQUAL+ factor model

The individual libraries participating in the survey can identify where their services need improvement in the view of their users. They can also compare their service quality with that of peer institutions in an effort to develop benchmarks and understanding of best practices across institutions. Based on the information they receive from their library users and participating libraries, libraries can provide services that are more closely aligned with user expectations. As library services are improved, it will help users to better reach their learning and research objectives.

LibQUAL+ is a tool for measuring library users perceptions of service quality and identifies gaps between desired, perceived and minimum expectations of service. It uses a scalable web interface and protocol to ask library users about their library service expectations.

LibQUAL+ helps the library to[8]:

1. Identify where their services need improvement in the view of their users.
2. Compare their service quality with that of others.
3. Provide services that are more close to user expectations.

The LibQUAL+ project is funded from US Dept. of Education's Fund for the improvement of Post-secondary Education, ARL and Texas A&M University and Fee from participating libraries. The latest version of the LibQUAL+

questionnaire contains the following 25 questions grouped in 4 service quality determinants, namely Access to information, Affect of service, Library as place and Personal control and use a 9-point Likert scale to mark user responses. The model questionnaire[9] used by ARL is given below:

Access to Information Dimension:	
	Question
3	Complete runs of journal titles
8	Timely document delivery/interlibrary loan
9	Interdisciplinary library needs being addressed
19	Convenient business hours
22	Comprehensive print collections

Affect of Service Dimension:	
1	Willingness to help users
4	Employees who are consistently courteous
11	Dependability in handling users' service problems
14	Giving users individual attention
15	Employees who deal with users in a caring fashion
17	Employees who have the knowledge to answer user questions
18	Readiness to respond to users' questions
20	Employees who instill confidence in users
24	Employees who understand the needs of their users

Library as Place Dimension:	
2	Space that facilitates quiet study
10	A haven for quiet and solitude
13	A place for reflection and creativity
21	A comfortable and inviting location
23	A contemplative environment

	Personal Control Dimension:
5	Making electronic resources accessible from my home or office
6	Modern equipment that lets me easily access the information I need
7	A library website enabling me to locate information on my own
12	Easy-to-use access tools that allow me to find things on my own
16	Making information easily accessible for indep ndent use
25	Convenient access to library collections

LibQUAL+ is based on the SERVQUAL model of assessing service quality in marketing research. As a beginning, a series of sixty interviews with a diverse set of library users, both students and faculty, was conducted at nine ARL libraries in 2000. Open ended and unstructured questions were used in the interviews. Each person interviewed was first asked to list the libraries that he/she had used so far. Then they were queried regarding their concept of library service quality. The dimensions of service quality identified in the SERVQUAL instrument were used as the basic set of issues.

A major focus of library service quality is the user. The interviews established that the user expects the library to provide service for all categories and levels of users, and to promote wide and easy access to all informational resources available in print, and electronic form. The users want to be self-reliant and confident in navigating the library for their purpose. Not only that, the user expect individualized attention from their library staff. They have expectation of courteous or knowledgeable service from their library staff. They expect a friendly encounter with library staff.

Users expect that library should give access to their print collections, full-text electronic resources, databases and inter-library lending services, as part of access to information. They expect that there should be ease of access and convenient working hours of operations. They expect an inter-library loan service in one week. Not only that, they expect document delivery system as an easy and fast one.

The study confirmed qualitatively that perceptions of quality are the most important indicators of satisfaction. The various factors that represent the dimensions of library service quality[10] are given in figure 11.2.

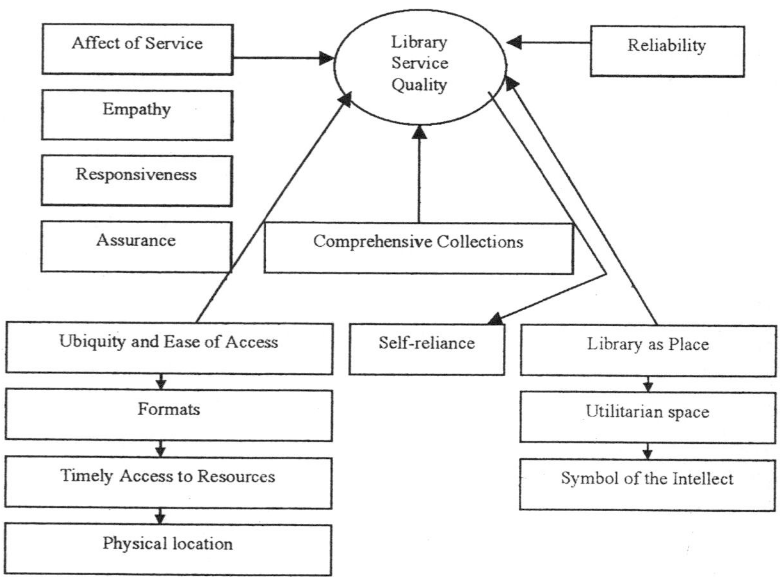

Figure 11.2. Factors involved in the Dimensions of Library Service Quality

The discussions on the five dimensions of service quality in the context of a library showed that all are significant components of library service quality. In addition to that, ubiquity and ease of access to collections, the library as place (utilitarian space and library as a symbol) and the self-reliance are found as component of library service quality.

Advantages of LibQUAL+ Study

LibQUAL+ is a well-established survey tool with a different methodology design, content and delivery mechanism. It is a standardized survey instrument used in many libraries. It is a web-based survey that reduces the cost of a survey like cost of printing, mailing, and data entry. LibQUAL+ has used a three-column response format of minimum, perceived and desired level of perception of library service quality.

LibQUAL+ instrument is a tool to learn what is important to customers and how they perceive the library services in relation to their expectations. It is the first attempt to move from the focus on inputs and production capabilities to outputs and outcomes. It is developed in the spirit of sharing benchmarking information among cooperating libraries. It provides information that can lead to widespread improvement in academic and research libraries in an international level. It enables the libraries to learn from one another and share successful approaches. It is a method of listening customers and redefines the library for them. It provides an opportunity to test how the customer defines satisfaction.

LibQUAL+ instrument suggests further research on the results of the user survey as it only indicates whether the overall library quality is good or not and whether there is any difference between the user perceptions and expectations about the library services. Therefore, it is highly necessary to conduct further research to explore the reasons for low, medium or high level of library service quality.

It provides an excellent opportunity for developing meaningful contacts and co-operations with customers. It provides opportunities to listen to the voices of customers, establish proactive caring relationship, customer cooperation in increasing the capacity of the libraries to meet the customers' expectations in future. It also gives a chance to listen the voice of library staff. In order to improve the service quality of a library, it is necessary to focus on performance, know how to measure progress, and help them develop the new knowledge skill needed to improve the service quality.

It provides an opportunity to hear the voice of processes, as the service is the result of a process and if service quality to be improved, its process should be improved first. The staff doing the process in the library can say much about it and so they must be included in the library process improvement programmes. The library management should listen to the voices of process staff before a process improvement program is enunciated.

LibQUAL+TM 2002

The continuous research on LibQUAL+ led to the development of LibQUAL+TM tool to assess the quality of libraries. LibQUAL+TM is a way of listening to users. It consists of 25 items, which measure perceptions of total service quality as well as four sub dimensions of perceived library quality, namely service affect, library as place, personal control, and information access. Service affect contains 9 item, library as place 5 items, personal control 6 items and information access 5 items. On each of these items, there are three levels of ratings used, namely minimally – acceptable service, desired service and perceived service.

With the help of LibQUAL+TM[11] instrument, the library can interpret the perceived level of service quality within the 'Zone of tolerance'. It uses a 9-point scale to measure the perceived library quality. LibQUAL+TM is an effort to create a culture of service quality assessment and service quality improvement within libraries.

A LibQUAL+TM Questionnaire is given as Appendix to this chapter. Similar type of questionnaires can be developed for the assessment of a library or a group of libraries. Such a tool suitable for libraries in developing countries is yet to develop.

References

1. Cook, C and Thompson, Bruce. Psychometric properties of scores. Library Trends, 49(4), 2001. p585-586.
2. Parasuraman, A. et al. A conceptual model of service quality and its implications for future research. Journal of Marketing. 49, 1985. pp45-48
3. Nitecki, D.A. 'Changing the concept and measure of service quality in academic libraries'. *Journal of Academic Librarianship*. 22(3), 1996. p181-190.
4. Cook, C and Heath, F. The Association of Research Libraries LibQYAL+ Project. *ARL News Letter*, 211, 2000. p12-14.
5. Cook and Thompson. Op. Cit. p586.
6. http://www.libqual.org/
7. Cook, C and Thompson, Bruce. Op. Cit. p601.
8. Nitecki, D.A and Hernon, P. Measuring service quality at Yale University's Libraries. *Journal of Academic Librarianship*, 26(4), 2000. p260.
9. http://www.libqual.org/
10. Cook and Heath. Users Perception of Library Service Quality. Library Trends, 49(4), 2001. p580.
11. Cook, C., et.al. 'LibQUAL+^{TM}: Service quality assessment in research libraries'. *IFLA Journal*, 4, 2001. p264-268

Appendix

LibQUAL+TM Questionnaire

Please rate the following statements by selecting your choices from the pull-down menus to indicate:

* **Minimum** – the number that represents the *minimum* level of service that you would find acceptable.
* **Desired** – the number tat represents the level of service that *you personally want.*
* **Perceived** – the number that represents the level of service that you believe our library currently provides.

You must EITHER rate all three columns OR identify the item as N/A

When it comes to...		My Minimum Service Level is Low High	My Desired Service Level is Low High	Perceived Service Performance is Low High	N/A
1.	Willingness to help users	1 2 3 4 5 6 7 8 9	1 2 3 4 5 6 7 8 9	1 2 3 4 5 6 7 8 9	N/A
2.	Space that facilitates quiet study	1 2 3 4 5 6 7 8 9	1 2 3 4 5 6 7 8 9	1 2 3 4 5 6 7 8 9	N/A
3.	Complete runs of journal titles	1 2 3 4 5 6 7 8 9	1 2 3 4 5 6 7 8 9	1 2 3 4 5 6 7 8 9	N/A
4.	Employees who are consistently courteous	1 2 3 4 5 6 7 8 9	1 2 3 4 5 6 7 8 9	1 2 3 4 5 6 7 8 9	N/A
5.	Making electronic resources accessible from my home or office	1 2 3 4 5 6 7 8 9	1 2 3 4 5 6 7 8 9	1 2 3 4 5 6 7 8 9	N/A
6.	Modern equipment that lets me easily access the information I need	1 2 3 4 5 6 7 8 9	1 2 3 4 5 6 7 8 9	1 2 3 4 5 6 7 8 9	N/A

7.	A library website enabling me to locate information on my own	1 2 3 4 5 6 7 8 9	1 2 3 4 5 6 7 8 9	1 2 3 4 5 6 7 8 9	N/A
8.	Timely document delivery/inter library loan	1 2 3 4 5 6 7 8 9	1 2 3 4 5 6 7 8 9	1 2 3 4 5 6 7 8 9	N/A
9.	Interdisciplinary library needs being addressed	1 2 3 4 5 6 7 8 9	1 2 3 4 5 6 7 8 9	1 2 3 4 5 6 7 8 9	N/A
10.	A haven for quiet and solitude	1 2 3 4 5 6 7 8 9	1 2 3 4 5 6 7 8 9	1 2 3 4 5 6 7 8 9	N/A
11.	Dependability in handling users' service problems	1 2 3 4 5 6 7 8 9	1 2 3 4 5 6 7 8 9	1 2 3 4 5 6 7 8 9	N/A
12.	Easy-to-use access tools that allow me to find things on my own	1 2 3 4 5 6 7 8 9	1 2 3 4 5 6 7 8 9	1 2 3 4 5 6 7 8 9	N/A
13.	A place for reflection and creativity	1 2 3 4 5 6 7 8 9	1 2 3 4 5 6 7 8 9	1 2 3 4 5 6 7 8 9	N/A
14.	Giving users individual attention	1 2 3 4 5 6 7 8 9	1 2 3 4 5 6 7 8 9	1 2 3 4 5 6 7 8 9	N/A
15.	Employees who deal with users in a caring fashion	1 2 3 4 5 6 7 8 9	1 2 3 4 5 6 7 8 9	1 2 3 4 5 6 7 8 9	N/A
16.	Making information easily accessible for independent use	1 2 3 4 5 6 7 8 9	1 2 3 4 5 6 7 8 9	1 2 3 4 5 6 7 8 9	N/A
17.	Employees who have the knowledge to	1 2 3 4 5 6 7 8 9	1 2 3 4 5 6 7 8 9	1 2 3 4 5 6 7 8 9	N/A

	answer user questions				
18.	Readiness to respond to users questions	1 2 3 4 5 6 7 8 9	1 2 3 4 5 6 7 8 9	1 2 3 4 5 6 7 8 9	N/A
19.	Convenient business hours	1 2 3 4 5 6 7 8 9	1 2 3 4 5 6 7 8 9	1 2 3 4 5 6 7 8 9	N/A
20.	Employees who instill confidence in users	1 2 3 4 5 6 7 8 9	1 2 3 4 5 6 7 8 9	1 2 3 4 5 6 7 8 9	N/A
21.	A comfortable and inviting location	1 2 3 4 5 6 7 8 9	1 2 3 4 5 6 7 8 9	1 2 3 4 5 6 7 8 9	N/A
22.	Comprehensive print collections	1 2 3 4 5 6 7 8 9	1 2 3 4 5 6 7 8 9	1 2 3 4 5 6 7 8 9	N/A
23.	A contemplative environment	1 2 3 4 5 6 7 8 9	1 2 3 4 5 6 7 8 9	1 2 3 4 5 6 7 8 9	N/A
24.	Employees who understand the needs of their users	1 2 3 4 5 6 7 8 9	1 2 3 4 5 6 7 8 9	1 2 3 4 5 6 7 8 9	N/A
25.	Convenient access to library collection	1 2 3 4 5 6 7 8 9	1 2 3 4 5 6 7 8 9	1 2 3 4 5 6 7 8 9	N/A

Please indicate the degree to which you agree with the following statements:		
1.	In general, I am satisfied with the way in which I am treated at the libraries	1 2 3 4 5 6 7 8 9 Strongly Disagree Strongly Agree
2.	In general, I am satisfied with library support for my learning, research and/or teaching needs.	1 2 3 4 5 6 7 8 9 Strongly Disagree Strongly Agree
3.	How would you rate the overall quality of the service provided by the library?	1 2 3 4 5 6 7 8 9 Extremely Poor Extremely Good

Please indicate your library usage patterns:

How often do you use resources on library premises?

* Daily
* Weekly
* Monthly
* Quarterly
* Never

How often do you use electronic library services remotely?

* Daily
* Weekly
* Monthly
* Quarterly
* Never

Please enter any comments about library services below.

....

....

....

....

....

....

12
Library Quality: A Review

A number of research studies on effectiveness, efficiency, satisfaction of users, and usefulness of services of libraries and information centers have been reported in professional literature. Most of these studies were aimed to assess the satisfaction of users or to evaluate the quality of library and information services offered. They used either existing methods for the study and research or devised new techniques for the purpose. Some of such significant studies are reviewed in this chapter.

User Satisfaction

Measuring library effectiveness is identified as one of the main purpose of studies conducted in libraries aimed to assess the level of satisfaction of users, as the satisfied users are the symbol of quality library services. Roshan Raina (1995)[1] conducted a study in Indian Institute of Management Library, Lucknow to see how far the student community was satisfied with the library facilities and services. It is reported that all the students were satisfied with the library collection, services and the information technology used in the library. But, they were not happy with the reading space, the environment, shelving of documents etc. Cullen and Calvert (1995)[2] studied the university library effectiveness in New Zealand and assessed the level of satisfaction of the user community. They reported that 'competence of library management' is the key indicator of library effectiveness to resource allocators, 'helpfulness and courtesy of staff' for library staff, 'expert staff assistance to users' for faculty, 'match of hours of opening with the user needs' for graduate students, and 'provision of multiple copies of documents in high demand' for undergraduate students.

User satisfaction surveys are regularly conducted in libraries in recent years to assess the level of satisfaction of users. Wilson and Orr (1995)[3] assessed the satisfaction of part-time students in a university with regard to the library facilities, collection, services and staff. They identified that the users had high satisfaction with the physical facilities and staff. At same time, Talbot and Martin (1996)[4], reported that the users in San Diego Libraries of the University of California were not satisfied with the printed collection, photostat service, opening hours, and physical facilities available in the library. It is to be noted that the users preferred printed document collection even in electronic era and good user education programme to exploit the library resources and services in a better manner. Hiller (2001)[5] reported that remote use of library resources and services was not a factor affecting the level of satisfaction of users and service quality. He reported that there was a difference in the focus of students and faculties with regard to the facilities, collection, services and staff. Faculty focused on the information resources and its access. On the other hand the students preferred the facilities.

Hernon and Altman (1996)[6] argued that higher level of service quality results in increased user satisfaction and viewed that there were two perspectives for viewing the user satisfaction of library services: 1. Service encounter satisfaction and 2. Overall service satisfaction. If all service transactions were up to their expectations, it would give raise to good perception and satisfaction with regard to the service quality and its determinants such as tangibles, reliability, responsiveness, assurance and empathy, an overall satisfaction to the users. On the other hand, Cullen (2001)[7] explored the relationship between service quality and user satisfaction in depth and stressed that the user satisfaction surveys could be used to assess the user satisfaction in micro and macro level through a model. He argued that the model could be used to assess the user satisfaction of electronic library services as well.

Quality Standards

The library of the University of Central Lancashire is reported as the first major library to implement ISO 9000. Brophy (1993)[8] shared his experience with the implementation of a quality standard in this large library. The basic aim of implementing ISO 9000 in the library was to provide highest quality library services to the users. There were three levels in implementation. At the strategic level, an overview of the library's performance and success in meeting strategic aims was done. At the operational level, the quality of service the individual user receives was analyzed. At the third level, monitoring, maintaining and improving quality was ensured.

Verma (2002)[9] studied the quality management approaches followed in leading libraries in India with special reference to ISO 9000 and found that total quality management approches were preferred to ISO 9000 and suggested that use of quality standards required more innovation and initiation or reorganisation process. Date and Gokhale (1999)[10] studied the ISO certified libraries in Mumbai and compared the results with that of non-certified libraries to understand the difference in the level of quality of services offered and to benchmark on low quality services. They argued that an attempt to implement quality standard in a library itself would improve the quality of library services.

Service Quality

Quinn (1997)[11] made a theoretical study about service quality concepts and its adaptability in academic libraries and found that the service quality concepts could very well be adapted to reference service, access services, collection development etc. and it would give more reputation to the library as well as good satisfaction to the users. He noted that the library researchers consider quality service as what the user expected and finding the best way to meet these expectations. Phipps (2001)[12] tested this argument among the users and staff of the Association of Research Libraries and reported that libraries must listen and act on the voices of the users to make them satisfied and improve the library service quality. Measuring the performance of processes and staff is also necessary to improve the services. Special methodologies like SERVQUAL, LibQUAL+ etc. can also be used for ascertaining the views of the users.

The Association of Research Libraries conducted a Symposium on measuring library service quality on 20-21 October 2000 in Washington, with an aim of discussing the need for identifying new tools for assessing service quality in libraries. About 180 experts in the area of performance measurement, organisational effectiveness and service quality attended the symposium. Kyrillidou (2001)[13] presented the proceedings of the symposium and provided the abstracts of the papers discussed.

The perceptions of the service quality of university libraries are found to be different to students and teachers. Chang and Hsieh (1996)[14] tested the service quality of student's and teacher's perception in China and found that there are significant differences between the two in service quality factors. The faculty viewed 'collections supporting research' as very important factor in service quality, but it was 'up-to-date equipment' for students. Jayasundara (2001)[15] studied the student's and teacher's perception of service quality in university libraries of Sri Lanka and reported that there are eight determinants to be assessed to measure service quality in academic libraries. On the other hand, Pors (1996)[16] compared the expectations and perceptions of students in Denmark and opined that the attitudes of students about their library services are very low compared to their expectations. Yang (2000)[17] surveyed the faculty of Texas A&M University to assess their perception about the library liaison programme and its impact on library services offered to them. The faculty observed that the liaison programme was necessary for them as it was beneficial to them to get quality services and information about forthcoming changes and developments in the library. On the other hand Cullen and Calvert (1993)[18] and Edwards and Browne (1995)[19] compared the user expectations and the librarians' perception about user expectations in detail and found that there were discrepancies between them. This would adversely affect the service quality.

SERVQUAL Studies

SERVQUAL is an internationally recognized tool for measuring service quality and it is heavily used in marketing research. Several researchers used the original SERVQUAL tool and its five quality determinants such as Tangibles, Reliability, Responsiveness, Assurance and Empathy to study the service quality of libraries.

Campbell et al (1995)[20] used this tool to study the service quality of Stirling District Council Library, Scotland. Among the five dimensions of service quality, tangibles and reliability are perceived low to its expectations. Coleman et al (1997)[21] observed that there were discrepancies in the quality of services offered in C. Evans Library of the Texas A & M University to their users and the one desired by its users. Similarly Abdul Majeed and Bavakutty (2002)[22] viewed that the users expected good collection (Tangibles) and personalised attention (Responsiveness) from libraries and there were discrepancies in the quality of services perceived by students and faculty. Simmonds and Andaleeb (2000)[23] viewed that the library resources and the staff of the Pennsylvania State University Library were not up-to the expectations of library users. They further analysed the service quality of other libraries in their area to identify the differences in quality as well as the techniques and methods used to improve the service quality and attract users. On the other hand, Nitecki (1996)[24] used SERVQUAL to measure the service quality of the reference service offered in academic libraries and to see how far this tool was suitable for assessing service quality in academic libraries. She noted that reference service providers should concentrate on both showing sincere interest in user problems and willingness to help users for increasing the service quality of reference service.

Many researchers like Nitecki and Hernon, Cook and Thompson, etc studied the applicability of SERVQUAL tool for measuring service quality of libraries and information centers. Nitecki and Hernon (2000)[25] analysed the SERVQUAL instrument for converting it to an instrument that reflects the expectations of a library and its users, to determine the feasibility of the change and to compare the results of studies conducted with other tools for measuring service quality and reported that, more items were to be added to SERVQUAL instrument to represent all activities and services of the library, but all its determinants are important in service quality measurement of libraries. Similarly Cook and Thompson (2000)[26] studied the reliability and validity of the SERVQUAL scores, and the importance of dimensions to evaluate the perceptions of library service quality and found that scores are less reliable on tangibles and assurance. They noted the chances for differences in validity and reliability of the scores in different library settings, namely academic, public and special libraries. Based on this view, they further conducted a study (2000)[27] to explore the feasibility of SERVQUAL in a research library setting and found that the original tool containing 22 items and five dimensions could very well be used to measure research library service quality.

The Reliability dimension in SERVQUAL tool was separately studied to see how far it could be used to understand the problem areas in library services. Jeannette Ho and Crowley (2003)[28] reported that finding of materials on shelf, arrangement of materials, circulation procedure, signage, and experience of using library catalogue were affecting reliability of services offered to users. They viewed that reliability dimension was an important dimension in library service quality.

Special Tools

Many researchers used special tools developed on the basis of the principles and structures of SERVQUAL tool instead of SERVQUAL itself. Hiller, Crossno, Philip and Hazlett, Landrum and Pybutok etc. developed such new tools. Hiller (2000)[29] studied the service quality of the University Library of Washington with a tool containing 41 items in three-column response format of minimum, perceived and desired level of service quality. Crossno et al (2001)[30] developed a new measuring tool, called Assessment of Customer Service in Academic Health Care Services(ACSAHL), which is shorter to the original SERVQUAL tool. Philip and Hazlett (2001)[31] used a new tool, called Pivotal-Core-Peripheral (P-C-P) attributes model to measure the service quality of information services offered in Northern Ireland libraries and found that it gave good results than the SERVQUAL method. Landrum and Prybutok (2003)[32] used a tool, developed on SERVQUAL principles, called ISYSCESS, to measure the variables associated with information system success. They reported that items on service quality, system quality, information quality and usefulness were necessary for measuring the success of a library or information system.

Some researchers developed their own tools for measuring service quality of libraries. Few of them tried for developing a common tool applicable for all types of libraries, and others developed a tool suitable to particular requirement. Hernon and Calvert (1996)[33] made an attempt to develop a common tool for measuring service quality in university libraries. They developed a self reporting data collection instrument containing 61 items for measuring service quality in university libraries in New Zealand. They opined that developing a generic instrument applicable to all libraries in all circumstances was not possible and so it was good to prepare an instrument considering all local requirements and objectives of the library.

Calvert (1998)[34] used a modified form of the tool developed by Hernon and Calvert to study the service quality of Polytechnic Libraries in Singapore. This tool contains 86 items which is given as appendix to this chapter. He argued that service quality changes over time and between cultures and countries. Calvert (2001)[35] himself and with Hernon (1997)[36] conducted further studies with the modified tool to produce global dimensions for user expectations of academic library service quality. Accordingly he identified five items commonly applicable in academic libraries of China and New Zealand. Such attempts will lead to the development of a general tool for measuring service quality of any type of libraries in the world.

Snoj and Petermanec (2001)[37] also developed a special tool for assessing the overall service quality in libraries in Slovania, which contains 45 items grouped under five quality dimensions, namely physical sorroundings, equipment and information technology, collection, information and library services, and staff. They reported that 'staff' is the important dimension affecting library service quality.

Dow (1998)[38] developed a special tool using educational impact as an alternative measure of library service quality based on Association of Higher Educations' Principles of Good Practice for Assessing Student Learning. He reported that it was a good tool for assessing the impact of library services on the teaching and learning activities of faculty and students based on a study conducted at River Campus Libraries of the University of Rochester. Similarly Doyle (1995)[39] developed the 'Perceptions of Library Service Questionnaire (PLSQ)', a tool for evaluating the students awareness and use of library services and staff support. PLSQ contains sixteen items for measuring user satisfaction. Banwet and Datta (2000)[40] developed a special tool containing service quality scale, service satisfaction scale, and service importance scale to assess the post-visit intentions of users. They reported that reliability of library services, service quality and user satisfaction were very important in post-visit intensions of users. On the other hand, Martensen and Grenhold (2003)[41] developed a structural equation model to measure users' perceived quality, satisfaction and loyalty quantitatively. They reported that, it was a cause and effect model suitable for identifying the problems for low satisfaction, loyalty and value to users.

Now attempts are on progress to assess the service quality of computerised, networked and web-based library and information services using traditional as well as web-based methods. Some of such studies have already been reported in Library and Information Science literature. Bertot and Ryan (2001)[42] studied the service quality of network based library services offered with the aim of identifying suitable service quality criteria. Accordingly, they identified technical infrastructure and extensiveness, technical infrastructure and service quality, information content and efficiency, information services and extensiveness, information services and efficiency, support, and extensiveness as service quality criteria suitable for libraries in a networked environment. Similarly Crowley et al (2002)[43] studied the service quality of Texas A&M University Library's web page and identified five themes, namely desire for research portals; access to research resources; use skill and knowledge; awareness of resources and services; and general attitudes towards libraries and research. On the other hand, Chao (2000)[44] studied the service quality of academic libraries on the web aiming to identify suitable criteria and develop an instrument for assessing the service quality of academic library websites. The study resulted in the development of a tool containing 16 criteria namely presentation; speed; heading and titles; search capability; special collections; content; graphic design; services etc. He argued that it was a good tool for measuring the service quality of all library websites accessible on internet.

LibQUAL+

LibQUAL is a measuring tool developed by Association of Research Libraries. The member libraries of the association as well as other libraries are using this tool for measuring the service quality of libraries. This tool is freely available on internet (http://www.libqual.org/) and reports on LibQUAL studies are regularly published in ARL News Letter. Cook and Thompson (2001)[45] studied the perceptions of users in acceptable, perceived and desired level of service quality and reported that serious measures were needed to improve the level of quality of library services as expected by the users. Similarly, Cook and Heath (2001)[46] reported that for users at every level of expertise, the extend to which libraries facilitate self reliant information seeking behaviour seemed to be related to their perceptions of library service quality and the perceptions of service quality were the most useful indicator for measuring library service quality.

On the other hand, Cook and Thompson (2001)[47] had investigated the psychometric properties of scores on thirty-four items of the LibQUAL+ questionnaire in Texas A&M University and other twelve universities in North America. They identified that all quality factors, namely affect of service, library as place, access to collection and reliability were important service quality dimensions. The LibQUAL+ scores were correlated highly with independent global ratings of library quality and there is no much difference in scores according to gender, user frequency of library use, user groups, disciplines etc.

Measuring the quality of library products and services is considered as a significant responsibility of a modern library. There are various tools developed, tested and used for this purpose. However, it is preferable to prepare and use a tool suitable to the library to be assessed.

References

1. Roshan Raina. An analysis of the students' feedback on the library resources, facilities and services at a national level management institute. *Annals of Library Science and Documentation.* 42(3), 1995. p106-112.
2. Cullen, Rowena and Calvert, Philip J. Stakeholder perceptions of university library effectiveness. *Journal of Academic Librarianship.* 21, 1995. p438-446.
3. Wilson, Carol and Orr, Noreen. User satisfaction with the library service among part-time students. *The New Review of Academic Librarianship.* 1,1995. p187-199.
4. Talbot, Dawn E. *et al.* From the users' perspective – the UCSD Libraries user survey project. *Journal of Academic Librarianship.* 24(5), 1998. p357-364.
5. Hiller, Steve. Assessing user needs, satisfaction and library performance at the University of Washington Libraries. *Library Trends.* 49(4), 2001. p605-625.
6. Hernon, P and Altman, E Service quality in academic libraries. N.J: Norwood, 1996.
7. Cullen, R. Perspectives on user satisfaction surveys. *Library Trends.* 49(4), 2001. p662-686.
8. Brophy, Peter. The quality program of the library and learning resources service at the University of Central Lancashire. *Aslib Information.* 21(6), 1993. p246-248.
9. Verma, R.K. Measuring quality management level with reference to ISO 9000 and TQM for special libraries in India. *Annals of Library Science and Information Studies.* 49(4), 2002. p141-163.

10. Date, Dhanashree A. and Gokhale, Pratibha A. Implementation of ISO 9000 in Industrial Libraries. *Library Science with a Slant to Documentation and Information Studies.* 36(2), 1999. p65-72.

11. Quinn, Brian. Adapting service quality concepts to academic libraries. *Journal of Academic Librarianship.* 23(5), 1997. p359-369.

12. Phipps, S. E. Beyond measuring service quality: learning from the voices of the customers, the staff, the processes, and the organization LibQUAL+. *Library Trends.* 49(4). 2001. p635-61.

13. Kyrillindou, Martha. Symposium on Measuring Library Service Quality, *ARL Bimonthly Report.* 215, 2001. p9-11.

14. Chang, P.L. and Hsieh, P.N. Evaluating university libraries' service quality: from user's point of view. *Bulletin of the Library Association of China.* 56, 1996. p49-68.

15. Jayasundara, Chaminda Chiran. An investigation into the determinants of service quality in University academic libraries of Sri Lanka: a mini survey for measuring user perception of service quality. *Journal of Educational Media and Library Sciences.* 38(4), 2001. p374-384.

16. Pors, N.O. Students' attitudes to the service quality of libraries. *Scandinavian Public Library Quarterly.* 29(2), 1996. p18-23.

17. Yang, Zheng Ye (Lan). University faculty's perception of a library liaison programme. *Journal of Academic Librarianship.* 26(2), 2000. p124-128.

18. Cullen, R and Calvert P (1993). Further dimensions of public library effectiveness. *Library and Information Science Research,* 18(2), 1993. p143-164.

19. Edwards, Susan and Browne, Mairead. Quality in Information Services: Do users and librarians differ in their expectations? *Library and Information Science Research.* 17, 1995. p163-182.

20. Campbell, S.J *et al.* A measurement of service. *Scottish Libraries.* 50, 1995. p10-11.

21. Coleman, Vicki *et al.* Towards a TQM Paradigm: Using SERVQUAL to Measure Library Service Quality. *College and Research Libraries.* 58(3), 1997. p237-245,250-251.

22. Abdul Majeed, K.C. and Bavakutty, M. Assessing the quality of information sources and information services in academic libraries. In *Information Access, Management and Exchange in Technological Age.* Ed. by Bavakutty, M *et al.* New Delhi: Ess Ess, 2002. p150-189.

23. Simmonds, Patience and Andaleeb, Syed Saad. Local experiences with user satisfaction surveys in Academic Libraries. *ARL Measuring Service Quality Symposium,* Washington DC, 2000.

24. Nitecki, D.A. 'Changing the concept and measure of service quality in academic libraries'. *Journal of Academic Librarianship.* 22(3), 1996. p181-190.

25. Niteki, Danuta A and Hernon, Peter. Service Quality at Yale University 's Libraries. *Journal of Academic Libraries.* 26(4), 2000. p259-273.

26. Cook, Colleen and Thompson, Bruce. Reliability and validity of Servqual scores used to evaluate perceptions of library service quality. *Journal of Academic Librarianship.* 26(4),2000. p248-259.

27. Cook, Colleen and Thompson, Bruce. Higher order factor analytic perspectives on users' perceptions of library service quality. *Library and Information Science Research.* 22(4), 2000. p393-404.

28. Jeannette Ho and Crowley, Gwyneth H. User perceptions of the 'reliability' of library services at Texas A&M University. *Journal of Academic Librarianship.* 29(2),2003. p82-87.

29. Hiller, Steve. Assessing user needs, satisfaction and library performance at the University of Washington. *ARL Measuring Service Quality Symposium,* Washington DC, 2000.

30. Crossno, J. E, *et al.* Assessment of customer service in academic health care libraries (ACSAHL): an instrument for measuring customer service ACSAHL vs SERVQUAL at University of Texas Southwestern Medical Center. *Bulletin of the Medical Library Association.* 89(2), 2001. p170-176.

31. Philip, George and Hazlett, Shirley-Ann. Evaluating the service quality of information services using a new P-C-P attributes model. *International Journal of Quality and Reliability Management.* 18(9), 2001. p900-916.

32. Landrum, Hollis L and Prybutok, V.R. Service quality and Success model for the information service industry. *European Journal of Operational Research.* 2003. p63-74.

33. Hernon, Peter and Calvert, Philip J. Methods for measuring service quality in university libraries in New Zealand. *Journal of Academic Librarianship.* 22,1996. p387-391.

34. Calvert, P.J. A different time, a different country: an instrument for measuring service quality in Singapore's polytechnic libraries. *Journal of Academic Librarianship.* 24(4), 1998. p296-303.

35. Calvert, Philip J. International variations in measuring customer expectations. *Library Trends.* 49(4), 2001. p732-757.

36. Calvert, P.J and Hernon, P. Surveying service quality within university libraries. *Journal of Academic Librarianship.* 23(5), 1997. p408-15.

37. Snoj, Boris and Petemanec, Zdenka. Let users judge the quality of faculty library services. *New Library World.* 102(1168), 2001. p314-324.

38. Dow, Ronald F. Using assessment criteria to determine library quality. *Journal of Academic Librarianship.* 24(4),1998. p277-291.

39. Doyle, Christine. The Perceptions of Library Service Questionnaire (PLSQ): the development of a reliable instrument to measure student perceptions of and satisfaction with quality of service in an academic library. *The New Review of Academic Librarianship.* 1, 1995. p139-159.

40. Banwet, D.K. and Datta, B. Effect of service quality on post-visit intentions : the case of a library. *Annals of Library Science and Documentation.* 47(2), 2000. p41-48.

41. Martensen, Anne and Grenhold, Lars. Improving library users' perceived quality, satisfaction and loyalty. *Journal of Academic Librarianship.* 29(3),2003. p140-147.

42. Phipps, S. E. Beyond measuring service quality: learning from the voices of the customers, the staff, the processes, and the organization LibQUAL+. *Library Trends.* 49(4). 2001. p635-61.

43. Crowley, Gwyneth H, *et al.* User perceptions of the library's web pages. *Journal of Academic Librarianship.* 28(4), 2002. p205-210.

44. Chao, Hungyune. Assessing the quality of academic libraries on the web: the development and testing of criteria. *Library and Information Science Research.* 24(2),2002. p169-194.

45. Cook, C. and Thompson, B. Psychometric properties of scores from the Web-based LibQUAL+ study of perceptions of library service quality. *Library Trends.* 49(4), 2001. p585-604.

46. Cook, Colleen and Heath, Fred M. Users' Perceptions of Library Service Quality: A LibQUAL+ Qualitative Study. *Library Trends.* 49(4), 2001. p548-584.

47. Cook, C. and Thompson, B. Psychometric properties of scores from the Web-based LibQUAL+ study of perceptions of library service quality. *Library Trends*. 49(4), 2001. p585-604.

Appendix

The Questionnaire used by Calvert

1. It is easy find where materials (books, journals, videos, maps, etc.) are shelved
2. The information I get from library materials is accurate
3. The library's Web pages contain correct and useful information about library services and materials
4. Information displayed on the computer catalog is clear and easy to follow
5. Study areas in the library are kept quiet.
6. Lighting in the building is adequate tó my needs
7. Catalog computers are in good working order
8. Documents I want are in their proper places on the shelves
9. The computer catalog is an accurate source of information about all documents held by the library
10. The range of materials held by the library meets my course needs
11. Instructions on remote access to the computer catalog are easy to follow
12. Directional signs in the library are clear, understandable, and helpful
13. Library materials are reshelved promptly after use
14. The library material I need is in good condition (e.g. not brittle or falling apart)
15. The toilets are clean
16. Internet, CD-ROM, and database computers are in good working order

17. The library purchases new materials which re relevant to my course needs
18. I can usually find a seat or study desk when I want one
19. I find the temperature in the building is comfortable
20. Computers for the library catalog are conveniently distributed throughout the library
21. Library staff give accurate answers to my questions
22. Library staff are approachable and welcoming
23. It is easy to find out in advance when the library will be open
24. I find the ventilation in the building is comfortable
25. When I connect remotely to the computer catalog I do not get a busy signal or get disconnected
26. The material I need from the course materials collection is usually available to me when I want it
27. Library staff are courteous and polite
28. I feel safe in the building
29. Library staff are available when I need them
30. Librarians provide teaching programs to help me make more effective use of the library
31. Staff communicate with me using terms I understand
32. I find displays of new materials helpful
33. The computer catalog has a "Help" option which I understand
34. Hours when the library are open match my schedule and needs
35. When I enter the library I can see where I can go for help
36. Library staff are friendly and easy to talk to
37. I find the humidity in the building is comfortable
38. The documents I need have not been mutilated (e.g.

torn pages or highlighted text)

39. Photocopiers are in good working order
40. I do not have to wait more than three minutes when I ask for assistance at a reference desk
41. Library staff offer suggestions where to look for information in other parts of the library
42. Library furniture is comfortable
43. I do not have to wait more then three minutes when I use the computer catalogue
44. There is an adequate supply of clean drinking water in the building
45. The library provides timely, accurate, and clear information about equipment not in working order
46. It is easy to make a compliment, complaint, or suggestions about library services or conditions.
47. The library acts promptly when I make a complaint
48. I do not have to wait more than three minutes when I use the course materials collection
49. Knowledgeable staff are available to assist whenever the library is open
50. There is a sufficient number of toilets in the building
51. When I request an item currently on loan to another person, I am told how long it will take to arrive
52. I do not have to wait more than three minutes when I borrow materials
53. Library staff are willing to leave the desk area to help me
54. Audio-visual equipment is in good working order
55. Library brochures and help sheets are helpful
56. Library furniture is designed to meet my practical needs

57. Accurate and helpful written instructions are available next to all equipment
58. The library has an attractive interior
59. Library staff encourage me to come back to ask for more assistance if I need it
60. I do not have to wait more than three minutes when I use Internet, CD-ROM, and database computers
61. Microfilm and microfiche readers are in good working order
62. When I request an item from a closed shelf, I am told how long it will take to arrive
63. When I request an item by interlibrary loan (ILL), I am told how long it will take to arrive
64. There are an adequate number of lockers in which I can store my personal belongings
65. Library staff demonstrate and teach the user of the Internet, CD-ROMs, and databases
66. Library staff understand what information I am looking for
67. Library staff offer suggestions on where to look for information outside the library
68. Computer printers are in good working order
69. Library staff do not refer me unduly from one service area to another for my enquiry to be answered
70. I do not have to wait more than three minutes when I use photocopiers
71. Library staff help me select appropriate electronic resources
72. Library staff mentions inter library loan, as a means to obtain material the library does not have.
73. Library staff personally help me to use electronic

resources

74. I do not have to wait more than three minutes when I phone the library for assistance or information
75. Library staff direct me to library broachers and help sheets
76. All public service desks throughout the library are served by knowledgeable staff
77. Library staff do not overwhelm me with too much information and detail
78. Library staff demonstrate cultural sensitivity
79. Library staff show me how to use toe computer catalog
80. There are places for me to use a laptop computer within the building
81. The library provides services such as staplers, hole punchers, pencil sharpeners, and giving change
82. I do not have to wait more than three minutes when I need prints from a computer
83. There is a sufficient number of group study rooms
84. I do not have to wait more then three minutes when I use microfilm and microfiche readers
85. There are study areas where talking is permitted
86. Library staff take me directly to documents I want instead of just pointing or telling me where to go

13
Quality of Libraries: Case Studies

Two studies of library service quality measurements using the SERVQUAL scale and suitably modified SERVQUAL scale appropriate to the library requirements were conducted. The results of these studies are discussed here.

CASE STUDY 1

Service quality measurement based on SERVQUAL was conducted in a leading academic library in Kerala State to assess the quality of the collection, services, staff, tools and techniques facilities etc. A questionnaire comprising 38 questions grouped under 5 service quality dimensions, namely Tangibles, Reliability, Responsiveness, Assurance and Empathy was used. The Tangibles include items on physical facilities, equipment, personnel, and communication materials. Reliability consists of items on the ability to perform the promised service dependably and accurately. Responsiveness consists of items on willingness to help customers and provide prompt services. Assurance consists of items on knowledge and courtesy of employees and their ability to convey trust and confidence. And Empathy consists of items on caring and individualized attention the firm provides to the customers.

The questionnaire, given as appendix (Appendix I), has two parts. Part I. consists of 19 items on user expectations and Part II consists of 19 items on user perceptions. The study used a sample of 65 users, 32 postgraduate students and 33 faculty members. Maximum attention was paid to give due representation to different disciplines and sex. The data were analyzed with simple statistical techniques like mean and standard deviation. The results of the study are as follows:

Quality of Libraries: User Expectations

Measuring the expectations of service quality of a library is significant as the quality is considered to be the gap between user expectations and their perceptions. The overall mean score (4.21) shows that the users have very high expectations about the academic library, and there are not much differences in the expectations of the individual users, as the standard deviation score is below 1.

It is observed that users expect 'adequate number of required books and journals' (mean score 4.82), 'willingness of staff to help the users' (mean score 4.68), 'easy access and convenient working hours' (mean score 4.62), 'excellent facilities and services and prompt service to users' (mean score 4.57) very high from an academic library. However, they do not expect 'personalized attention to users' (mean score 3.2), 'users' confidence to depend on staff' (mean score 3.52), 'response of the staff to user queries' (mean score 3.78), 'modern building and furniture' (mean score 3.85) much.

However, there are differences in the expectations of users with regard to 'personal attention' (standard deviation score 1.45), 'staff response on user queries' (standard deviation score 1.26), 'user confidence to depend on staff' (standard deviation score 1.24), 'modern building and furniture' (standard deviation score 1.11), and 'attractive display of books, journals and other documents (standard deviation score 1.04) among the users.

The mean score, rank and the standard deviation score of user expectations of all the 19 items are given in Table 13.1.

Table 13.1. Quality of Libraries: User Expectations: Item wise Analysis

Sl.No.	Items	Mean	SD	Rank
1	Modern building and furniture are required for a good library	3.85	1.11	16
2	A good library will provide excellent facilities and services	4.57	0.75	4
3	Required books and journals in adequate numbers will be available in a good library	4.82	0.50	1
4	The books, journals and other documents will be attractively displayed in a good library	4.14	1.04	12
5	A good library will do all those that are promised to do	4.02	0.91	15
6	In a good library, the staff will assist the user for locating a document.	4.52	0.81	6
7	A good library will provide right book the very first time	4.18	0.92	11
8	Proper records with accurate information will always be available in a good library	4.28	0.98	9
9	In a good library, the staff will always be willing to help the users	4.68	0.66	2
10	The staff in a good library will give prompt service to users	4.57	0.66	5
11	The staff in a good library tells precisely when the document requested would be available	4.25	0.66	10
12	The staff in a good library will inform the user as soon as the requested document is available	4.38	0.63	7
13	The staff in a good library will immediately respond to users	3.78	1.26	17
14	The behaviour of staff in a good library will develop confidence in users	4.34	0.85	8
15	The staff of a good library will have proper knowledge to answer user's questions	4.12	1.01	13
16	Users of a good library feel free to depend on library staff for some help	3.52	1.24	18

17	The staff in a good library will give personalized attention to the users	3.20	1.45	19
18	A good library will have easy access and convenient working hours	4.62	0.60	3
19	The staff in a good library will understand the specific needs of the users	4.11	0.90	14

Further analysis of these items according to SERVQUAL dimensions namely Tangibles, Reliability, Responsiveness, Assurance and Empathy shows that, among the five dimensions of service quality, Tangibles scored the highest (mean score 4.34) and Empathy the least (mean score 3.97). The details are given in Table 13.2.

Table 13.2. Quality of Libraries: User Expectations: Dimensions wise Analysis

Sl. No	*Dimensions*	*Mean*	*Rank*	*SD*
1	Reliability	4.25	3	0.58
2	Assurance	3.99	4	0.70
3	Tangibles	4.34	1	0.57
4	Empathy	3.97	5	0.70
5	Responsiveness	4.33	2	0.48

The mean score of each dimension indicates that users have very high expectations and there are no considerable differences in the expectations of individual users, as the standard deviation scores are below 1. The mean scores of individual items under each dimensions shows that the items belonging to Tangibles, Responsiveness and Reliability are highly expected than others.

Quality of Libraries: User Perceptions

User perception is viewed as the experience or feeling of the user about the library services provided to them. The overall mean, and standard deviation scores of all the items of user perceptions are 3.45, and 1.08 respectively. In general, the perceptions of the users are not good and the standard deviation score (above 1) indicates that there are variations among the individual users' perceptions.

Analysis of the 19 items showed that the 'staffs were always willing to help the users' scored the highest (mean score 3.92) and the 'staffs understand the specific needs of the users' the least (mean score 3.03). The mean score, standard deviation score and the rank of the level of perception of all the 19 items are given in Table 13.3.

Table 13.3. Quality of Libraries: User Perceptions: Items wise Analysis

Sl.No.	Item	Mean	SD	Rank
1	My Library has modern building and furniture	3.12	1.05	18
2	My library provides me excellent facilities and services	3.40.	1.21	10
3	Required books and journals in adequate number are available in my library.	3.26	1.22	14
4	The books, journals and other documents are attractively displayed in my library	3.54	1.05	8
5	My library does all those that are promised to do.	3.31	1.09	13
6	My library assists the user for locating a document needed.	3.68	1.03	5
7	My library provides me the right book the very first time	3.26	1.14	15
8	Proper records with accurate information are always available in my library.	3.60	1.03	7
9	The staff in my library is always willing to help me	3.92	0.96	1
10	The staff in my library gives me prompt service	3.77	1.01	4
11	The staff in my library tells me precisely when the document requested is available	3.32	1.08	12

12	The staff in my library informs me as soon as the document requested is available	3.43	1.06	9
13	The staff in my library immediately respond to my requests	3.38	1.18	11
14	The behaviour of staff in my library gives me confidence in library matters	3.63	0.96	6
15	The staff in my library has the proper knowledge to answer my questions	3.22	1.27	16
16	I feel free and comfortable to depend on my library staff for some help	3.78	1.02	3
17	The staff in my library gives me personalized attention	3.18	1.04	17
18	My library has easy access and convenient working hours	3.80	1.06	2
19	The staff in my library understands my specific needs	3.03	1.09	19

The item wise analysis of user perceptions shows that users' perceptions of all the items are low as the mean scores are below 4. It is found that 'willingness of staff to help the users' (mean score 3.92) and 'easy access and working hours' (mean score 3.8) are perceived high and 'building and furniture available' (mean score 3.12) and 'understanding the specific needs of users by library staff' (mean score 3.03) very low among the items.

Further analysis of the items of perceptions according to the dimensions namely Tangibles, Reliability, Responsiveness, Assurance and Empathy shows that 'Responsiveness' is perceived the highest (mean score 3.57) and 'Tangibles' scored the least (mean score 3.33). These indicate that the library staff is always ready to respond to the questions of users, but the users are not very much satisfied with the Tangibles such as building and furniture, collection, services and facilities. The mean and standard deviation scores of the user perceptions of the five quality dimensions are given in Table 13.4.

Table 13.4. Quality of Libraries: User Perceptions: Dimensions wise Analysis

Sl. No	*Dimensions*	*Mean*	*Rank*	*SD*
1	Reliability	3.46	3	0.81
2	Assurance	3.54	2	0.88
3	Tangibles	3.33	5	0.86
4	Empathy	3.34	4	0.92
5	Responsiveness	3.57	1	0.82

The mean score of each dimension shows that the perceptions of users about the service quality dimensions are very low. On the other hand, the standard deviation score indicates that the perceptions of individual users do not vary significantly.

Library Quality

Service quality of a library is assumed as the gap between the user's perceptions and expectations of quality items and dimensions. If the perception is above or equal to the expectations, it is said that there is quality, otherwise not.

The users perceptions about the library collection, services and facilities (overall mean score 3.46) are below to their expectations (overall mean score 4.18). The users' expectations are very high. Therefore, there is a wide gap (gap score –0.71) between the two, which indicates the low quality of the library, its collection, services, staff etc. The gap between user perceptions and expectations on all the 19 items are given in Table 13.5.

Table 13.5. Quality of Libraries: Item wise Analysis

Sl. No	*Item*	*Mean (Perception)*	*Mean (Expectation)*	*Quality Gap*	*Rank*
1	Modern building and furniture	3.12	3.85	-0.73	8
2	Excellent facilities and services	3.4	4.57	-1.17	18
3	Adequate number of books and journals	3.26	4.82	-1.56	19
4	Attractive display of documents	3.54	4.14	-0.6	4
5	Doing things in right time	3.31	4.02	-0.71	6
6	Help to locate documents	3.68	4.52	-0.84	12
7	Provision of right book in time	3.26	4.18	-0.92	14
8	Availability of error free record	3.6	4.28	-0.68	5
9	Willingness to help	3.92	4.68	-0.76	9
10	Prompt service	3.77	4.57	-0.8	10
11	Inform the correct time of the availability of requested document	3.32	4.25	-0.93	15
12	Inform the availability of requested document in time	3.43	4.38	-0.95	16
13	Immediate response to user queries	3.38	3.78	-0.4	3
14	Develop confidence in users	3.63	4.34	-0.71	7
15	Knowledge to answer queries	3.22	4.12	-0.9	13
16	Trust on staff	3.78	3.52	0.26	1
17	Individual personal attention	3.18	3.2	-0.02	2
18	Easy access and convenient working hours	3.8	4.62	-0.82	11
19	Understanding the specific needs of the users	3.03	4.11	-1.08	17

The item wise analysis shows that except in two cases, the quality of the library investigated is very low. It is observed from the table that 'confidence on staff' has a positive gap score (gap score +0.26), showing good quality of the staff who promise confidence and 'personalised attention' (gap score –0.02) has very small negative gap score showing quality equal to user expectations. On the other hand, highest gap score is marked on 'excellent facilities and service' (gap score –1.56), 'adequate number of books and journals' (gap score –1.17), and 'understanding of user needs well' (gap score –1.08) which shows least quality to them.

The analysis of the dimension shows that the gap between the perceptions and expectations about 'Assurance' is equal to zero. However, the gap is the highest in the case of 'Tangibles'. The mean score of perceptions, expectations, the gap scores between the two and the rank of all the five quality dimensions are given in Table 13.6.

Table 13.6. Quality of a Library: Dimension wise Analysis

Sl.No	*Dimensions*	*Mean (Perception)*	*Mean (Expectation)*	*Quality Gap*	*Rank*
1	Reliability	3.462	4.25	-0.78	3
2	Assurance	3.543	3.543	0	1
3	Tangibles	3.33	4.345	-1.01	5
4	Empathy	3.336	3.976	-0.64	2
5	Responsiveness	3.61	4.47	-0.86	4

This study is conducted using the dimensions of original SERVQUAL instrument, which, it is criticised, do not cover several significant aspects of the library. Therefore, suitable modifications are being suggested to the SERVQUAL tool to get reliable data pertaining to the service quality of libraries.

CASE STUDY II

In order to get more comprehensive idea about the level of quality of libraries, researchers in Library and Information field have suggested modifications to the SERVQUAL tool to suit to the local requirements of the library. A study was conducted in a leading academic library in Kerala State, India to assess the quality of physical facilities, collection, staff, tools and techniques used and services offered in the library using a modified SERVQUAL tool, .

This tool comprised 80 items grouped under five-quality dimensions, namely Physical Facilities, Library Collection, Library Staff, Technical Processes, and Library Service. Physical Facilities include items on location, layout, reader space, lighting and ventilation, neatness and cleanliness of the library premises, and furniture. Library Collection consists of items on textbooks, reference books, journals, user needs, display of documents, library accessibility, lending, and provision of documents on request. Library Staff includes items on user help, timely work, provision of information about the availability of requested documents to users, correctness of information given to users, response on users' queries, users confidence, staff's knowledge to answer user queries, personal attention given to users, and understanding of user needs. Technical Processes contains items on acquisition of documents, its technical processing, arrangement, reshelving, rectification, library catalogue, and loan process, and Library Service includes number of loaned documents to users, loan period, personal help, xerox service, exhibition of new arrivals, working hours, user education, user study, library atmosphere, and payment for service.

The questionnaire contains two parts. Part I include 40 items on user expectations and Part II contains 40 items on user perceptions. The questionnaire used is given as appendix (Appendix II) to this chapter.

The study used a sample of 221 users, of which 175 are postgraduate students and 36 are faculty members. Maximum attention is paid to give due representation to different disciplines (Arts 89, Science 112 and Commerce 20) and sex (Male 81 and Female 130). The responses received are analyzed with simple statistical techniques like mean and standard deviation. The results of the study are as follows:

Quality of Libraries: User Expectations

Users expect good physical facilities, collection, services, staff and technology in their libraries. They are very significant in measuring the service quality, as quality of a library is measured on the basis of the gap between user expectations and perceptions. It is found from the table 13.7 that 'good collection of reference books', 'good lighting and ventilation', 'neat and clean library premises', 'good reader space', and 'proper catalogue' are highly expected from a good academic library. However, 'documents on loan for as many days the user needs', 'all documents on loan', 'personal attention of the staff' and 'maximum personal help' are the least expected items by the users from an academic library. An examination of the users' expectations indicates that they expect those items that are generally possible and experienced so far. The mean score, rank and the standard deviation score of all the items in the questionnaire are given in the table 13.7.

Table 13.7. Quality of Libraries: User Expectations: Item wise Analysis

Sl.No.	*Item*	*Mean*	*Rank*	*Std.Dev*
Physical Facilities				
1	Good library is easily accessible	4.439	14	0.682
2	Good layout is necessary for a good library	4.344	18	0.687
3	Sufficient space for users is needed in a good library	4.570	4	0.588
4	Good library needs good lighting and ventilation	4.611	2	0.550
5	Good library should be clean, tidy and hygienic	4.593	3	0.601
6	Good library needs comfortable furniture	4.294	22	0.667
	Average	**4.475**		**0.629**

Library Collection				
7	Good collection of textbooks is needed in a good library	4.471	9	0.684
8	Good collection of journals is required in a good library	4.448	13	0.613
9	Good collection of reference books is needed in a good library	4.652	1	0.596
10	Good library study users' needs while acquiring documents	4.380	16	0.633
11	Good library displays new documents attractively	4.181	29	0.735
12	Good library offers open access to the collection	4.005	34	0.845
13	All documents in a good library are lent out for home reading	3.439	39	1.161
14	Good library provides documents at the very first time	4.068	33	0.874
	Average	**4.206**		**0.768**
Library Staff				
15	Staff in a good library help to locate documents needed	4.516	7	0.658
16	Staff in a good library do their work in time	3.991	35	0.929
17	Staff in a good library inform the availability of documents requested	4.321	21	0.757
18	Staff in a good library give accurate information on request	4.452	10	0.670
19	Staff in a good library immediately respond to user queries	4.100	32	0.868
20	Staff in a good library develop confidence in users	4.176	30	0.787
21	Staff in a good library have sufficient knowledge to answer queries	4.281	23	0.765
22	Staff in a good library provide personal attention	3.738	38	0.901
23	Staff in a good library understand user needs well	3.977	36	0.927
	Average	**4.172**		**0.807**

Technical Processes				
24	Good library acquires new documents in time	4.281	24	0.765
25	Good library releases the new documents for service in time	4.339	19	0.693
26	Good library arranges documents in an easily retrievable order	4.452	11	0.697
27	Good library re-shelves the documents in time	4.326	20	0.788
28	Good library keeps the documents on shelf correctly	4.525	6	0.671
29	Good library has a proper catalogue	4.529	5	0.671
30	Good library does issue and return process quickly	4.208	27	0.816
	Average	**4.380**		**0.729**
Library Service				
31	Good library issues sufficient number of documents on loan	4.240	26	0.764
32	Good library issues documents for sufficient period	3.294	40	1.213
33	Good library offers reference help	3.896	37	0.886
34	Good library offers xerox service	4.204	28	0.738
35	Good library exhibits list of new documents	4.353	17	0.612
36	Good library has convenient working hours	4.403	15	0.736
37	Good library conducts user education programme	4.172	31	0.796
38	Good library has regular interaction with users	4.253	25	0.660
39	Good library provides good atmosphere for serious reading	4.502	8	0.685
40	Good library offers services on free of charge	4.452	12	0.649
	Average	**4.177**		**0.774**

The overall mean score (4.282) as well as the standard deviation (0.741) shows that the users expect almost all items very high and there is no much variations in the views of users in this regard. The item wise analysis shows that, the mean scores of large majority of items are above 4, which shows high expectations and the standard deviations of all the items, except 'documents on loan for as many days the user needs', and 'all documents on loan', have scores less than one which show negligible variations in the opinions of users.

User Expectations: Dimensions wise Analysis

Further analysis of these items according to the quality dimensions, namely Physical facilities, Library collection, Library staff, Technical processes, and Library service shows that all the dimensions are expected very high (mean scores above 4) and the users have more or less the same opinion about them, as the standard deviation score is below 1. The expectation score, rank and the standard deviation score of these dimensions are given in table 13.8.

Table 13.8. Quality of Libraries: User Expectations: Dimension wise Analysis

Sl.No	*Dimension*	*Mean*	*Rank*	*Std.Dev*
1	Physical Facilities	4.475	1	0.629
2	Library Collection	4.206	3	0.768
3	Library Staff	4.172	5	0.807
4	Technical Processes	4.38	2	0.729
5	Library Service	4.177	4	0.774
	Overall	**4.282**		**0.741**

From the table it is observed that the dimension 'physical facilities' has the highest mean score and followed by 'technical processes'. On the other hand, 'library staff' and 'library service' are expected low compared to other dimensions.

The item wise analysis of these dimensions shows that, 'good lighting and ventilation' and 'clean, tidy and hygienic condition of the library' in 'physical facilities', 'collection of reference books' and 'textbooks' in 'library collection', 'help to locate documents' and 'correct information on request' in 'library staff', 'keeping of documents in correct order on the shelves' and 'arrangement of documents in an easily retrievable order' in 'technical processes', and 'convenient working hours' and 'exhibition of list of new documents' in 'library services' are expected very high.

Where as, 'the comfortable furniture' and 'layout' in 'physical facilities', 'all documents on loan' and 'open access' to the collection in 'library collection', 'personal attention' and 'understanding of user needs' in 'library staff', 'acquisition of new documents' and 'reshelving of documents in time' in 'technical processes', and 'issue of documents for sufficient period' and 'reference help' in 'library service' are expected very low.

Quality of Libraries: User Perception

The analysis of user perceptions shows that the users have low perception about the library (overall mean score 3.584), and there are negligible variations in their perceptions (over all standard deviation score 0.97). The item wise analysis of the perceptions of users indicates that the items included under the dimension, 'Physical Facilities', such as 'neatness and cleanliness' (mean score 4.344), 'reader space' (mean score 4.294), 'lighting and ventilation' (mean score 4.235), 'layout' (mean score 4.118), 'location' (mean score 4.068), and 'comfortable furniture' (mean score 4.014) are perceived very high. Where as, the items like 'open access' (mean score 2.905), 'un limited loan period' (mean score 3.054), 'understanding of user needs' (mean score 3.127), 'all documents on loan' (mean score 3.127), 'xerox service' (mean score 3.131) etc. are perceived low.

The users' perception seem to be very realistic, as the library is presently functioning in an attractive building having large reader space, enough furniture, lighting and ventilation, tiled floor area etc. At the same time, the library does not offer open access to all, issues textbooks for 14 days and others for over-night, does not issue all documents on loan, and there is delay in getting xerox service and so these items are perceived very low.

The table 13.9 gives the mean score, rank and the standard deviation score of perceptions of users.

Table 13.9. Quality of Libraries: User Perception: Item wise Analysis

Sl.No.	*Item*	*Mean*	*Rank*	*SD*
Physical Facilities				
1	My library is easily accessible	4.068	5	0.894
2	My library has a good layout	4.118	4	0.861
3	My library has sufficient reader space	4.294	2	0.762
4	My library has good lighting and ventilation	4.235	3	0.878
5	My library is neat and clean	4.344	1	0.687
6	My library has comfortable furniture	4.014	6	0.902
	Average	**4.179**		**0.831**
Library Collection				
7	My library has adequate number of books	3.421	25	1.175
8	My library has good collection of journals	3.498	19	0.923
9	My library has good collection of reference books	3.534	18	1.038
10	My library studies user requirements while acquiring new books	3.321	30	1.045
11	My library displays the documents attractively	3.484	20	0.980
12	My library offers open access	2.905	40	1.138
13	My library lends out all documents for home reading	3.127	37	1.045

14	My library provides required documents the very first time	3.376	27	1.040
	Average	**3.333**		**1.048**

Library Staff

15	My library staff helps me to locate documents	3.584	16	0.976
16	My library staff does their works in time	3.710	12	0.862
17	My library staff informs me the availability of documents requested	3.484	21	0.994
18	My library staff gives me accurate information on request	3.575	17	1.023
19	My library staff responds immediately to my queries	3.620	14	0.949
20	My library staff develops confidence in users	3.484	22	0.994
21	My library staff has sufficient knowledge to answer my queries	3.285	31	1.150
22	My library staff gives me good personal attention	3.204	34	0.990
23	My library staff understand my needs very well	3.127	38	1.032
	Average	**3.453**		**0.997**

Technical Processes

24	My library acquires new documents in time	3.439	23	0.945
25	My library makes the new books ready for service fast	3.267	33	0.994
26	My library arranges the documents in an easily retrievable order	3.430	24	1.144
27	My library reshelf the documents as soon as it is returned/ used	3.335	28	1.003
28	My library always keep the documents on shelf in correct order	3.176	35	1.128
29	My library has a proper catalogue	3.692	13	0.975
30	My library does the issue and return of documents very fast	3.783	10	0.846
	Average	**3.446**		**1.005**

Library Service

31	My library issues sufficient number of documents required	3.276	32	1.112
32	My library issues documents for as many days the user requires	3.054	39	1.077
33	My library offers good reference help	3.407	26	0.913
34	My library offers Xerox service	3.131	36	1.197
35	My library exhibits list of new documents acquired	3.620	15	0.991
36	My library has convenient working hours	3.787	9	0.956
37	My library conducts user education programme	3.719	11	1.001
38	My library always keep good interaction with users	3.330	29	1.097
39	My library provides good atmosphere for serious reading	3.914	7	0.961
40	My library provides services on free of charge	3.846	8	0.828
	Average	**3.508**		**1.013**

User Perceptions: Dimension wise Analysis

Further analysis of the user perception items according to the quality dimension shows that Physical Facilities (mean score 4.179) followed by Library Service (mean score 3.508) are perceived high and others are perceived (mean scores below 3.5) very low. There are variations in the perceptions of three quality dimensions, namely Library Collection, Technical Processes, and Library Service among the users, as the standard deviation scores are more than 1.

The table 13.10 shows the mean score, rank and standard deviation score of the five dimensions under study.

Table 13.10. Quality of Libraries: User Perceptions: Dimension wise analysis

Sl.No	*Dimension*	*Mean*	*Rank*	*SD*
1	Physical Facilities	4.179	1	0.831
2	Library Collection	3.333	5	1.048
3	Library Staff	3.453	3	0.997
4	Technical Processes	3.446	4	1.005
5	Library Service	3.508	2	1.013
	Overall	3.584		0.979

The item wise analysis of these dimensions shows that, 'neatness and cleanliness', and sufficient reader space' in 'Physical Facilities', 'adequate reference book collection', and 'display of documents' in 'Library Collection', 'performing of their work in time', and 'quick response to user queries' in 'Library Staff', 'fast loan procedure', and 'properly arranged catalogue' in 'Technical Processes', and 'good atmosphere for serious reading', and 'services on free of cost' in 'Library Service' are perceived high.

However 'comfortable furniture', and 'location' in 'Physical Facilities', 'open access', and 'all documents on loan' in 'Library Collection', 'understanding specific needs of users', and 'personal attention' in 'Library Staff', 'correct order of documents on shelf', and 'making the new documents ready for service' in 'Technical Processes' and 'issuing of documents for sufficient period', and 'xerox service' in 'Library Service' are perceived very low.

Library Quality

The library quality is the gap between the user perceptions and expectations. The overall mean score of user perception is 3.584 and the user expectation is 4.282, the gap being -0.698. As such the user perceptions are much lesser than their expectations. This establishes that the quality of the library under study is not up to the expectations of the users.

The item wise analysis of library quality shows that, 'good lay out' (gap score –0.226), 'loan period' (gap score – 0.24), 'neatness and cleanliness' (gap score –0.249), 'reader space' gap score (-0.276), and 'comfortable furniture' (gap score –0.28) have lowest gap scores. Where as, 'correct order of documents on shelves' (gap score –1.349), 'good collection of reference books' (gap score -1.118), 'easy access to collection' (gap score –1.1), 'adequate xerox service' (gap score –1.073), and 'study of user needs in acquisition' (gap score –1.059) have highest gap scores showing very poor condition of the library. Among these, low quality of 'adequate reference collection' and 'proper order of documents on shelves' may affect the academic purpose of using the library by the teachers and the postgraduate students.

The table 13.11 shows the mean scores of perceptions and expectations, the gap scores between the two, and the rank of all the items included in the tool used to assess the quality of the library.

Table 13.11. Quality of Libraries: Item wise Analysis

Sl. No.	*Item*	*Perception Mean*	*Expectation Mean*	*Gap Score*	*Rank*
Physical Facilities					
1	Easily accessible location	4.068	4.439	-0.371	8
2	Good layout	4.118	4.344	-0.226	1
3	Sufficient Reader Space	4.294	4.570	-0.276	4
4	Good lighting and ventilation	4.235	4.611	-0.376	9
5	Cleanliness	4.344	4.593	-0.249	3
6	Comfortable furniture	4.014	4.294	-0.280	5
	Average	**4.179**	**4.475**	**-0.296**	
Library Collection					
7	Adequate collection of textbooks	3.421	4.471	-1.050	34
8	Good collection of journals	3.498	4.448	-0.950	29

9	Good collection of reference books	3.534	4.652	-1.118	39
10	Study of user needs for acquisition	3.321	4.38	-1.059	35
11	Display of new documents	3.484	4.181	-0.697	20
12	Easy access to collection	2.905	4.005	-1.100	38
13	All documents on Loan	3.127	3.439	-0.312	7
14	Provision of correct document in time	3.376	4.068	-0.692	18
	Average	**3.333**	**4.206**	**-0.872**	

Library Staff

15	Help of staff to locate documents	3.584	4.516	-0.932	28
16	Completion of the works in time	3.71	3.991	-0.281	6
17	Quick provision of information about the availability of requested documents	3.484	4.321	-0.837	22
18	Provision of accurate information on request	3.575	4.452	-0.877	26
19	Immediate response on user queries	3.62	4.100	-0.480	12
20	Development of confidence on staff	3.484	4.176	-0.692	19
21	Knowledge to answer user queries	3.285	4.281	-0.996	32
22	Provision of individual personal attention	3.204	3.738	-0.534	14
23	Understanding user needs well	3.127	3.977	-0.850	25
	Average	**3.453**	**4.172**	**-0.720**	

Technical Processes

24	Acquisition of new documents in time	3.439	4.281	-0.842	24
25	Fast release of new documents for service	3.267	4.339	-1.072	36
26	Proper arrangement of documents on shelf	3.43	4.452	-1.022	33

27	Immediate re-shelving	3.335	4.326	-0.991	31
28	Correct order of documents on the shelf	3.176	4.525	-1.349	40
29	Proper library catalogue	3.692	4.529	-0.837	23
30	Speed of issue and return process	3.783	4.208	-0.425	10
	Average	**3.446**	**4.380**	**-0.934**	
Library Service					
31	Issue of sufficient number of documents	3.276	4.240	-0.964	30
32	Sufficient period of loan	3.054	3.294	-0.240	2
33	Good reference help	3.407	3.896	-0.489	13
34	Adequate xerox service	3.131	4.204	-1.073	37
35	Exhibition of list of new arrivals	3.62	4.353	-0.733	21
36	Good working hours	3.787	4.403	-0.616	17
37	Provision of user education	3.719	4.172	-0.453	11
38	Regular interaction with users	3.33	4.253	-0.923	27
39	Good atmosphere for serious reading	3.914	4.502	-0.588	15
40	Service on free of charge	3.846	4.452	-0.606	16
	Average	**3.508**	**4.177**	**-0.669**	

Quality of Libraries: Dimension wise Analysis

The quality assessment of the dimensions shows that Physical Facilities have the lowest gap score (–0.296), followed by Library Service (gap score –0.669). The 'Technical Processes' and 'Library Collection' have the highest gap scores of -0.934 and –0.872 respectively. The scores of expectation, perception, and the gap between the two of the five quality dimensions are given in table 13.12.

Table 13.12. Quality of Libraries: Dimension wise Analysis

Sl.No	Dimension	Perception Mean	Expectation Mean	Gap Score	Rank
1	Physical Facilities	4.179	4.475	-0.296	1
2	Library Collection	3.333	4.206	-0.872	4
3	Library Staff	3.453	4.172	-0.720	3
4	Technical Processes	3.446	4.380	-0.934	5
5	Library Service	3.508	4.177	-0.669	2
	Overall	**3.584**	**4.282**	**-0.698**	

Further analysis of the items included in each dimension shows that, 'good lay out' (gap score –0.226) and 'neatness and cleanliness' (gap score –0.249) in 'Physical Facilities', 'all documents on loan' (gap score –0.312), and 'provision of correct document in time' (gap score –0.692) in 'Library Collection', 'completion of work in time' (gap score –0.281) and 'immediate response on user queries' (gap score –0.48) in 'Library Staff', 'speedy issue and return process' (gap score –0.425) and 'proper library catalogue' (gap score –0.837) in 'Technical Processes', and 'sufficient loan period' (gap score –0.24) and 'provision of user education' (gap score –0.453) in 'Library Service' have lowest gap score showing comparatively a better position in the available quality of the library.

However, 'good lighting and ventilation' (gap score –0.376) and 'easily accessible location' (gap score –0.371) in 'Physical Facilities', 'good collection of reference books' (gap score –1.118) and 'easy access to collection' (gap score –1.1) in 'Library Collection', 'knowledge to answer user queries' (gap score –0.996) and 'help to locate documents' (gap score –0.932) in 'Library Staff', 'correct order of documents on shelves' (gap score –1.349) and 'fast release of new documents for service' (gap score –1.072) in 'Technical Processes' and 'adequate xerox service' (gap score –1.073) and 'issue of sufficient number of documents' (gap score –0.964) in

'Library Services' have the highest gap score showing the poor condition of these aspects in the library.

The users' assessment of the library seem to be realistic, as it is observed that the 'physical facilities' of the library studied are better compared to other quality dimensions. Similarly, the library has a 'good layout', 'issues documents for sufficient period' (textbooks for 14 days and reference books and journals for overnight), the library premises are 'neat and clean', and has 'good reader space' and 'comfortable furniture'. On the other hand, it is true that there are heavy misplacement of documents due to open access, the collection of reference books are inadequate as well as out-dated, great delay in getting xerox service due to heavy demand and delay in releasing new documents for use due to inadequate professional staff to process them quickly and the library do not weigh the needs of students while acquiring new documents in the library.

The results of the two case studies using two different tools namely, SERVQUAL and suitably modified SERVQUAL to measure the service quality of one and the same library reveal that the second study is more comprehensive and elaborate. This establishes the fact that it is necessary to make use of special tool suitable to the library to be measured for assessing the quality of the library.

Appendix I

PART A : Expectations About A good Library

Following are the statements describing the features of a good library. I would like to know your views on a good library. Please tick mark (✓) your response on each of the statement in the column given.

SD = Strongly Disagree

D = Disagree

N = Neither Agree nor Disagree

A = Agree

SA = Strongly Agree.

1. Modern building and furniture are required for a good library

   SD D N A SA

2. A good library will provide excellent facilities and services

   SD D N A SA

3. Required books and journals in adequate number will be available in a good library

   SD D N A SA

4. The books, journals and other documents will be attractively displayed in a good library

   SD D N A SA

5. A good library will do all those that are promised to do

   SD D N A SA

6. A good library will assist the user for locating a document.

   SD D N A SA

7. A good library will provide right book the very first time

   SD D N A SA

8. Proper records with accurate information will always be available in a good library

   SD D N A SA

9. The staff in a good library will always be willing to help the users

   SD D N A SA

10. The staff in a good library will give prompt service to users

    SD D N A SA

11. The staff in a good library tells precisely when the document requested would be available

    SD D N A SA

12. The staff in a good library will inform the user as soon as the requested document is available

    SD D N A SA

13. The staff in a good library will not delay respond to users

    SD D N A SA

14. The behaviour of staff in a good library will develop confidence in users

    SD D N A SA

15. The staff of a good library will have proper knowledge to answer user's questions

    SD D N A SA

16. Users of a good library feel free to depend on library staff for some help

    SD D N A SA

17. The staff in a good library will give personalized attention to the users

SD D N A SA

18. A good library will have easy access and convenient working hours

SD D N A SA

19. The staff in a good library will understand the specific needs of the users

SD D N A SA

PART B : Perceptions About Your Library

Following are the statements describing various features of your library. I would like to know your views on these features. Please tick mark (✓) your response on each of the statement in the column given.

SD = Strongly Disagree
D = Disagree
N = Neither Agree nor Disagree
A = Agree
SA = Strongly Agree.

1. My Library has modern building and furniture

SD D N A SA

2. My library provides me excellent facilities and services

SD D N A SA

3. Required books and journals in adequate number are available in my library.

SD D N A SA

4. The books, journals and other documents are attractively displayed in my library

SD D N A SA

5. My library does all those that are promised to do.

SD D N A SA

6. My library assists the user for locating a document needed.

   SD D N A SA

7. My library provides me the right book the very first time

   SD D N A SA

8. Proper records with accurate information are always available in my library.

   SD D N A SA

9. The staff in my library is always willing to help me

   SD D N A SA

10. The staff in my library gives me prompt service

    SD D N A SA

11. The staff in my library tells me precisely when the document requested is available

    SD D N A SA

12. The staff in my library informs me as soon as the document requested is available

    SD D N A SA

13. The staff in my library immediately responds to my requests

    SD D N A SA

14. The behaviour of staff in my library gives me confidence in library matters

    SD D N A SA

15. The staff in my library has the proper knowledge to answer my questions

    SD D N A SA

16. I feel free and comfortable to depend my library staff for some help

    SD D N A SA

17. The staff in my library gives me personalized attention

    SD D N A SA

18. My library has easy access and convenient working hours

    SD D N A SA

19. The staff in my library understands my specific needs

    SD D N A SA

Appendix II

PART A : Expectations About A good Library

Following are the statements describing the features of a good library. I would like to know your views on a good library. Please tick mark (✓) your response on each of the statement in the column given.

SD = Strongly Disagree
D = Disagree
N = Neither Agree nor Disagree
A = Agree
SA = Strongly Agree.

A. Physical Facilities

1. A good library is easily accessible.

SD D N A SA

2. A good layout is necessary for a good library.

SD D N A SA

3. Sufficient space for readers is required in a good library.

SD D N A SA

4. A good library needs good lighting and ventilation.

SD D N A SA

5. A good library is clean, tidy and hygienic.

SD D N A SA

6. A good library needs comfortable furniture.

SD D N A SA

B. Library Collection

7. Adequate collection of books are available in a good library.

SD D N A SA

8. Adequate collection of journals are available in a good library.

   SD D N A SA

9. Adequate collection of reference books are available in a good library.

   SD D N A SA

10. A good library study the users' requirements while acquiring new books.

    SD D N A SA

11. A good library displays Books, Journals and other documents attractively.

    SD D N A SA

12. A good library offers open access to its collection.

    SD D N A SA

13. All documents in a good library are lent out for home reading.

    SD D N A SA

14. A good library provides required documents to readers the very first time.

    SD D N A SA

C. **Library Staff**

15. Staff in a good library helps the users when they fail to locate a document needed.

    SD D N A SA

16. The staff in a good library does their work in time.

    SD D N A SA

17. The staff in a good library informs the reader about the availability of a document requested.

    SD D N A SA

18. The staff in a good library gives correct information to users on request.

SD D N A SA

19. The staff in a good library immediately responds to user's queries.

SD D N A SA

20. The behaviour of staff in a good library develops confidence in users.

SD D N A SA

21. The staff in a good library has sufficient knowledge to answer the users' questions.

SD D N A SA

22. The staff in a good library gives personal attention to the users.

SD D N A SA

23. The staff in a good library understands the specific needs of users.

SD D N A SA

D. Technical Processes

24. A good library acquires new documents in time.

SD D N A SA

25. A good library processes and makes available the new documents to the users very fast.

SD D N A SA

26. A good library arranges the documents in an easily retrievable order.

SD D N A SA

27. A good library replaces/ re-shelves the returned documents on the shelves immediately.

SD D N A SA

28. A good library keeps the documents always in correct order.

SD D N A SA

29. A good library has a proper catalogue.

SD D N A SA

30. A good library does the issue and return process quickly.

SD D N A SA

E. Library Service

31. A good library issues sufficient number of documents a user needs.

SD D N A SA

32. A good library issues documents for as many days a user needs.

SD D N A SA

33. A good library gives maximum personal help to the users.

SD D N A SA

34. A good library provides Xerox service to the users.

SD D N A SA

35. A good library regularly exhibits the list of new documents acquired.

SD D N A SA

36. A good library has convenient working hours.

SD D N A SA

37. The librarian in a good library educates the users how to use the library well.

SD D N A SA

38. The librarian in a good library regularly interacts with the users.

SD D N A SA

39. A good library provides good atmosphere for serious reading inside the library.

SD D N A SA

40. A good library provides services on free of cost.

SD D N A SA

PART B : Perceptions About Your Library

Following are the statements describing various features of your library. I would like to know your views on these features. Please tick mark (✓) your response on each of the statement in the column given.

SD = Strongly Disagree
D = Disagree
N = Neither Agree nor Disagree
A = Agree
SA = Strongly Agree.

A. Physical Facilities

1. My library is in an easily accessible location.

SD D N A SA

2. My library has a good layout.

SD D N A SA

3. My library has adequate space for readers.

SD D N A SA

4. My library has good lighting and ventilation.

SD D N A SA

5. My library is clean, tidy and hygienic.

SD D N A SA

6. My library has comfortable furniture.

SD D N A SA

B. Library Collection

7. My library has adequate collection of books required.

SD D N A SA

8. My library has adequate collection of journals required.

SD D N A SA

9. My library has adequate collection of reference books required.

SD D N A SA

10. My library considers my needs while acquiring new documents.

SD D N A SA

11. My library displays documents in an attractive manner.

SD D N A SA

12. My library offers open access to me to all documents.

SD D N A SA

13. My library lends out all documents to me for home reading.

SD D N A SA

14. My library provides me required documents the very first time.

SD D N A SA

C. Library Staff

15. My library staff helps me when I fail to locate a needed document.

SD D N A SA

16. My library staff does their work in time.

SD D N A SA

17. My library staff informs me about the availability of the document requested.

    SD D N A SA

18. My library staff gives me correct information on request.

    SD D N A SA

19. My library staff immediately responds to my queries.

    SD D N A SA

20. The behavior of my library staff gives me confidence.

    SD D N A SA

21. My library staff has sufficient knowledge to answer my queries.

    SD D N A SA

22. My library staff gives me due personal attention.

    SD D N A SA

23. My library staff understands my specific needs well.

    SD D N A SA

D. Technical Processes

24. My library acquires new documents in time.

    SD D N A SA

25. Newly acquired documents in my library are processed and made available to me very fast.

    SD D N A SA

26. My library arranges the documents in an easily retrievable order.

    SD D N A SA

27. My library replaces/reshelves returned documents on the shelves immediately.

    SD D N A SA

28. My library keeps the documents always in correct order.

SD D N A SA

29. My library has a proper catalogue.

SD D N A SA

30. My library does the issue and return process quickly.

SD D N A SA

E. **Library Service**

31. My library issues sufficient number of documents I need.

SD D N A SA

32. My library issues documents for as many days I need.

SD D N A SA

33. My library gives me maximum personal help.

SD D N A SA

34. My library provides me xerox service.

SD D N A SA

35. My library regularly exhibits list of new documents acquired.

SD D N A SA

36. My library has convenient working hours.

SD D N A SA

37. My librarian educates me how to use the library well.

SD D N A SA

38. My librarian regularly interacts with me.

SD D N A SA

39. My library gives me good atmosphere for serious reading inside the library.

SD D N A SA

40. My library gives me services on free of cost.

SD D N A SA

Bibliography

Articles

Abbot, Chritine. Performance indicators in a quality context. *The Law Librarian*. 25(4), 1994. pp205-208.

Abdul Majeed, K.C. and Bavakutty, M. Assessing the quality of information sources and services in academic libraries. *In* Information Access, Management and Exchange in Technological Age. Ed. by Bavakutty *et al.* New Delhi: Ess Ess, 2002. pp150-189.

Alemna, A.A. Library Evaluation: Some options for Academic Libraries. *Aslib Proceedings*. 51(7), 1999. pp242-247.

Allen, Ferne C. Benchmarking: Practical Aspects for Information Professionals. *Special Libraries*. 84, 1993. pp123-130.

Altman, E and Hernon, P. Service Quality and Customer Satisfaction do Matter. *American Libraries*. 29(7), 1998. pp53-55.

Aluri, Rao. Improving Reference Service: The Case for Using A Continuous Quality Improvement Method. *RQ*. 33, 1994. pp220-236.

Andaleeb, S.S. and Simmonds, P.L. Explaining user satisfaction with academic libraries. *College and Research Libraries*. 59(2), 1998. pp156-167.

Anderson, E.W. and Fornell, C. A customer satisfaction research prospective. In Service quality: New Directions

Andrews, J. An exploitation of Students Library Use Problem. *Library Review*. 40(1), 1991. pp5-14.

Applegate, R. Models of User Satisfaction: Understanding

False Positives. *RQ.* 32(4), 1993. pp525-539.

Armstrong, B. Customer focus: obtaining customer input. *Australian Library Journal.* 43(2), 1994. pp108-117.

Arnau, R.C., Thompson, R.L., & Cook, C. Do different response formats change the latent structure of responses?: An empirical investigation using taxonometric analysis. *Educational and Psychological Measurement,* 61, 2001. pp23-44.

Association of College and Research Libraries. Standards for college libraries. *College and Research Libraries News.* 56(4), 1995. pp245-257.

Bankapur, Vinayak and Mansur, Sunil. Total Quality Management for Library and Information System. *University News* 39(28), 2001. pp 8-10.

Banwet, D.K. and Datta, B. Effect of service quality on post-visit intentions : the case of a library. *Annals of Library Science and Documentation.* 47(2),2000. p41-48.

Berkley, B.J. and Gupta, A. Improving service quality with information technology. *International Journal of Information Management.* 14(2), 1994. pp109-121.

Bertot, J.C, *et al.* Developing national library network statistics and performance measures for U.S. public libraries. *Performance measurement and Metrics : Internation Journal for Library and Information Services.* 1(1),2000. p15-42.

Bertot, John Carlo. Measuring service quality in the networked environment. *Library Trends.* 49(4), 2001. pp758-775.

Bharpur Singh and M.P. Satija. College librarian's self perception of readers services in their own libraries. *CLIS Observer.* 13(3-4), 1996. p20-24.

Bicknell, Tracy. Focusing on Quality Reference Service. *Journal of Academic Librarianship.* 20(2),1994. p77-81.

Brophy, Peter et al. Quality Management: A University Approach. *Aslib Informaiton.* 21(6), 1993. pp246-248.

Brophy, Peter. The quality program of the library and learning resources service at the University of Central Lancashire. *Aslib Information.* 21(6),1993. p246-248.

Burger, Kenneth W and Hines, Richard W. What does the user really want?: The library user survey project at Duke University. *Journal of Academic Librarianship.* 20(5/6),1994. p306-309.

Byrne, A. CAUL's Interest in Performance Measures. *Australian Academic and Research Libraries.* 28(4), 1997. pp252-258.

Calvert, P. and Cullen, R. Further dimensions of Public Library Effectiveness: The Second Stage of the Newzeland Study. *Library and Information Science Research.* 16(2), 1994. p87-104.

Calvert, P.J and Hernon, P. Surveying service quality within university libraries. *Journal of Academic Librarianship.* 23(5),1997. p408-15.

Calvert, P.J. A different time, a different country: an instrument for measuring service quality in Singapore's polytechnic libraries. *Journal of Academic Librarianship.* 24(4),1998. p296-303.

Calvert, P.J. International variations in measuring customer expectations. *Library Trends.* 49(4), 2001. pp732-757.

Calvert, P.J. Measuring service quality: from theory to practice. *Australian Academic and Research Libraries.* 28(3), 1997. pp198-204.

Campbell, S.J. et.al. A measurement of service. *Scottish Libraries.* 50, 1995. pp10-11.

Chang, P.L. and Hsieh, P.N. Evaluating university libraries' service quality: from user's point of view. *Bulletin of the Library Association of China.* 56,1996. p49-68.

Chao, Hungyune. Assessing the quality of academic libraries on the web: the development and testing of criteria. *Library and Information Science Research.* 24(2),2002. p169-194.

Cheng, G.Y.T. The use of benchmarking in improving the library service quality of devolved management. *Journal of the Hong Kong Library Association.* 18, 1996. pp1-14.

Clack, M.E. Organisational development and TQM: the Harward College Library's experience. *Journal of Library Administration.* 18(1-2), 1993. pp29-43.

Clover, D. Committing to customer service: Development of a service charter at the open polytechnic library. *New Zealand Libraries.* 48(12), 1997. pp239-243.

Coleman, P. and Jarred, A.D. Regional association criteria and the standards for college libraries. *Journal of Academic Librarianship.* 20(5/6), 1994. pp273-284.

Coleman, Vicki *et al.* Towards a TQM Paradigm: Using SERVQUAL to Measure Library Service Quality. *College And Research Libraries.* 58(3),1997. p237-245,250-251.

Cook, C and Heath, F. The Association of Research Libraries LibQual+TM Project. *ARL Newsletter.*

Cook, C (Guest Ed.). (2002). The maturation of assessment in academic libraries: The role of LibQUAL+TM (special issue). *Performance Measurement and Metrics,* 3(2), 34-112.

Cook, C and Heath, F. The Association of Research Libraries LibQUAL+TM Project: An update. *ARL Newsletter: A Bimonthly Report on Research Library Issues and Actions from ARL, CNI, and SPARC,* 211, 2000. pp12-14.

Cook, C and Heath, F. Users' perceptions of library service quality: A "LibQUAL+TM" qualitative study.

Cook, C and Heath, F. SERVQUAL and the quest for new measures. *Journal of Library Administration*, 35(4), 2002. pp37-40.

Cook, C and Heath, F. The ARL LibQUAL+TM pilot project: An update. *Journal of Library Administration*, 35(4), 2002. pp47-54.

Cook, C and Heath, F., Thompson, B., & Thompson, R.L. LibQUAL+TM: Service quality assessment in research libraries. *IFLA Journal*, 4, 2001. pp264-268.

Cook, C and Thompson, B. Higher-order factor analytic perspectives on users' perceptions of library service quality. *Library Information Science Research*, 22, 2000. pp393-404.

Cook, C and Thompson, B. Reliability and validity of SERVQUAL scores used to evaluate perceptions of library service quality. *Journal of Academic Librarianship*, 26, 2000. pp248-258.

Cook, C and Thompson, B. Psychometric properties of scores from the Web-based LibQUAL+TM study of perceptions of library service quality. *Library Trends*, 49, 2001. pp585-604.

Cook, C and Thompson, B. Scaling for the LibQUAL+TM instrument: A comparison of desired, perceived and minimum expectation responses versus perceived only.

Cook, C et.al Score norms for improving library service quality: A LibQUAL+TM study. *Portal: Libraries and the Academy*, 2, 2002. pp13-26.

Cook, C, et.al. " Zones of tolerance" in perceptions of library service quality: A LibQUAL+TM study. *Portal: Libraries and the Academy*, 3, 2003. pp113-123.

Cook, C, et.al. : One instrument in the New Measures toolbox. *ARL Newsletter: A Bimonthly Report on Research*

Library Issues andActions from ARL, CNI, and SPARC, 212, 2000. pp4-7.

Cook, C, et. al. Users' hierarchical perspectives on library service quality: A "LibQUAL+^{TM}" study. *College and Research Libraries,* 62, 2001. pp147-153.

Cook, C, et.al. LibQUAL+^{TM}: One instrument in the new measures toolbox. *Journal of Library Administration,* 35(4), 2002. pp41-46.

Cook, C, et.al. A meta-analysis of response rates inWeb- or Internet-based surveys. *Educational and Psychological Measurement,* 60, 2000. pp821-836.

Cook, C, et.al.The forging of consensus: A methodological approach to service quality assessment in research libraries—theLibQUAL+^{TM} experience. In J. Stein, M. Kyrillidou & D. Davis (Eds.), *Proceedings of the 4th Northumbria International Conference on Performance Measurement in Libraries and Information Services.* Washington,DC: Association of Research Libraries, 2002. pp93-104.

Cook, C, et.al. The search for new measures: The ARL "LibQUAL+^{TM}" study—a preliminary report. *Portal: Libraries and the Academy,* 1, 2001. pp103-112.

Cook, C, et.al. Score reliability in Web or Internet-based surveys: Unnumbered graphic rating scales versus Likert-type scales. *Educational and Psychological Measurement,* 61, 2001. pp 697-706.

Cook, Colleen and Heath, Fred M. SERVQUAL and the Quest for New Measures. *ARL Newsletter.* 207, 1999. pp12-13.

Cook, Colleen and Heath, Fred M. Users' Perceptions of Library Service Quality: A LibQUAL+ Qualitative Study. *Library Trends.* 49(4),2001. p548-584.

Cook, Colleen and Thompson, B. *Library and Information Science Research.* 22(4), 2001. pp393-404.

Cook, Colleen and Thompson, B. *Library Trends.* 49(4),2001. p585-604.

Cook, Colleen and Thompson, Bruce. Reliability and Validity of SERVQUAL Scores Used to Evaluate Perceptions of Library Service Quality. pp248-258.

Cook, Colleen and Thompson, Bruce. Scaling for the LibQUAL + TM Instrument: A comparison of desired, perceived, and minimum expectation responses verses perceived. *4th Northumbria International Conference on Measuring Service Quality,* Pittsburgh, Pensilvania, USA, 2001.

Cook, Colleen et.al. SERVQUAL: A client based approach to developing performance indicators. In Proceedings of the 3rd Northumbria International Conference on Performance Measurement in Libraries and Information Services.

Cook, Colleen. et al. Users' hierarchical perspectives on library service quality: A LibQUAL+ Study. *College and Research Libraries.* 62(2), 2001. pp147-153.

Cook, Colleen. et.al. LibQUAL+: One instrument in the new measures toolbox. *ARL Newsletter.* 212, 2000. pp4-7.

Cook, Coollen et al. A new culture of assessment: Preliminary report on the ARL SERVQUAL survey. In 66th IFLA Council and General conference, 2000. pp13-18.

Crossno, J. E, *et al.* Assessment of customer service in academic health care libraries (ACSAHL): an instrument for measuring customer service ACSAHL vs SERVQUAL at University of Texas Southwestern Medical Center. *Bulletin of the Medical Library Association.* 89(2),2001. pp170-176.

Crowley, Gwyneth H, et.al. User perceptions of the library's web pages. *Journal of Academic Librarianship.* 28(4), 2002. pp205-210.

Cullen, R. and Calvert, P. Further dimensions of Public Library Effectiveness: Report on a Parallel Newzeland Study. *Library and Information Science Research.* 15(2), 1993. pp143-164.

Cullen, R. and Calvert, P. Newzeland University Libraries Effectiveness Project: Dimensions and Concepts of Organisational Effectiveness. *Library and Information Science Research.* 18(2), 1996. pp99-119.

Cullen, R. Perspectives on user satisfaction surveys. *Library Trends,* 49 (4). pp662-686.

Cullen, Rowena and Calvert, Philip J. Stakeholder perceptions of university library effectiveness. *Journal of Academic Librarianship.* 21, 1995. pp438-446.

D'Elia, George and Walsh, Sandra. User Satisfaction with Library Services. *Library Quarterly.* 53, 1983. pp110-111.

Date, Danasree A and Gokhale, Pratibha A. Implementation of ISO 9000 in Industrial Libraries: A Case Study. *Library Science with a Slant to Documentation and Information Studies.* 36(2), 1999. pp65-72.

Dawes, Susan. A Service of Quality. *Aslib Information.* 20(6), 1992. pp250-252.

Dawson, Andy. Quality First: The Taywood Information Centre and BS 5750. *Aslib Proceedings.* 20(3), 1992. pp112-113.

De Jager, K. Library use and academic achievement. *South African Journal of Library and Information Science.* 65(1), 1997. pp26-30.

Dobbs, Gwen and Swinney, Victoria. Embracing Assessment:

New measures for Academic Libraries. OKACRL Annual Conference 2001.

Dole, Wand. LibQUAL+TM and the small academic library. *Performance Measurement and Metrics.* 3(2), 2002. pp85-95.

Dow, Ronald F. Using assessment criteria to determine library quality. *Journal of Academic Librarianship.* 24(4), 1998. pp277-291.

Doyle, Christine. The perceptions of library service questionnaire (PLSQ): the development of a reliable instrument to measure student perceptions of and satisfaction with quality of service in an academic library. *The New Review of Academic Librarianship.* 1, 1995. pp139-159.

Edwards, S and Browne, M. Quality in information services: Do users and librarians differ in their expectations?. *Library and Information Science Research.* 17(2), 1995. pp163-182.

Ferguson, J.M. and Zawacki, R.A. Service Quality: A Critical Success Factor for IS Organisations. *Information Strategy.* 9(2), 1993. pp24-30.

Fojt, M. Strategies for service quality 2. *Library Review.* 44(5), 1995. pp2-72.

Fredenburg, Anne M. Quality Assurance: Establishing a Programme for Special Libraries. *Special Libraries.* 79, 1988. pp277-284.

Garlick, M. Measuring Customer Satisfaction: Myth or Reality. *Australian Public Libraries and Information Services.* 11(2), 1998. pp61-74.

Gilchrist, Alan. Quality Issues in the Information Sector: Old ideas, New Pressures. In Technology and Competence: Proceedings of the 8th Nordic Conference on Information and Documentation, 1992. pp9-16.

Gupta, Dinesh K. A focus on Customers: Imperative for Managing Quality in Library and Information Services. In *Delivering Service Quality: Managerial Challenges for the 21st Century*. Ed by Raghavachary and Ramani. New Delhi: Macmillan, 2000. pp401-406.

Hansel, Patsy J. Quality is not Necessarily Quality: A Challenge to Librarians to Develop Meaningful Standards of Performance for Library Reference Services. *North Carolina Libraries*. 48, 1990. pp184-188.

Harwood, N and Bydder, J. Student expectations of, and satisfaction with, the University Library. *Journal of Academic Librarianship*. 24(2), 1998. pp161-171.

Heath, F, et.al. ARL Index and other validity correlates of LibQUAL+TM scores. *Portal: Libraries and the Academy*, 2, 2002. pp27-42.

Hernon, Peter and Altman, E. Service quality in academic libraries. *Journal of Academic Librarianship*. 22(4), 1996. pp314-315.

Hernon, Peter and Altman, E. Service quality in academic libraries. *College and Research Libraries*. 58(2), 1997. pp191-192.

Hernon, Peter and Calvert, P.J. Methods for measuring service quality in university libraries in New Zealand. *Journal of Academic Librarianship*. 22(5), 1996. pp387-391.

Hernon, Peter and Nitecki, Danuta. Service quality: a concept not fully explored. *Library Trends*. 49(4), 2001. pp687-708.

Hernon, Peter. Assessment of Library Services: An Examination of Service Quality and Outcomes Assessment. OKACRL Annual Conference 2001.Boekhorst, Peter Te. Measuring quality: the IFLA guidelines for performance measurement in academic libraries. *IFLA Journal*. 21(4), 1995. pp276-281.

Hernon, Peter. et.al. Service quality and customer satisfaction: an assessment and future directions. *Journal of Academic Librarianship*. 25(2), 1999. pp9-17.

Hiller, Steve. Assessing User Needs, Satisfaction and Library performance at the University of Washington. *ARL Measuring Service Quality Symposium*, Washington DC, 2000.

Hiller, Steve. Assessing user needs, satisfaction and library performance at the University of Washington Libraries. *Library Trends*. 49(4), 2001. pp605-625.

Jayasundara, Chaminda Chiran. An Investigation into the Determination of Service Quality in University Academic Libraries of Sri Lanka. *Journal of Educational Media and Library Sciences*. 38(4), 2001. pp374-384.

Jeannette Ho and Crowley, Gwyneth H. User perceptions of the 'reliability' of library services at Texas A&M University. *Journal of Academic Librarianship*. 29(2), 2003. pp82-87.

Jha, Kamal Narayan, et al. Application of ISO 9000 for Library and Information Services. *Annals of Library Science & Documentation*. 44(3), 1997. pp81-85.

Johannsen, Carl Gustav. The Use of Quality Control Principles and Methods in Library and Information Science and Practice. *Libri*. 42(4), 1992. pp283-295.

Johnson, Dine Tobin. Focus on the Library Customer. *Library Trends*. 43(4), 1995. pp318-325.

Johnson, Sheila Grant. Assessing Library Services: The Ideal and the Real. *OKACRL Annual Conference*, 2001.

Jurow, S. and Bernard, S.B. Integrating total quality management in a library setting. *Journal of Academic Librarianship*. 18(1-2), 1993. pp14-21.

Kania, A.M. Academic library standards and performance

measures. *College and Research Libraries*. 49(1), 1988. pp16-23.

Kaser, D. Standards for college libraries. *Library Trends*. 31(1), 1982. pp7-19.

Kelsey, Kathleen Dodge and Bond, Julie A. A model for measuring customer satisfaction within an academic centre of excellence. *Managing Service Quality*. 11(5), 2001. pp359-367.

Kettinger, W.J. and Lee, C.C. Exploring a 'gap' model of information services quality. *Information Resources Management Journal*. 8(3), 1995. pp5-16.

Kettinger, W.J. and Lee, C.C. Perceived Service Quality and User Satisfaction with the Information Services Function. *Decision Sciences*. 25(5), 1994. pp737-766.

Kettinger, W.J. and Lee, C.C. Pragmatic Perspectives on the Measurement of Information Systems Service Quality. *MIS Quarterly*. 21(2), 1997. pp223-240.

Koenig, Michael E. D, et.al. User Perceptions of the Effect of the Outsourcing of US Government Libraries. *IFLA Journal*. 25, (2), 1999, p40-52.

Koivu, T. and Schonberg, R. The quality project in Finnish Libraries. *Scandinavian Public Library Quarterly*. 30(3), 1997. pp12-18.

Kyrillidou, M., & Hipps, K. (2002). Symposium on measuring library service quality. *Journal of Library Administration*, 35(4), 2002. pp55-62.

Kyrillidou, Martha and Kaylyn, Hipps. Symposium on measuring library service quality. *ARL Bimonthly Report*. 215, 2001. pp9-11.

Lakos, A. Building a culture of assessment in academic libraries: obstacles and possibilities. In Living the future II conference, 1998. pp30-41.

Landrum, Hollis L and Prybutok, V.R. A Service quality and

Success model for the information service industry. *European Journal of Operational Research.* 2004

Larson, C.A. Customers first: Using process involvement to improve service quality and efficiency. *Reference Service Review.* 26(1), 1998. pp51-60.

Lilley, E. and Usherwood, B. Wanting it all: The relationship between expectations and the public's perceptions of public library services. *Library Management.* 21(1-2), 2000. pp13-24.

Lincoln, Yvonna S. Insights into library services and users from qualitative research. *Library and Information Science Research.* 24(1), 2002. pp3-16.

Mackey, Terry. Think Quality: The Deming Approach Does Work in Libraries. *Library Journal.* 1992. pp57-61.

Maddox-Swan, R. Measuring service quality in information services environment. *College and University Media Review.* 5(1), 1998. pp29-43.

Markless, S and Streatfield, D. Developing Performance and Impact Indicators and Targets in Public and Education Libraries. *International Journal of Information Management.* 21, 2001. pp167-179.

Martensen, Anne and Grenhold, Lars. Improving library users' perceived quality, satisfaction and loyalty. *Journal of Academic Librarianship.* 29(3),2003. p140-147.

Mc Neil, Beth and Giescke, Joan. Using LibQUAL+TM to improve services to library constituents: a preliminary report on the University of Nebraska-Lincoln experience. *Performance Measurement and Metrics.* 3(2), 2002. pp96-100.

Millson-Martula, C and Menon, V. Customer expectations: concepts and reality for academic library services. *College and Research Libraries.* 56(1), 1995. pp33-47.

Myres, B.L. et al. A comprehensive model for assessing the quality and productivity of the information systems function. *Information Resources Management Journal.* 10(1), 1997. pp6-25.

Nitecki, D.A. Assessment of service quality in academic library: Focus on the applicability of SERVQUAL. In *Proceedings of the 2nd Northumbria International Conference on Performance Measurement in libraries and information services.* Newcastle: University of Northumbria, 1998. pp181-196.

Nitecki, D.A. Changing the concept and measure of service quality in academic libraries. *Journal of Academic Librarianship.* 22(3), 1996. pp181-190.

Nitecki, D.A. Service quality in academic libraries. In Encyclopedia of Library and Information Science. Ed by A. Kent and C. Hall. New York: Dekker, 1999. pp219-232.

Nitecki, Danuta and Franklin, B. New Measures for Research Libraries. *Journal of Academic Librarianship.* 25(6), 1999. pp484-487.

Nitecki, Danuta. et al. Measuring service quality in Yale University's Libraries. *Journal of Academic Librarianship.* 26(4), 2000. pp259-273.

Perkins, G.H. and Yuan, H. Genesis of a Web based Satisfaction Survey in an Academic Library: The Western Kentucky University Libraries' Experience. *Library Administration and Management.* 14(3), 2000. pp159-166.

Philip, G and Stewart, J. Assessment of the Service Quality of A Cancer Information Service Using a new P-C-P Attributes Model. *Managing Service Quality.* 9(3), 1999. pp167-179.

Philip, G and Stewart, J. Involving Mental Health Information Service Users in Evaluating Service Quality.

International Journal of Health Care Quality Assurance. 12(5), 1999. pp199-209.

Philip, George and Hazlett, Shirley-Ann. Evaluating the service quality of information services using a new P-C-P attributes model. *International Journal of Quality and Reliability Management.* 18 (9), 2001. pp900-916.

Philip, George and Hazlett, Shirley-Ann. Service quality of industrial information services. *British Library Research and Innovation Report.* 32, 1996. pp1-118.

Phipps, S.E. Beyond measuring service quality: learning from the voices of the customers, the staff, the processes, and the organization LibQUAL+. *Library Trends.* 49(4), 2001. pp635-661.

Phipps, S.E. Performance Measurement as a methodology for Assessing Team and Individual Performance: The University of Arizona Library Experience. In *Proceedings of the 3rd Northumbria International Conference on Performance Measurement in Libraries and Information Services.* 1999. pp113-117.

Pinter, Chris. Customers and Academic Library Services. In *Providing Customer Oriented Services in Academic Libraries.* Ed by Chris Pinter and Maxine Mellin. London: Sconul, 1996. pp1-24.

Pitt, L.F. et al. Service Quality: A Measure of Information Systems Effectiveness. *MIS Quarterly.* 19(2), 1995. pp173-187.

Poll, Roswitha. Performance, processes and costs: measuring service quality with the balance scoreboard. *Library Trends.* 49(4), 2001. pp709-717.

Pors, N.O. Students' attitudes to the service quality of libraries. *Scandinavian Public Library Quarterly.* 29(2), 1996. pp18-23.

Quinn, B. Adapting service quality concepts to academic

libraries. *Journal of Academic Librarianship.* 23, (5), 1997. pp359-369.

Remenyi, D.S.J and Money, A.H. Service quality and correspondence analysis in determining problems with the effective use of computer services. *European Journal of Information Systems.* 3(1),1994. p2-12.

Riggs, D.E. Managing Quality: total quality management in libraries. *Library Administration and Management.* 7(2), 1993. pp73-78.

Roshan Raina. An analysis of the students' feedback on the library resources, facilities and services at a national level management institute. *Annals of Library Science and Documentation.* 42(3),1995. p106-112.

Rowley, J. Managing quality in information services. *Information services & Use.* 16(1), 1996. pp51-61.

Rowley, J. New perspectives on service quality. *Library Association Record.* 98(8), 1996.pp416-418.

Sandelands. E. Strategies for service qualitv. *Library Review.* 43(5), 1994. pp2-72.

Seay, Thomas. Et.al. Measuring and improving the quality of public services: a hybrid approach. *Library Trends.* 44(3), 1996. pp464-490.

Shaughnessy, T.W. Benchmarking, total quality management and libraries. *Library Administration and Management.* 7(1), 1993. pp7-12.

Shaughnessy, Thomas W. Assessing library effectiveness. *Journal of Library Administration.* 12(1), 1990. pp1-8.

Simmonds, Patience and Andaleeb, Syed Saad. Local experiences with user satisfaction surveys in Academic Libraries. *ARL Measuring Service Quality Symposium,* Washington DC, 2000.

Simmonds, Patience L and Andaleeb, Syed Saad. Usage of academic libraries: The role of service quality, resources and user characteristics. *Library Trends.* 49(4), 2001. pp626-634.

Snoj, Boris and Petemanec, Zdenka. Let users judge the quality of faculty library services. *New Library World.* 102 (1168), 2001. pp314-324.

Snyder, C. A. Measuring library service quality with a focus on the LibQUAL+TM project: An interview with Fred Heath. *Library Administration & Management,* 16, 2002. pp4-7.

Stein, J. Feedback from a Captive Audience: Reflections of the Results of a SERVQUAL Survey. *In Proceedings of the 2nd Northambria International Conference on Performance Measurement in Libraries and Information services.* New Castle: University of Northambria, 1997. pp207-222.

Strategies for service quality. *New Library World.* 95(1113), 1994. pp1-39.

Talbot, Dawn E. *et al.* From the users' perspective – the UCSD Libraries user survey project. *Journal of Academic Librarianship.* 24(5),1998. p357-364.

Thompson, B. Representativeness versus response rate: It ain't the response rate!. Paper presented at the Association of Research Libraries (ARL) *Measuring Service Quality Symposium on the New Culture of Assessment*: Measuring Service Quality, Washington, DC, 2000.

Thompson, B and Cook, C.Stability of the reliability of LibQUAL+TM scores: A "Reliability Generalization" meta-analysis study. *Educational and Psychological Measurement,* 62, 2000. pp735-743.

Thompson, B, et. al. The LibQUAL+TM gap measurement model: The bad, the ugly, and the good of gap measurement. *Performance Measurement and Metrics,* 1, 2000. pp165-178.

Thompson, B, et.al. How many dimensions does it take to measure users' perceptions of libraries?: A "LibQUAL+^{TM}" study. *Portal: Libraries and the Academy*, 1, 2001. pp29-138.

Thompson, B, et. al. Structure of perceptions of service quality in libraries: A LibQUAL+^{TM} study. *Structural Equation Modeling*, 2004.

Thompson, B, et.al. Reliability and structure of LibQUAL+^{TM} scores. *Portal: Libraries and the Academy*, 2, 2002. pp3-12.

Thompson, R.L. Scalable Web-based user survey research across institutions: The LibQUAL+^{TM} experience. Paper presented at the Association of Research Libraries (ARL) *Measuring Service Quality Symposium on the New Culture of Assessment*: Measuring Service Quality, Washington, DC, 2001.

Van Dyke, T.P. et al. Cautions on the Use of the SERVQUAL Measure to Assess the Quality of Information System Services. *Decision Sciences*. 30(3), 1999. pp877-891.

Van Dyke, T.P. et al. Measuring Information System Service Quality: Concerns on the Use of the SERVQUAL Questionnaire. *MIS Quarterly*. 21(2), 1997. pp195-208.

Van House, N.A. Output measures in libraries. *Library Trends*. 38(2), 1989. pp268-279.

Verma, R.K. Measuring quality management level with reference to ISO 9000 and TQM for special libraries in India. *Annals of Library Science and Information Studies*. 49(4), 2002. pp141-163.

Wall, Tom B. LibQUAL + TM as transformative experience. *Performance Measurement and Metrics*. 3(2), 2002. pp43-48.

Watson, R.T. et.al. User satisfaction and service quality if IS department: closing the gaps. *Journal of Information*

Technology. 8(4), 1993. pp257-265.

Webb, Sylvia P. Pursuing quality in special libraries. *Library Review*. 44(7), 1995. pp5-7.

White, M.D. and Abels, E.G. Measuring service quality in special libraries: lessons from service marketing. *Special Libraries*. 86(1), 1995. pp36-45.

Whitehall, T. Quality in library and information service. *Library Management*. 13(5), 1992. pp26-35.

Whitlatch, Jo Bell. Unobtrusive studies and the Quality of Academic Library Reference Services. *College and Research Libraries*. 50, 1989. pp181-194.

Wilson, Carol and Orr, Noreen. User satisfaction with the library service among part-time students. *The New Review of Academic Librarianship*. 1, 1995, pp187-199.

Wilson, I. Building the User Centred Library. *RQ*. 34(3), 1995. pp297-302.

Winworth, Ian. Innovative United Kingdon approaches to measuring service quality. *Library Trends*. 49(4), 2001. pp718-731.

Yang, Zheng Ye (Lan). University faculty's perception of a library liaison programme. *Journal of Academic Librarianship*. 26(2),2000. p124-128.

Books

Abbott, Christie. Performance measurement in library and information services. London: Aslib, 1994.

ARL Symposium on the New Culture of Assessment: Measuring Service Quality, Washington DC, 2000.

Blagdon, John and Harrington, John. How good is your library. London: Aslib, 1990.

Brophy, Peter and Kate, Coulling. Quality management for information and library managers. Aldershot: Aslib Gower, 1996.

Brekke, Elaine. User Surveys in ARL Libraries. Washington DC: ARL, 1995.

Ellis, Debbie and Norton, Bob. Implementing BS5750 ISO 9000 in Libraries. London: Aslib, 1993.

FID. ISO 9000 for libraries and information centers: A guide. The Hague: FID, 1996.

Ford, Geoffrey and Mc Dougall. Performance assessment in academic libraries. London: British Library Board, 1992.

Foreman, L Ed. Developing quality in Libraries: Culture and measurement for information services. London: HMSO, 1992.

Hernon, P and Altman, E. Assessing service quality: Satisfying the expectations of library customers. Chicago: ALA, 1998.

Hernon, P and Altman, E. Service quality in academic libraries. Norwood, N.J: Ablex, 1996.

Hernon, P and Whiteman, J. Delivering satisfaction and service quality: A customer based approach for libraries. Chicago: ALA, 2001.

Mc Donald, J. A and Micikas, I.B. Academic Library: The dimensions of their effectiveness. Westfort: Greenwood Press, 1994.

Pinter, Chris and Melling, Maxine, ed. Providing Customer Oriented Services in Academic Libraries. London: Sconul, 1996.

Poll, R and te Boekhoerst, P. Measuring quality: International guidelines for performance measurement in academic libraries. Munchen: K.G. Saur, 1996.

Proceedings of the 2nd Northumbria International Conference on Performance measurement in libraries and information centers. Newcastle: University of Northumbria, 1998.

Proceedings of the 3rd Northumbria International Conference on Performance measurement in libraries and information centers. Newcastle: University of Northumbria, 2000.

Symposium on Measuring Library Service Quality,2001.

Van House, N. et al. Measuring academic library performance: A practical approach. Chicago: ALA, 1990.

Dissertations and Theses

Cook, Colleen. A mixed-methods approach to the identification and measurement of library service quality constructs: LibQUAL+TM. College Station: Texas A & M University, 2001.

Hebert, F. The quality of interlibrary borrowing services in large urban public libraries in Canada. Toronto: University of Toronto, 1993.

Maddox-Swan, R. Perceived Performance and Disconfirmation of Expectations as Measures of Customer Satisfaction with Information Services in the Academic Library. Florida State University, 1998.

Nitecki, D.A. An assessment of the applicability of SERVQUAL dimensions as a customer based criterion for evaluating quality of an academic library. Maryland : University of Maryland, 1995.

Index